A-Z DARTFORD

CON

Key to Map Pages

Map Pages   4-   onwards

REFE

Motorway	**M25**	Car Park (selected)	**P**
A Road	**A226**	Church or Chapel	†
B Road	**B262**	Fire Station	■
Dual Carriageway		Hospital	**H**
One-way Street Traffic flow on A roads is indicated by a heavy line on the drivers' left.	➡	House Numbers (A & B Roads only)	2 33
Junction Names	DARTFORD HEATH	Information Centre	**i**
Restricted Access		National Grid Reference	550
Pedestrianized Road		Police Station	▲
Track & Footpath		Post Office	★
Residential Walkway		Toilet: without facilities for the Disabled with facilities for the Disabled Disabled facilities only	▽ ▽ ▽
Railway	Station / Level Crossing / Tunnel	Educational Establishment	
Built-up Area	BOND ST	Hospital or Hospice	
Local Authority Boundary	— · — · ·	Industrial Building	
Posttown Boundary		Leisure or Recreational Facility	
Postcode Boundary (within posttown)	— — —	Place of Interest	
Map Continuation	▲ 12	Public Building	
		Shopping Centre or Market	
		Other Selected Buildings	

SCALE

1:19,000
3⅓ inches (8.47 cm) to 1 mile
5.26 cm to 1 kilometre

0	¼	½	¾ Mile

| 0 | 250 | 500 | 750 Metres | 1 Kilometre |

Copyright of Geographers' A-Z Map Company Limited

Head Office :
Fairfield Road, Borough Green, Sevenoaks, Kent TN15 8PP
Telephone: 01732 781000 (General Enquiries & Trade Sales)
01732 783422 (Retail Sales)

www.a-zmaps.co.uk

Copyright © Geographers' A-Z Map Co. Ltd.

Ordnance Survey® This product includes mapping data licensed from Ordnance Survey® with the permission of the Controller of Her Majesty's Stationery Office.

KEY TO MAP PAGES

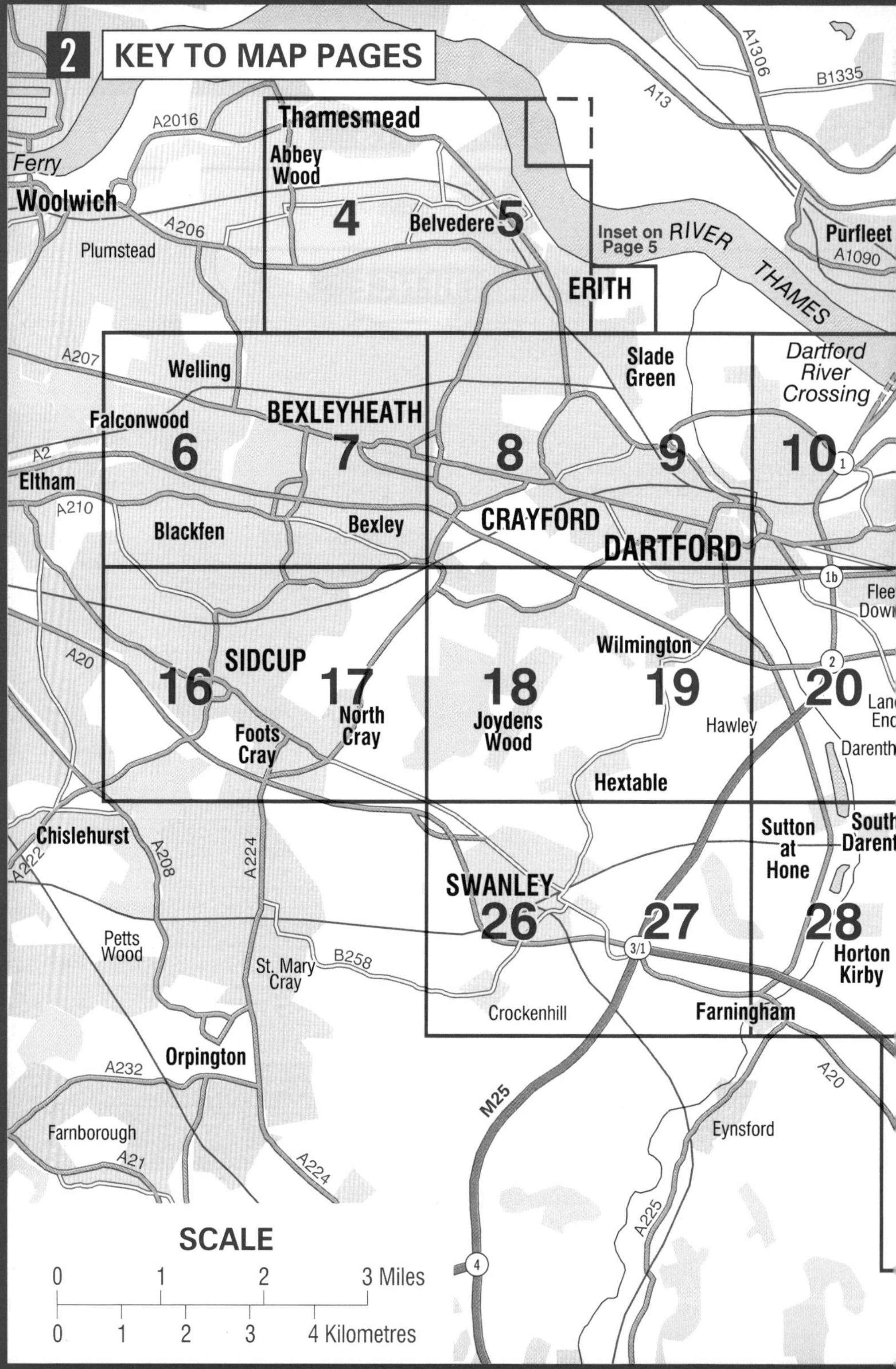

Thamesmead
Abbey Wood
4
Belvedere
5
Woolwich
Ferry
A2016
A206
Plumstead
Inset on Page 5
RIVER THAMES
ERITH
A13
A1306
B1335
Purfleet
A1090
A207
Welling
Falconwood
BEXLEYHEATH
6
7
8
9
10
Slade Green
Dartford River Crossing
A2
Eltham
A210
Blackfen
Bexley
CRAYFORD
DARTFORD
1
1b
2
Flee Dow
A20
SIDCUP
16
17
18
19
20
Wilmington
North Cray
Joydens Wood
Hawley
Lan Enc
Darenth
Foots Cray
Hextable
Chislehurst
A222
A208
A224
Sutton at Hone
South Darent
SWANLEY
26
27
28
3/1
Horton Kirby
Petts Wood
St. Mary Cray
B258
Crockenhill
Farningham
Orpington
A232
A20
M25
Farnborough
A21
A224
Eynsford
A225
4
SCALE
0 1 2 3 Miles
0 1 2 3 4 Kilometres

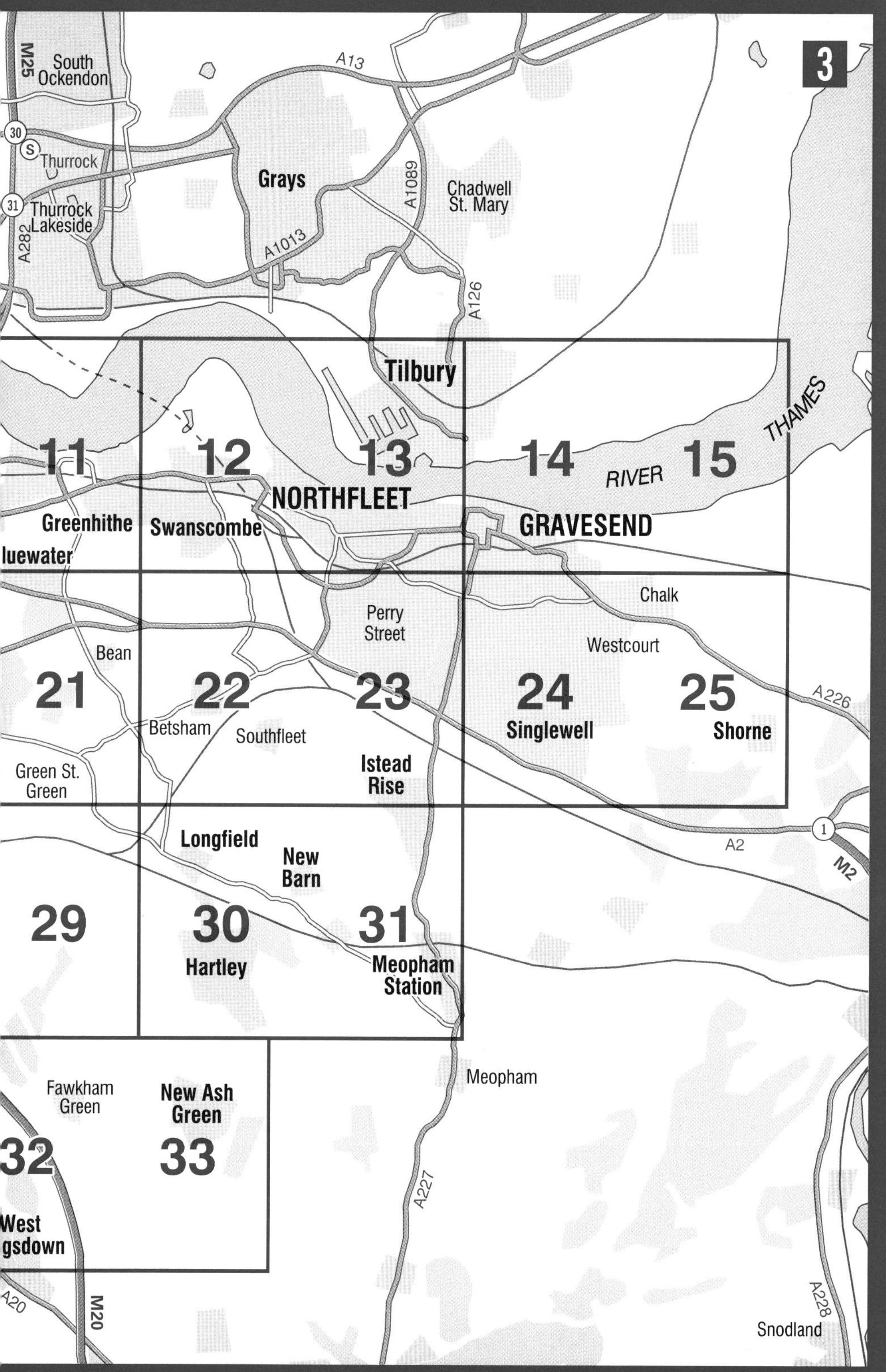

3

M25
South
Ockendon

A13

30 (S)
Thurrock

31
Thurrock
Lakeside

A282

Grays

A1089

A1013

Chadwell
St. Mary

A126

Tilbury

THAMES

11 **12** **13** **14** *RIVER* **15**

NORTHFLEET

Greenhithe   Swanscombe   **GRAVESEND**

luewater

Chalk

Perry
Street

Westcourt

Bean

21 **22** **23** **24** **25**

Betsham   Southfleet   **Singlewell**   **Shorne**

A226

Green St.
Green

**Istead
Rise**

1

Longfield   **New**
Barn

A2

M2

29 **30** **31**

Hartley   **Meopham
Station**

Meopham

32 Fawkham
Green

**New Ash
Green**

33

West
gsdown

A20   M20

A227

A228

Snodland

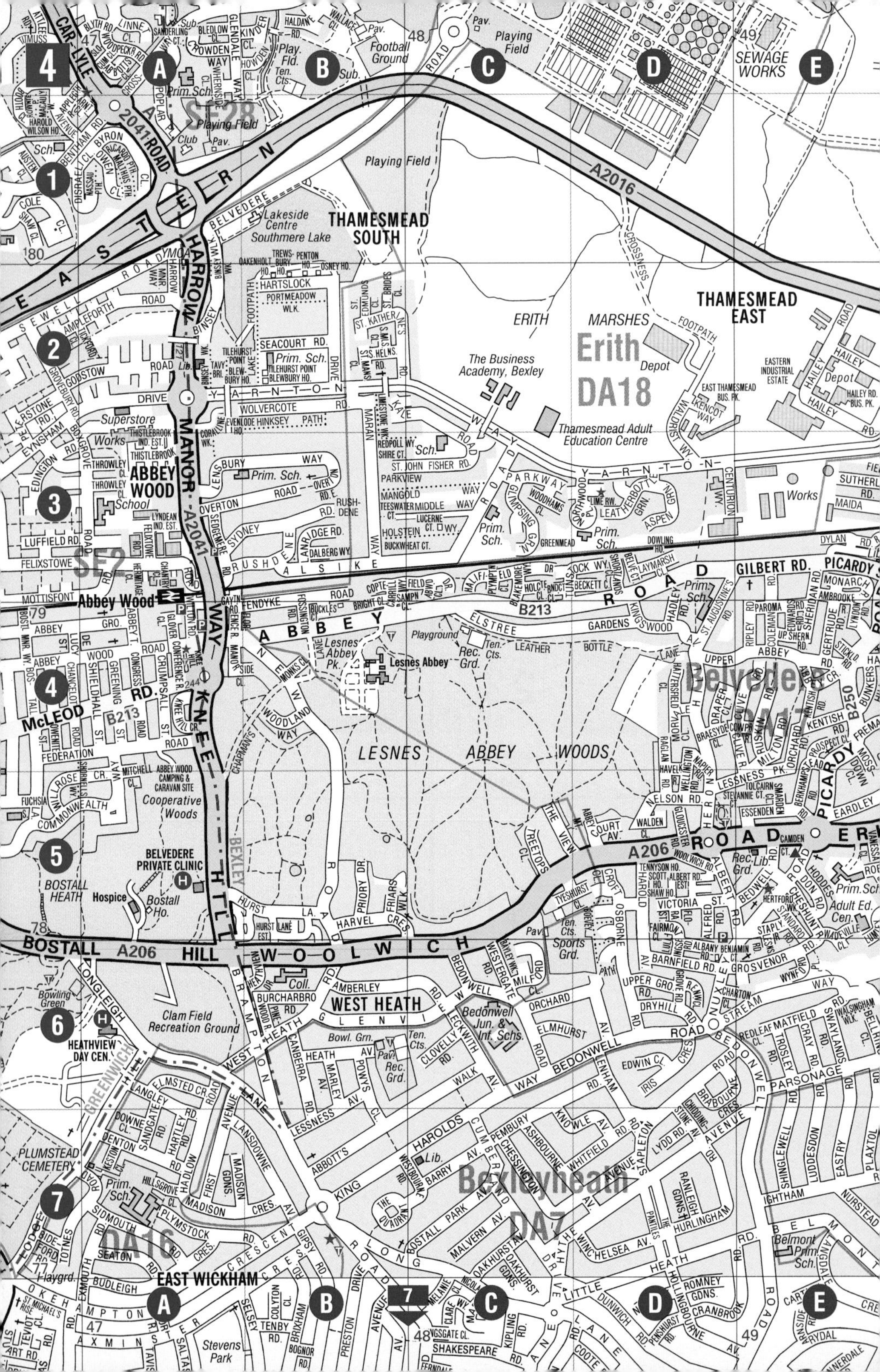

A
B
C
D
E
1
2
3
4
5
6
7
47
48
49
180
79
78
77
SEWAGE WORKS
Football Ground
Playing Field
SE28
Playing Field
EASTERN
A2016
THAMESMEAD SOUTH
Lakeside Centre
Southmere Lake
THAMESMEAD EAST
ERITH
MARSHES
Erith
DA18
The Business Academy, Bexley
Thamesmead Adult Education Centre
EASTERN INDUSTRIAL ESTATE
EAST THAMESMEAD BUS. PK.
HAILEY RD. BUS. PK.
Depot
YARNTON WAY
HARROW MANOR WAY
A2041
ABBEY WOOD
Abbey Wood
SE2
Superstore
Works
School
Prim. Sch.
ABBEY ROAD
B213
GILBERT RD.
PICARDY
Belvedere
DA17
B250
Lesnes Abbey
Lesnes Abbey Pk.
Playground
Rec. Grd.
LESNES ABBEY WOODS
McLEOD RD.
FEDERATION
ABBEY WOOD CAMPING & CARAVAN SITE
Cooperative Woods
BELVEDERE PRIVATE CLINIC
Hospice
Bostall Ho.
BOSTALL HEATH
BOSTALL HILL
A206
WOOLWICH ROAD
KNEE HILL
BEXLEY
Bowling Green
HEATHVIEW DAY CEN.
Clam Field Recreation Ground
WEST HEATH
Coll.
Bowl. Grn.
Rec. Grd.
Bedonwell Jun. & Inf. Schs.
Sports Grd.
BEDONWELL
PLUMSTEAD CEMETERY
GREENWICH
Bexleyheath
DA7
DA16
EAST WICKHAM
Stevens Park
Lib.
Belmont Prim. Sch.
LONG LANE
BOSTALL PARK AV.
HEATH
ABBOTT'S
KING
HAROLDS
UPPER
7

5
INSET
RIVER THAMES
Erith DA8
Rainham RM13
BELVEDERE
HILLSIDE
ERITH
LESSNESS HEATH
NORTHUMBERLAND HEATH
NORTH END
Erith DA8
Erith Yacht Club
Slade Green Jun. & Inf. Schs.
Erith & Dist. Hosp.
Erith Sports Centre
Erith Stadium
Bexley College
Trinity Sch. Belvedere
Jenningtree Point
Coldharbour Point
ERITH REACH
HAVERING
BEXLEY
BRONZE AGE WAY
A2016
A206
A220
B253
B213
FRASER ROAD
BEXLEY ROAD
QUEEN'S ROAD
NORTHEND RD.
MANORWAY
PICARDY

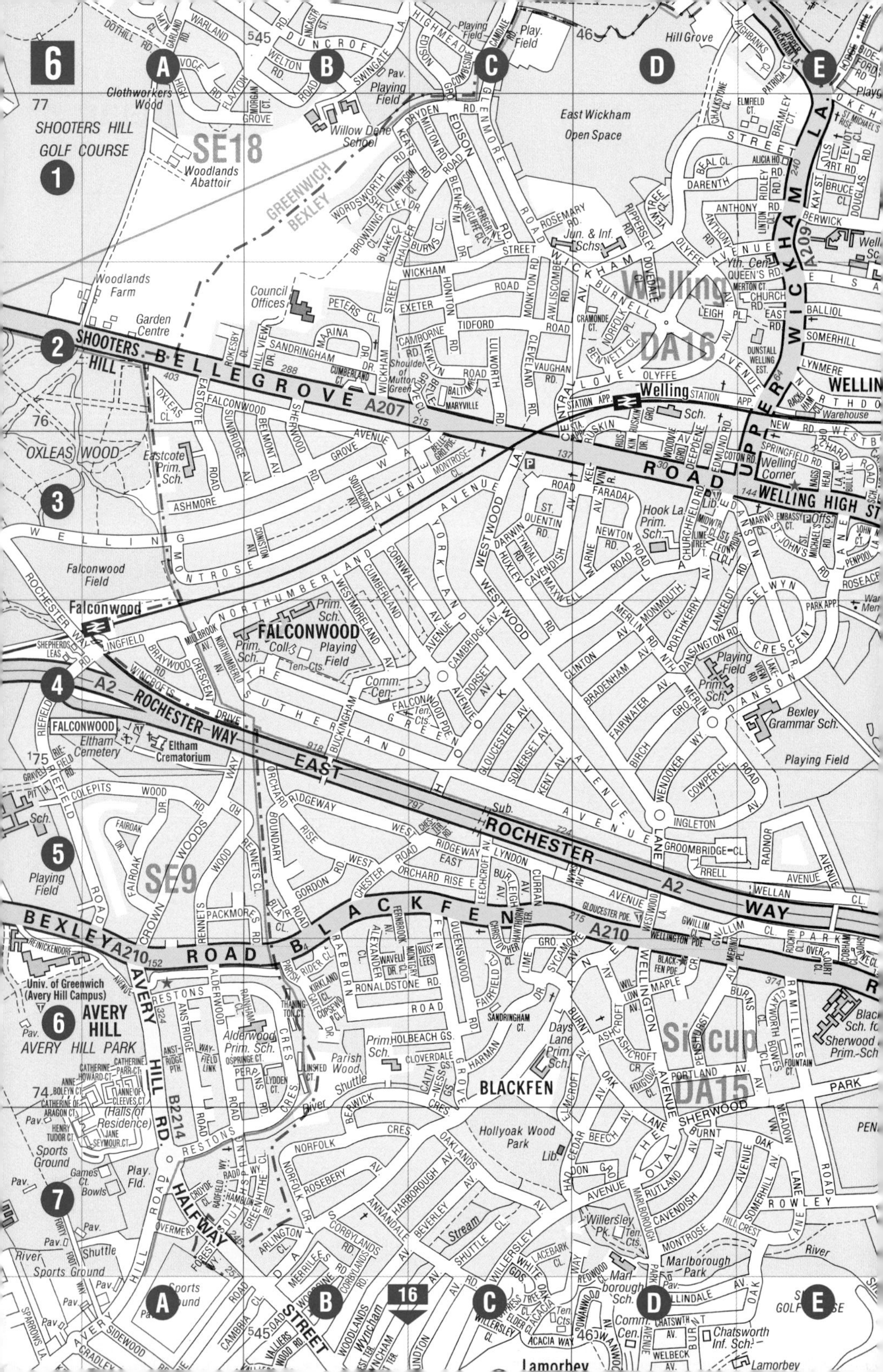
SHOOTERS HILL GOLF COURSE
Clothworkers Wood
SE18
Woodlands Abattoir
Willow Dene School
GREENWICH
BEXLEY
East Wickham Open Space
Hill Grove
Woodlands Farm
Garden Centre
Council Offices
SHOOTERS HILL
BELLEGROVE A207
OXLEAS WOOD
Eastcote Prim. Sch.
Welling
DA16
WELLING HIGH ST
UPPER WICKHAM LA.
A209
Welling Corner
Hook La. Prim. Sch.
Falconwood Field
Falconwood
FALCONWOOD
Falconwood Playing Field
A2 ROCHESTER WAY
Eltham Cemetery
Eltham Crematorium
Bexley Grammar Sch.
Playing Field
EAST ROCHESTER WAY
SE9
BEXLEY ROAD A210
BLACKFEN ROAD
Univ. of Greenwich (Avery Hill Campus)
AVERY HILL
AVERY HILL PARK
Alderwood Prim. Sch.
Parish Wood
Days Lane Prim. Sch.
BLACKFEN
Sidcup
DA15
Hollyoak Wood Park
Sports Ground
Willersley Pk.
Marlborough Park
Marlborough Sch.
Chatsworth Inf. Sch.
Lamorbey
16

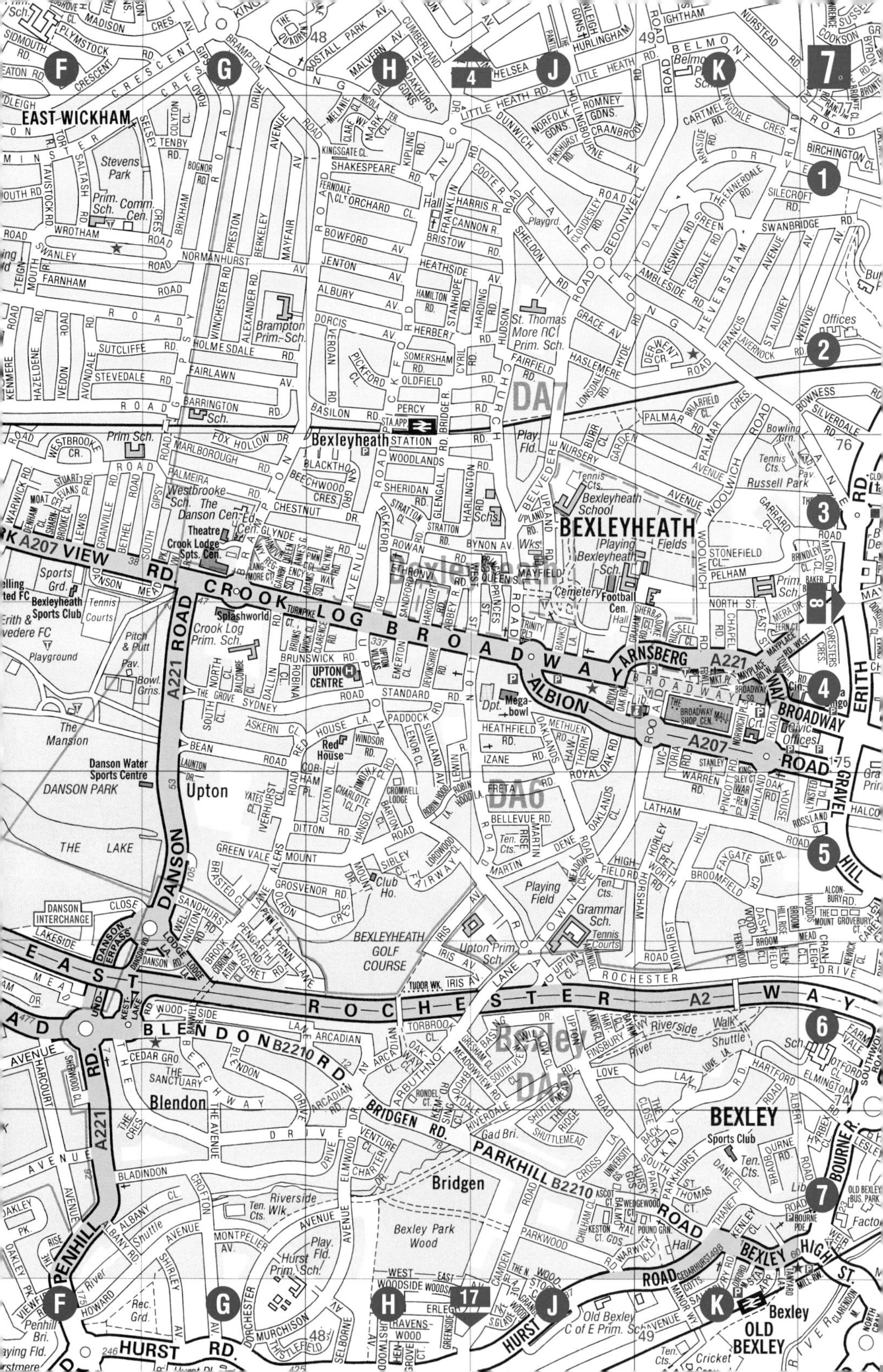

F
G
H
J
K
7
4
48
49
EAST WICKHAM
Stevens Park
Prim. Sch.
Comm. Cen.
SIDMOUTH RD.
PLYMSTOCK RD.
CRESCENT
MADISON CRES.
BRAMPTON
TAVISTOCK RD.
SALTASH RD.
TORTER
SELSEY CRES.
COLYTON RD.
TENBY RD.
BOGNOR RD.
BRIXHAM
WROTHAM ROAD
SWANLEY ROAD
NORMANHURST
FARNHAM ROAD
SUTCLIFFE RD.
STEVEDALE RD.
HOLMESDALE RD.
FAIRLAWN AV.
BARRINGTON RD.
HAZELDENE
IVEDON
AVONDALE
PRESTON
BERKELEY
MAYFAIR
AVENUE
WINCHESTER RD
ALEXANDER RD
Brampton Prim. Sch.
BOSTALL PARK AV.
CUMBERLAND AV.
MALVERN AV.
OAKHURST GDNS.
KINGSGATE CL.
SHAKESPEARE
KIPLING
ORCHARD CL.
BOWFORD AV.
JENTON AV.
ALBURY AV.
DORCIS AV.
VERONA
PICKFORD CL.
BASILON RD.
PERCY
Hall
HARRIS R.
CANNON R.
BRISTOW
HEATHSIDE AV.
HAMILTON RD.
STANHOPE
HARDING
HERBERT
SOMERSHAM RD.
OLDFIELD
BRIDGE R.
CYRIL
LITTLE HEATH RD.
DUNWICH
COOTE R.
FRANKLIN
HURLINGHAM
CHELSEA
NORFOLK GDNS.
ROMNEY GDNS.
CRANBROOK
HOLLINGBOURNE AV.
PENSHURST RD.
Playgrd.
SHELDON
CLOUDESLEY RD.
BEDONWELL
ROAD
GRACE AV.
St. Thomas More RC Prim. Sch.
FAIRFIELD
HASLEMERE
LONSDALE RD.
HYDE
DERWENT CR.
IGHTHAM
NURSTEAD
BELMONT
Belmont Prim. Sch.
CARTMEL
LANGDALE CRES.
ARNSIDE
DRIVE
THE GREEN
KESWICK RD.
ESKDALE RD.
AMBLESIDE RD.
HEVERSHAM
ENNERDALE RD.
SILECROFT
SWANBRIDGE RD.
AVENUE
ST. AUDREY AV.
WENVOE
FRANCIS
LAVERNOCK RD.
Offices
BIRCHINGTON CL.
1
2
3
5
6
DA7
DA6
DA5
BOWNESS
SILVERDALE RD.
PALMAR RD.
BRIARFIELD CL.
PALMAR CRES.
Bowling Grn.
Tennis Cts.
Pav.
Russell Park
76
GARRARD CL.
BRINDLEY CL.
MASON RD.
ERITH
Bexleyheath STATION
STA. APP.
WOODLANDS
BLACKTHORN
BEECHWOOD CRES.
SHERIDAN
GLENGALL
HARLINGTON RD.
STRATTON
Schs.
BYNON AV.
MAYFIELD
Play. Fld.
NURSERY
BURR CL.
GARDEN
AVENUE
BELVEDERE
UPLAND
Tennis Cts.
Bexleyheath School
BEXLEYHEATH
Playing Fields
Bexleyheath Sch.
Cemetery
Football Cen.
Hall
WOOLWICH ROAD
STONEFIELD CL.
PELHAM
NORTH ST.
CHAPEL
Prim. Sch.
MERA DR.
FERN CT.
MAYPLACE RD. WEST
FORESTERS CRES.
Prim Sch.
WESTBROOKE CR.
FOX HOLLOW DR.
MARLBOROUGH RD.
PALMEIRA
Westbrooke Sch.
The Danson Cen. Ed.
Cen.
Theatre
Crook Lodge Spts. Cen.
CHESTNUT DR.
GIPSY
SOUTH
BETHEL
GRANVILLE
LEWIS
WARWICK RD.
DENHAM
MOAT CT
EVANS
STUART CL.
BROOKE CL.
A207 VIEW RD.
38
Sports Grd.
DANSON MEAD
Bexleyheath Sports Club
Tennis Courts
Playground
Pitch & Putt
Pav.
Bowl. Grns.
The Mansion
Danson Water Sports Centre
DANSON PARK
THE LAKE
A221 ROAD
DANSON
53
105
47
CROOK LOG BROADWAY
Splashworld
Crook Log Prim. Sch.
TURNPIKE CT.
CLARENCE
BRUNSWICK RD.
UPTON VILLAS
337
UPTON CENTRE
ROBINA
DALLIN
NORTH CL.
BALCOMBE CL.
THE GROVE
SYDNEY ROAD
STANDARD RD.
SOUTH CL.
ASKERN CL.
BEAN ROAD
LAUNTON DR.
Upton
YATES CL.
IVERHURST
RED HOUSE LA.
Red House
WINDSOR RD.
COBHAM PL.
CUXTON CL.
CHARLOTTE CL.
TIMOTHY CL.
CROMWELL LODGE
BARTON ROAD
PADDOCK
LENOR CL.
SUNLAND AV.
LEWIN
ROBIN HOOD LA.
ROBIN HOOD
DITTON RD.
HANSOL
GREEN VALE
MOUNT
ALERS
BRASTED CL.
SIBLEY
Club Ho.
GROSVENOR RD.
LORDWOOD CL.
FAIRWAY
BEXLEYHEATH GOLF COURSE
SANDHURST RD.
WELLINGTON RD.
PENGARTH RD.
PENN LA.
OLRON CRES.
MARGARET RD.
BROOK
DANSON LA.
LODGE
ETHRONVI
SANDFORD
HARCOURT
ABBEY R.
PRINCES
QUEEN'S
WEST ST.
EMERTON CL.
DEVONSHIRE RD.
UPTON
ROWAN
ALBION
ARNSBERG WAY
A221
BROADWAY
MKT. PL.
THE BROADWAY SHOP. CEN.
MALL
NORWICH PL.
BROADWAY
Civic Offices
A207 ROAD
175
GRAVEL HILL
Mega-bowl
Dpt.
HEATHFIELD RD.
OAKLANDS
METHUEN RD.
HAWTHORN RD.
IZANE RD.
ROYAL OAK RD
FRETA RD.
BELLEVUE RD.
MARTIN RISE
Ten. Cts.
MARTIN DENE
ROAD
VICTORIA RD.
STANLEY
WARREN RD.
PINCOTT RD.
HIGHLAND
OAK RD
HOUSE
LYNSTED CL.
ROSSLAND CL.
LATHAM
HILL
FAYGATE CR.
GATE CL.
BROOMFIELD
ALCONBURY RD.
HORLEY CL.
PETWORTH CL.
HORSHAM
HIGHFIELD RD
Ten. Cts.
Playing Field
Grammar Sch.
Tennis Courts
TOWN
MEADOW
MIDHURST
Upton Prim. Sch.
IRIS AV.
IRIS
TUDOR WK.
ROCHESTER DRIVE
ROCHESTER WAY
A2
THE MOUNT
GROVEBURY CT.
BROOM
HILL RISE
DASH WOOD CL.
CRANLEIGH
MEAD
NEWICK CL.
DANSON INTERCHANGE
CLOSE
LAKESIDE
DANSON UNDERPASS
EAST
MEAD
DR.
477
AVENUE
HARCOURT
SHERWOOD CL.
RD.
A221
KEST. LAKE
WOODSIDE
BLENDON B2210 RD.
BLENDON
CEDAR GRO.
THE SANCTUARY
Blendon
BEECHWAY
BLENDON DRIVE
ARCADIAN
TORBROOK CL.
ARCADIAN AV.
Riverside Walk
River
Shuttle
Sch.
HARTFORD RD.
ELMINGTON CL.
FINSBURY WY
LOVE LA.
LOVE LANE
BRIDGEN RD.
ARBUTHNOT
MEADOWVIEW RD.
SOUTH VIEW
RIVERDALE
SHUTTLEMEAD
THE RIDGE
Gad Bri.
PARKHILL B2210
CROSS
UNIVERSITY
HURST
BACK LA.
THE CLOSE
BEXLEY
Sports Club
Ten. Cts.
DANE CL.
ST. THOMAS CT.
SOUTH PARK
PARKHURST
BOURNE R.
BRADBOURNE
Lib.
7
OLD BEXLEY BUS. PARK
Factory
WEIR
ROAD
BEXLEY HIGH ST.
60
THE AVENUE
THE CRES.
AVENUE
BLADINDON
76
DRIVE
ELMWOOD
VENTURE
CHARTER
78
Bridgen
Riverside Wlk.
Ten. Cts.
Bexley Park Wood
CROFTON
ALBANY CL.
Shuttle
AVENUE
MONTPELIER AV.
SHIRLEY
Hurst Prim. Sch.
Play. Fld.
AVENUE
PARKWOOD
CAMDEN
WEST
WOODSIDE
WOODSIDE
EAST
17
ERLEG
RAVENSWOOD
HENGROVE CT.
GREENSIDE
SELBORNE
MURCHISON
THISTLEFIELD
DORCHESTER
48
HURST RD.
246
HOWARD
River
Rec. Grd.
Penhill Bri.
Playing Fld.
PENHILL
RISE
OAKLEY PK.
VIEWFIELD
175
OAKLEY PK.
HURST
THE N. WOOD
Old Bexley C of E Prim. Sch.
AVENUE
49
Ten. Cts.
Cricket
Bexley
OLD BEXLEY
RIVER
CHILHAM CL.
KESTON CT.
GDNS.
WEDGEWOOD CT.
POUND GRN.
Hall
WARWICK CL.
CEDARHURST
MANOR WY
498
THANET
KENLEY CL.
ROAD
BOURNE PDE.
MILL RW.

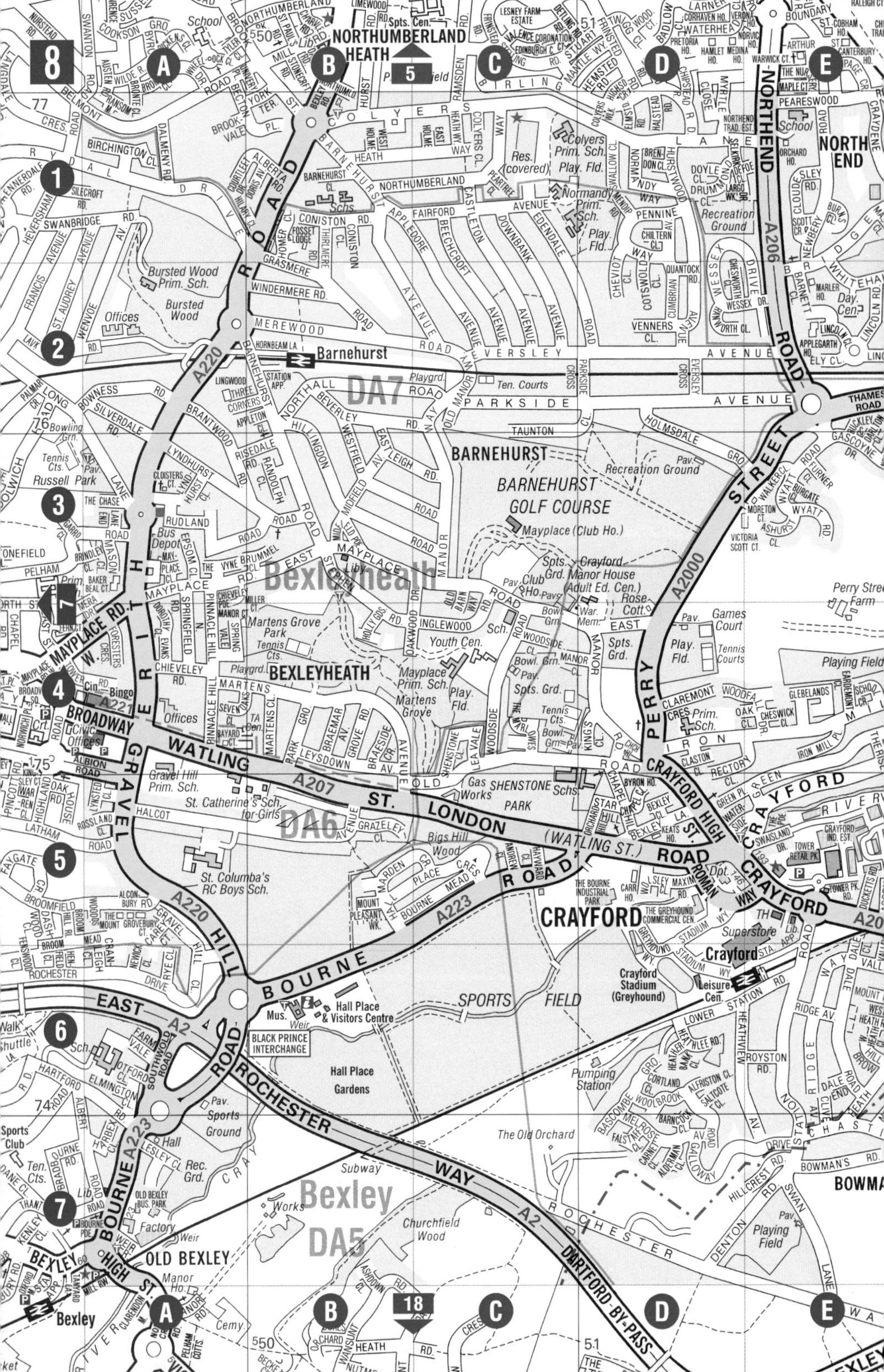
NORTHUMBERLAND HEATH
5
A
B
C
D
E
1
2
3
4
5
6
7
NORTHEND ROAD
A206
NORTH END
Colyers Prim. Sch.
Normandy Prim. Sch.
Recreation Ground
Barnehurst
DA7
PARKSIDE AVENUE
EVERSLEY AVENUE
BARNEHURST
BARNEHURST GOLF COURSE
Mayplace (Club Ho.)
Crayford Manor House (Adult Ed. Cen.)
PERRY STREET
A2000
Bexleyheath
BEXLEYHEATH
Martens Grove Park
Mayplace Prim. Sch.
BROADWAY
A221
WATLING ST.
A207
LONDON ROAD
(WATLING ST.)
Civic Offices
Gravel Hill Prim. Sch.
St. Catherine's Sch. for Girls
DA6
St. Columba's RC Boys Sch.
SHENSTONE PARK
CRAYFORD HIGH ST.
CRAYFORD
Crayford
Crayford Stadium (Greyhound)
Leisure Cen.
BOURNE ROAD
A223
A220
GRAVEL HILL
EAST ROCHESTER WAY
A2
BLACK PRINCE INTERCHANGE
Hall Place & Visitors Centre
Hall Place Gardens
SPORTS FIELD
Pumping Station
The Old Orchard
Bexley DA5
Churchfield Wood
OLD BEXLEY
BEXLEY
Bexley
DARTFORD BY-PASS
18
Bursted Wood Prim. Sch.
Bursted Wood
Russell Park
Playing Field
Perry Street Farm

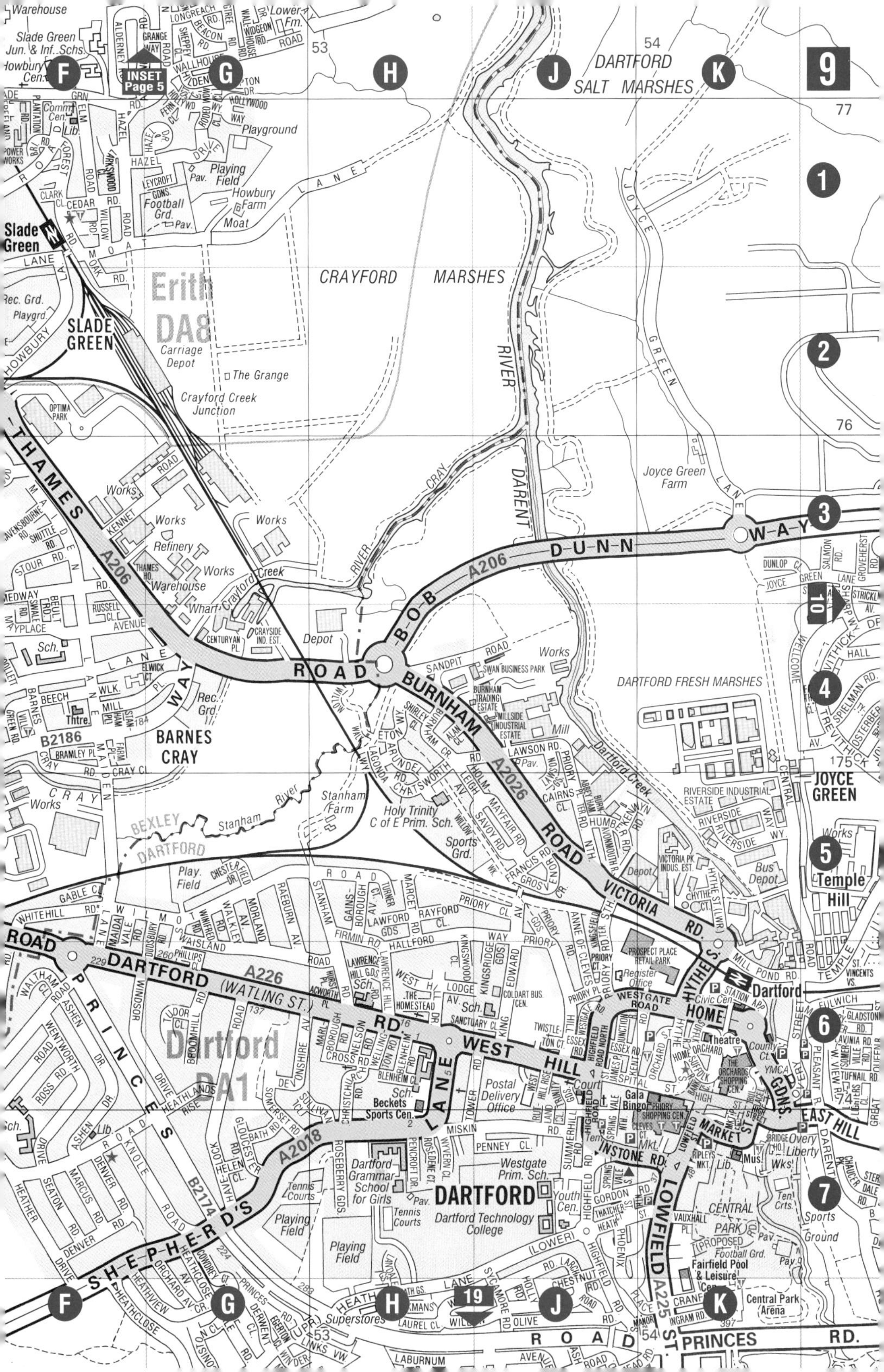

9
F
G
H
J
K
1
2
3
4
5
6
7
53
54
77
76
175
74
INSET Page 5
10
19
DARTFORD SALT MARSHES
CRAYFORD MARSHES
DARTFORD FRESH MARSHES
Erith DA8
Dartford DA1
SLADE GREEN
Slade Green
BARNES CRAY
JOYCE GREEN
Temple Hill
DARTFORD
Dartford
BEXLEY
DARTFORD
Warehouse
Slade Green Jun. & Inf. Schs.
Howbury Cen.
Lower Fm.
Playground
Playing Field
Howbury Farm
Moat
Football Grd.
Pav.
Comm. Cen.
Lib.
Power Works
Rec. Grd.
Playgrd.
Carriage Depot
The Grange
Crayford Creek Junction
Optima Park
Works
Refinery
Warehouse
Wharf
Crayford Creek
Crayside Ind. Est.
Depot
Thames Ho.
Sch.
Thtre.
Rec. Grd.
Joyce Green Farm
Swan Business Park
Burnham Trading Estate
Millside Industrial Estate
Mill
Dartford Creek
Riverside Industrial Estate
Victoria Pk. Indus. Est.
Bus Depot
Stanham Farm
Stanham River
Holy Trinity C of E Prim. Sch.
Sports Grd.
Play. Field
Prospect Place Retail Park
Register Office
Civic Cen.
Theatre
The Orchards Shopping Cen.
County Ct.
YMCA
Priory Shopping Cen.
Gala Bingo
Court
Mkt.
Lib.
Mus.
Overy Liberty Wks.
Ripleys Mkt.
Beckets Sports Cen.
Postal Delivery Office
Westgate Prim. Sch.
Dartford Grammar School for Girls
Tennis Courts
Playing Field
Dartford Technology College
Youth Cen.
Central Park
Football Grd.
Fairfield Pool & Leisure Cen.
Central Park Arena
Ten. Crts.
Sports Ground
Superstores
Coldart Bus. Cen.
The Homestead
A206
A2026
A226
A2018
A225
B2186
B2174
THAMES ROAD
BOB DUNN WAY
BURNHAM ROAD
VICTORIA RD.
DARTFORD RD. (WATLING ST.)
WEST HILL
EAST HILL
HIGH ST.
LOWFIELD ST.
PRINCES RD.
SHEPHERD'S LANE
HYTHE ST.
HOME GDNS.
MARKET ST.
WESTGATE ROAD
MILL POND RD.
JOYCE GREEN LANE
MOAT LANE
HOWBURY LANE
CRAYFORD WAY
MAIDEN LANE
BARNES CRAY
MAYPLACE
CRAY RD.
RIVER DARENT
RIVER CRAY
PRINCES
KNOLE ROAD
DENVER RD.
HEATH LANE
ROAD
TEMPLE HILL

DARTFORD SALT MARSHES
LONG REACH
RIVER
Pier
Jetty
Works
Power Station
LITTLEBROOK BUSINESS CENTRE
DA1
DA2
Dartford
BOB DUNN WAY
A206
A282
BOULEVARD
CROSSWAYS
QUEEN ELIZABETH II BRIDGE
DARTFORD
Toll Booths
Depot
CROSSWAYS 25 BUSINESS PARK
EDISON'S PARK
Warehouse
Junction 1a
LITTLEBROOK INTERCHANGE
APPROACH ROAD
DARTFORD TUNNEL APPROACH
COTTON LANE
B2228
Recreation Ground
Bowls & Social Club
LITTLEBROOK HOSP.
ARCHERY HO.
STONE HOUSE HOSP.
Resource Cen.
JOYCE GREEN
Temple Hill
NEW TOWN
LONDON ROAD
BRENT
EAST HILL
A226
THE PARK
A296
WATLING STREET
B2500
John's Hole
Junc.1b
PRINCES RD. INTERCHANGE
PRINCES ROAD
A225
LIVINGSTONE HOSP.
Sports Ground
DARTFORD
Central Park Arena
Hesketh Park
Princes Golf
CHALK PIT (DISUSED)
9
20

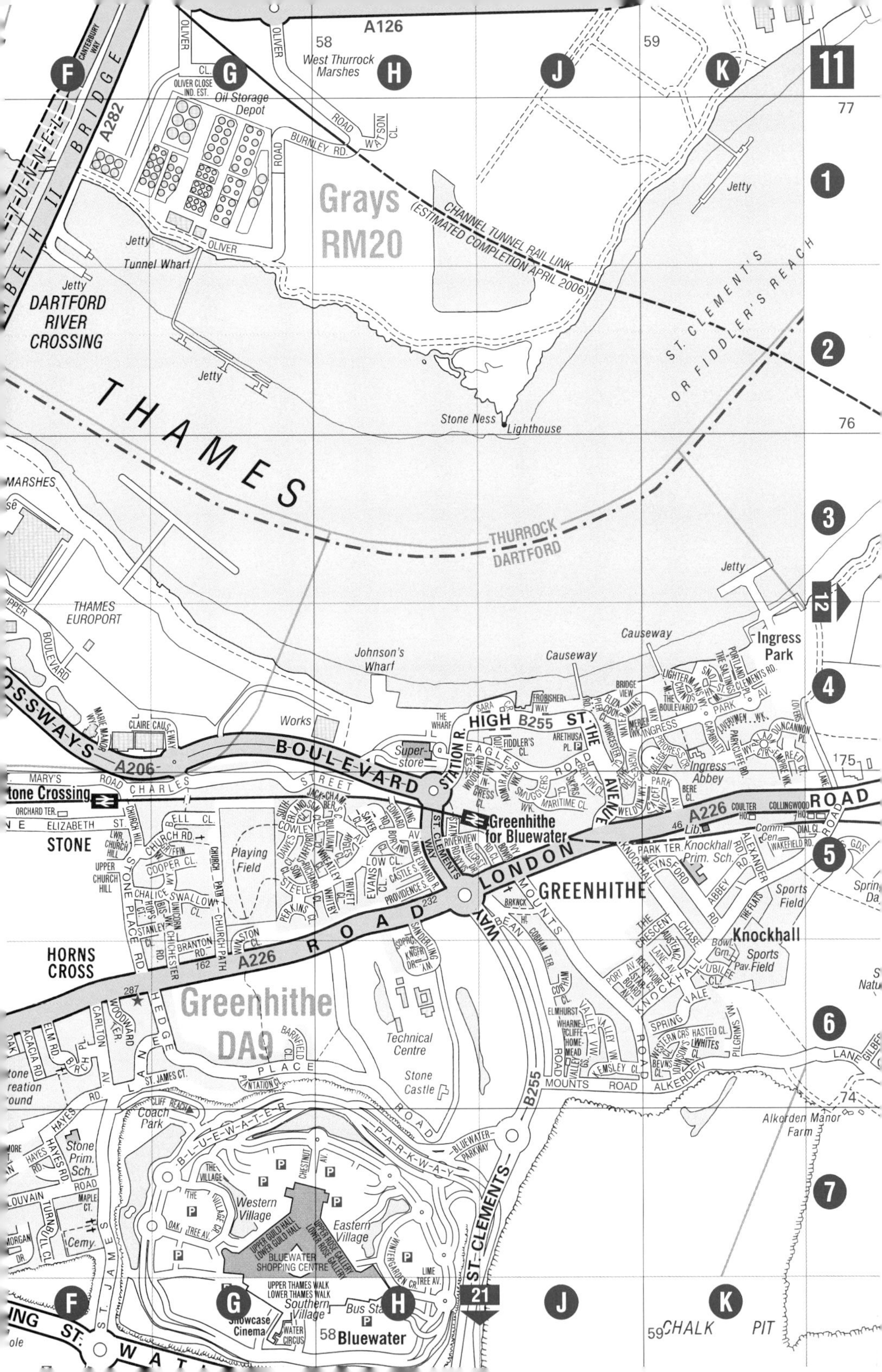

11
A126
58
59
77
76
175
74
West Thurrock Marshes
Oil Storage Depot
OLIVER CLOSE IND. EST.
OLIVER CL.
OLIVER ROAD
WATSON CL.
BURNLEY RD.
OLIVER
Jetty
Tunnel Wharf
DARTFORD RIVER CROSSING
QUEEN ELIZABETH II BRIDGE
A282
CANTERBURY WAY
Grays RM20
CHANNEL TUNNEL RAIL LINK (ESTIMATED COMPLETION APRIL 2006)
ST. CLEMENT'S OR FIDDLER'S REACH
THAMES
Stone Ness
Lighthouse
THURROCK
DARTFORD
MARSHES
THAMES EUROPORT
UPPER BOULEVARD
CROSSWAYS
A206
BOULEVARD
CLAIRE CAUSEWAY
MARIE MANOR WY.
Works
Johnson's Wharf
Causeway
Ingress Park
Ingress Abbey
HIGH B255 ST.
THE WHARF
STATION R.
Superstore
FIDDLER'S CL.
ARETHUSA PL.
THE AVENUE
INGRESS PARK AV.
SMUGGLERS WAY
MARITIME CL.
WELDON WY.
LOVERS LANE
DUNCANNON PL.
EMPIRE WK.
REED CL.
PORTLAND PL.
THE SALTINGS
ST. CLEMENTS RD.
CAPABILITY WY.
Stone Crossing
MARY'S ROAD
CHARLES STREET
ORCHARD TER.
ELIZABETH ST.
STONE
CHURCH HILL
LWR. CHURCH HILL
UPPER CHURCH HILL
BELL CL.
CHURCH RD.
COOPER CL.
SWALLOW CL.
CHALICE WY.
STONE PLACE RD.
STANLEY CL.
BRANTON RD.
CHURCH PATH
Playing Field
COWLEY AV.
KING EDWARD R.
PROVIDENCE S.
EVANS CL.
LOW CL.
TRIVETT CL.
WHITBY
ST. CLEMENTS WAY
Greenhithe for Bluewater
RIVERVIEW
LONDON
ROAD
A226
232
162
287
HORNS CROSS
GREENHITHE
MOUNTS ROAD
BEAN
COBHAM TER.
SANDERLING WY.
Greenhithe DA9
Technical Centre
Stone Castle
BARNFIELD
PLACE
PLANTATION CL.
ST. JAMES CT.
HEDGE
LANE
WOODWARD TER.
CARLTON AV.
ELM RD.
ACACIA RD.
BIRCH PL.
COULTER HO.
COLLINGWOOD HO.
Lib.
Comm. Cen.
WAKEFIELD RD.
DIAL CL.
PARK TER.
Knockhall Prim. Sch.
EYNSFORD
KNOCKHALL
ALEXANDER RD.
ABBEY RD.
THE FLATS
Sports Field
Knockhall
Knockhall Sports Field
Bowl. Grn.
Pav.
THE CRESCENT
CHASE
JUBILEE
VALE
PORT AV.
SPRING VALE
WESTERN CRS
HASTED CL.
WHITES CL.
PILGRIMS WA.
BEVNS CL.
ELMHURST
WHARNECLIFFE
HOMEMEAD
VALLEY VW.
EMSLEY CL.
MOUNTS ROAD
ALKERDEN LANE
Alkerden Manor Farm
B255
BLUEWATER PARKWAY
CLIFF REACH
Coach Park
HAYES RD.
Stone Prim. Sch.
LOUVAIN
TURNBULL CL.
MAPLE CT.
Cemy.
THE VILLAGE
Western Village
OAK TREE AV.
CHESTNUT AV.
Eastern Village
WINTERGARDEN CR.
LIME TREE AV.
UPPER GUILD HALL
LOWER GUILD HALL
UPPER ROSE GALLERY
LOWER ROSE GALLERY
BLUEWATER SHOPPING CENTRE
UPPER THAMES WALK
LOWER THAMES WALK
Southern Village
Bus Sta
Showcase Cinema
WATER CIRCUS
58 Bluewater
ST. CLEMENTS WAY
21
12
ST. JAMES
WATLING ST.
59 CHALK PIT
F
G
H
J
K
1
2
3
4
5
6
7

RIVER
THURROCK
DARTFORD
ST. CLEMENT'S OR FIDDLER'S REACH
NORTHFLEET HOPE
Thurrock Yacht Club
Grays Beach Riverside Park
Boating Pool
Causeway
Jetty
Lighthouse
Radar Sta.
Broadness Salt Marshes
DARTFORD
GRAVESHAM
Pier
Bell Wharf
Swanscombe Marshes
CHANNEL TUNNEL RAIL LINK (EST. COMP. APRIL 2006)
Sewage Works
Botany Marshes
MANOR WAY
GREEN MANOR WAY
LOWER ROAD
MANOR (BOTANY ROAD) WAY
Depot
Wharf
Works
Tower Wharf
Warehouses
Ingress Park
DA9
Works
NORTHFLEET INDUSTRIAL ESTATE
KENT KRAFT INDUSTRIAL ESTATE
SWANSCOMBE BUSINESS CEN.
Resr.
Gravesend & Northfleet FC
LONDON ROAD
A226
GALLEY HILL ROAD
HIGH ST.
GALLEY HILL INDUSTRIAL ESTATE
EBBSFLEET INDUSTRIAL ESTATE
Swanscombe
Springfield Lodge Day Nursery
Sports Field
Knockhall
Sports Pav. Field
Swanscombe Leisure Cen.
Skull Site Nature Reserve
Recreation Ground
SWANSCOMBE
STANHOPE RD.
B259
SOUTHFLEET ROAD
Ten. Ct.
Rec. Grd.
Cemy.
Lib.
Swan Valley Comm. Sch.
The Sweyne Jun. & Inf. Sch.
Alkerden Manor Farm
Swanscombe
DA10
Ebbsfleet (Due Open 2007)
College
Tennis Cts.
Wks.
STONEBRIDGE RD.
THAMES WAY
Northfleet
Ebbsfleet
Sewage Works
CHALK PIT
560
61
77
76
75
74
A B C D E
1 2 3 4 5 6 7
11
22

13
TILBURY MARSHES
Tilbury FC Ground
Tilbury North Junction
Rail Container Terminal
Superstore
DOCK ROAD
PARK WAY
Tilbury Go-Karting Track
Playing Field
The Gateway Comm. Coll.
A126
ST. CHADS ROAD
LEIGHTON GDS.
MELBA GDS.
RAPHAEL
SULLIVAN RD.
ELGAR GDS.
GAINSBOROUGH AV.
King George's Field
Mills
Grain Terminal
Warehouse
TILBURY DOCKS
No. 1 Gate Main Entrance
Warehouses
Works
ST. ANDREW'S ROAD
A1089
FERRY ROAD
Tilbury
Tilbury Town
RM18
LEICESTER ROAD
FAIRFAX
DARWIN
ADELAIDE
CALCUTTA
STEPHENSON AV.
CHRISTCHURCH ROAD
TORONTO RD.
OTTAWA RD.
QUEBEC RD.
MANOR RD.
CIVIC SQ.
MONTREAL RD.
NEWTON
HUME
DOCK RD.
TILBURY
Aggregates Terminal
Cement Terminal
Bulk Metal Terminal
Northfleet Hope Container Terminal
Rolling Lift Bridge
Locks
TILBURY FREE PORT
Tilbury Ness
Swing Bridge
Jetty
Pier
RIVERSIDE APPROACH
RIVERSIDE RAIL FREIGHT TERMINAL
FORTRESS DISTRIBUTION PARK
LONDON INTERNATIONAL CRUISE TERMINAL
Tilbury Landing Stage
175
14
THURROCK
GRAVESHAM
T H A M E S
Ferry (Passenger)
GRAVESEND
NORTHFLEET
Wharf
Depot
ROSHERVILLE
Gravesend
HALL ROAD
THE HILL
LONDON ROAD
B2175
DOVER ROAD
DA11
OVERCLIFFE
ROAD
WAY
A226
B261
B256
STUART RD.
BATH ST.
WEST ST.
Superstores
AMF Bowl. Alley
Imperial Bus. Est.
Gravesend
DARNLEY
LENNOX AV.
PELHAM ROAD
WROTHAM RD.
Recreation Ground
SPRINGHEAD RD.
THAMES WAY
PERRY STREET
23
School
F G H J K
1 2 3 4 5 6 7

TILBURY
Tilbury RM18
RIVER
GRAVESEND
Gravesend
MILTON
DENTON
Tilbury Fort
Tilbury Power Station
Sewage Works
Works
Walton Common
West Tilbury Marshes
Parsonage Common
Tilbury Manor Jun. Sch. & Manor Inf. Sch.
Playing Field
Tilbury Leisure Cen.
RIVERSIDE RAIL FREIGHT TERMINAL
FORTRESS DISTRIBUTION PARK
LONDON INTERNATIONAL CRUISE TERMINAL
Tilbury Landing Stage
Ferry (Passenger)
Wharf
Quay
Causeway
Bill Meroy Creek
Jetty
Royal Terrace Pier
Town Pier
St. Andrew's Gds.
Chantry Heritage Cen.
Riverside Leisure Area
Canal Basin
Timber Yard
London Port Health Authority
Denton Wharf
Slipways
Denton Marshes
Sewage Works
CANAL INDUSTRIAL PARK
Sports Ground
St. John's RC Sch.
A226
A227
MILTON ROAD
E. MILTON RD.
ROCHESTER RD.
WROTHAM RD.
DOCK RD.
ST. CHADS RD.
MONTREAL RD.
FORT ROAD
HIGHWAY
FEENAN HIGHWAY
CIVIC SQ.
LONDON RD.
BRENNAN RD.
SANDHURST RD.
PORTSEA RD.
STEPHENSON AV.
GAINSBOROUGH AV.
DICKENS AV.
BATH ST.
WEST ST.
THE TER.
PARROCK ST.
WINDMILL ST.
DARNLEY RD.
ROYAL PIER RD.
GORDON PROMENADE
WHARF RD.
DENTON
Westcott Marsh
A
B
C
D
E
1
2
3
4
5
6
7
13
24
565
66
175
76
74

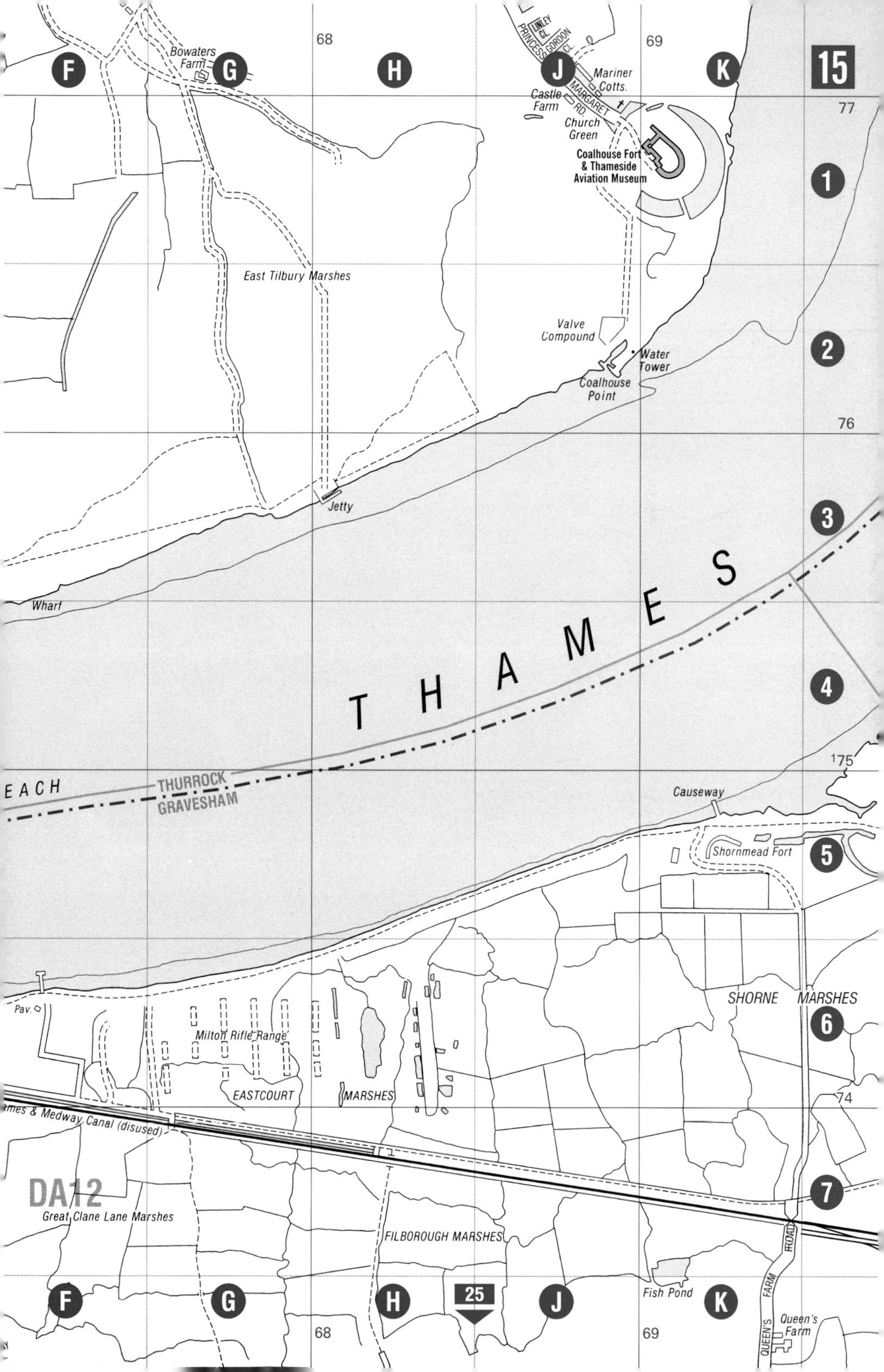

F
G
Bowaters
Farm
68
H
69
J
K
15
77
1

LUMLEY CL.
PRINCESS GORDON CL.
MARGARET RD
Mariner
Cotts.
Castle
Farm
Church
Green
Coalhouse Fort
& Thameside
Aviation Museum

East Tilbury Marshes

Valve
Compound
Water
Tower
Coalhouse
Point

2

76

3

Jetty

Wharf

T H A M E S

4

175

E A C H
THURROCK
GRAVESHAM

Causeway

Shornmead Fort

5

SHORNE   MARSHES

6

74

Pav.

Milton Rifle Range

EASTCOURT   MARSHES

mes & Medway Canal (disused)

DA12
Great Clane Lane Marshes

FILBOROUGH MARSHES

Fish Pond

QUEEN'S FARM ROAD
Queen's
Farm

F
68
G
H
25
J
69
K
7

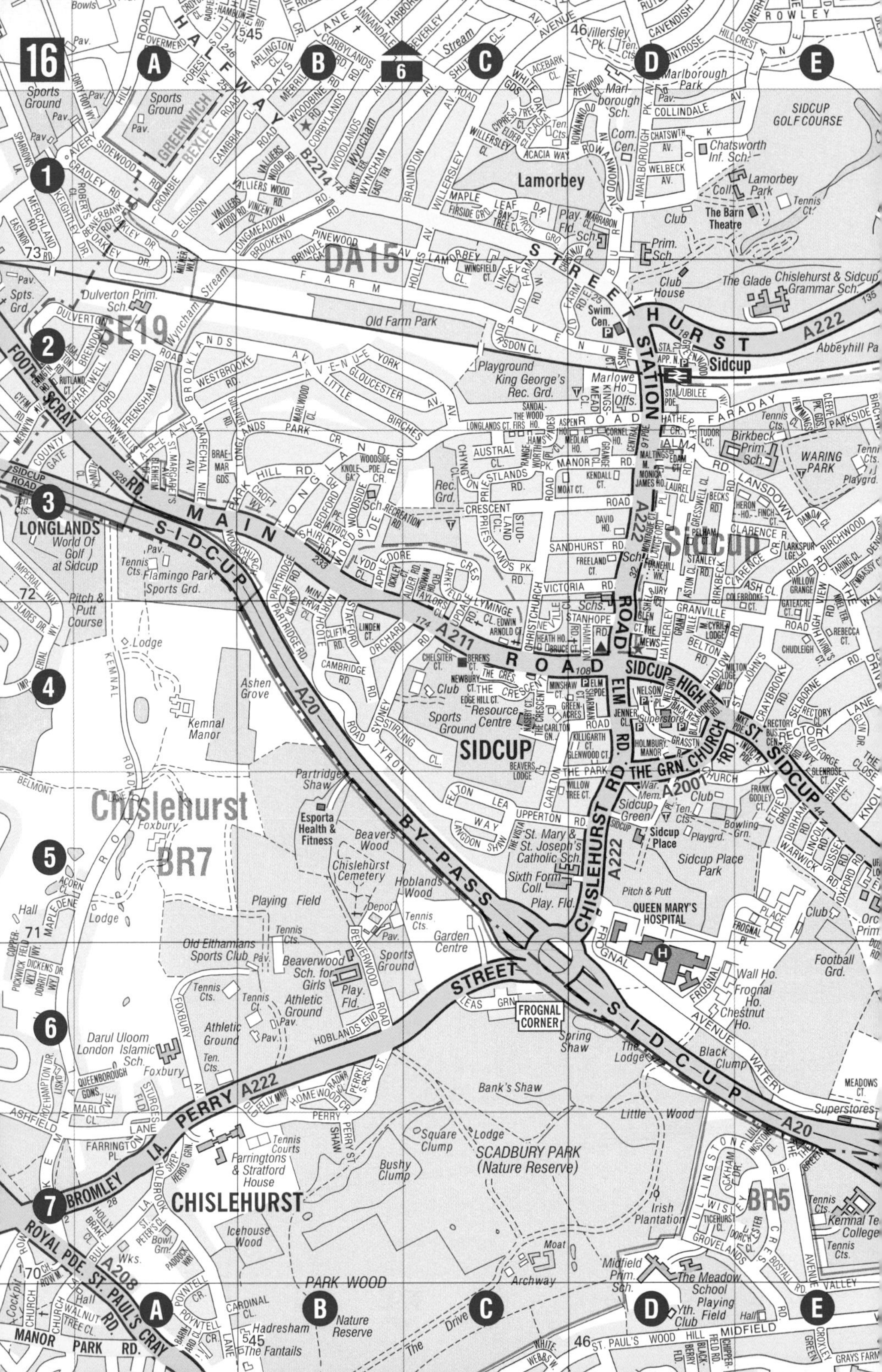

A
B
C
D
E
6
1
2
3
4
5
6
7
Lamorbey
DA15
SE19
Sidcup
SIDCUP
Chislehurst
BR7
CHISLEHURST
BR5
LONGLANDS
SIDCUP GOLF COURSE
Old Farm Park
King George's Rec. Grd.
QUEEN MARY'S HOSPITAL
SCADBURY PARK (Nature Reserve)
FROGNAL CORNER
Sidcup Place Park
Kemnal Manor
Ashen Grove
Chislehurst Cemetery
Hoblands Wood
Beavers Wood
Partridge Shaw
Esporta Health & Fitness
Flamingo Park Sports Grd.
World Of Golf at Sidcup
Pitch & Putt Course
Farringtons & Stratford House
Icehouse Wood
Irish Plantation
Little Wood
Bank's Shaw
Square Clump
Bushy Clump
PARK WOOD Nature Reserve
Chislehurst & Sidcup Grammar Sch.
The Barn Theatre
Lamorbey Park
Kemnal Tech. College
A20
A222
A211
A208
A2001
B2214
SIDCUP BY-PASS
MAIN ROAD
STATION ROAD
HURST ROAD
CHISLEHURST RD.
PERRY STREET
BROMLEY LA.
ROYAL PDE.
ST. PAUL'S CRAY RD.
FOOTS CRAY RD.
SIDCUP HIGH ST.
HALFWAY STREET
MANOR PARK RD.
45
46
70
71
72
73

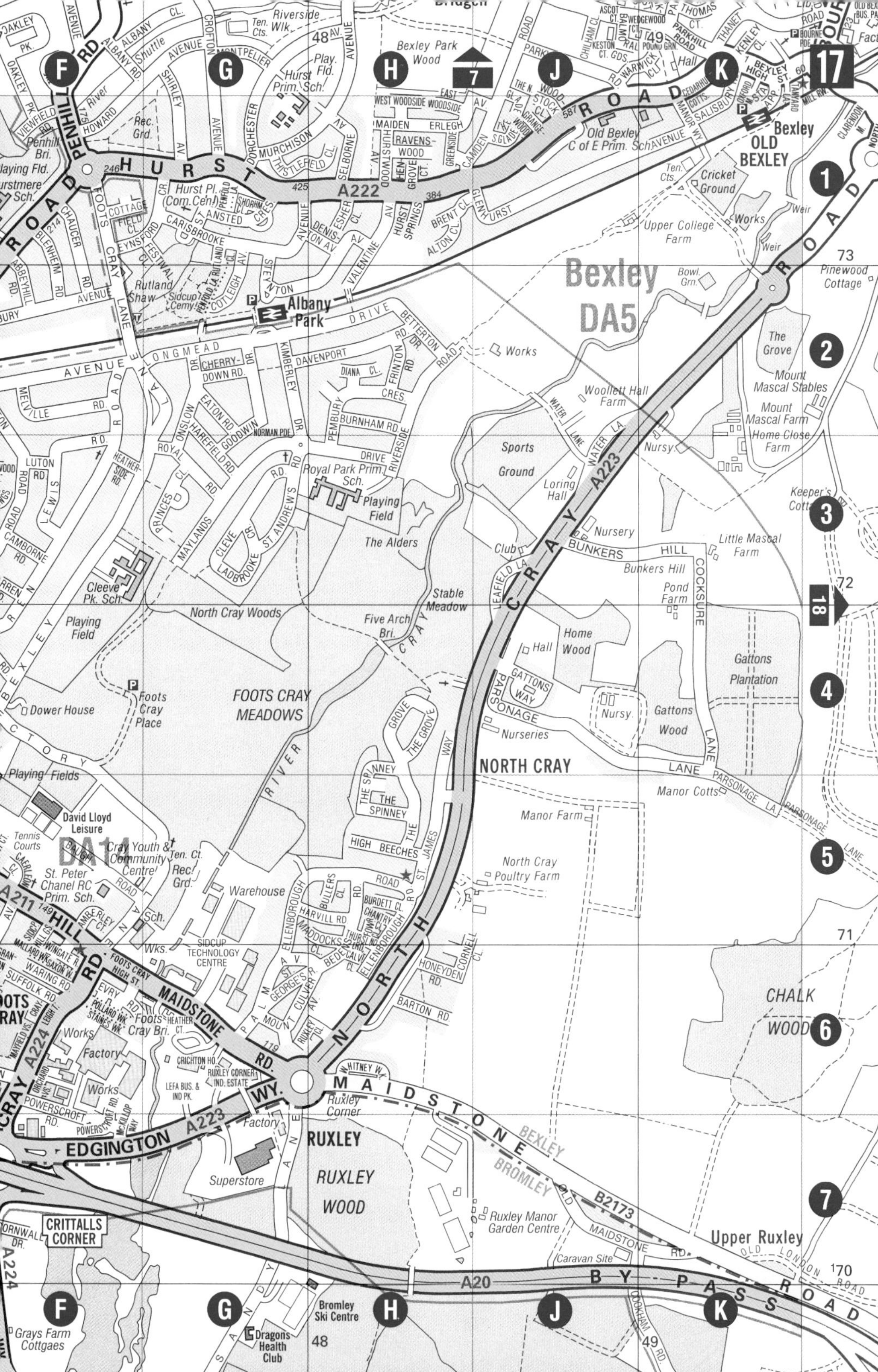

17
Bexley DA5
OLD BEXLEY
Bexley
HURST ROAD
A222
Albany Park
NORTH CRAY ROAD
A223
North Cray Woods
FOOTS CRAY MEADOWS
NORTH CRAY
Foots Cray Place
Dower House
David Lloyd Leisure
DA14
MAIDSTONE RD.
EDGINGTON WY.
RUXLEY
RUXLEY WOOD
Ruxley Corner
Superstore
CRITTALLS CORNER
A20
BY PASS ROAD
Bromley Ski Centre
Dragons Health Club
Grays Farm Cottgaes
CHALK WOOD
Upper Ruxley
Ruxley Manor Garden Centre
B2173
BEXLEY
BROMLEY
Gattons Plantation
Gattons Wood
Home Wood
Bunkers Hill
Pond Farm
Little Mascal Farm
Mount Mascal Stables
Mount Mascal Farm
Home Close Farm
The Grove
Pinewood Cottage
Upper College Farm
Cricket Ground
Woollett Hall Farm
Sports Ground
Loring Hall
Royal Park Prim. Sch.
Cleeve Pk. Sch.
Bexley Park Wood
Hurst Prim. Sch.
Old Bexley C of E Prim. Sch.
North Cray Poultry Farm
Manor Farm
Manor Cotts.
Sidcup Technology Centre
Warehouse
St. Peter Chanel RC Prim. Sch.
Cray Youth & Community Centre
Five Arch Bri.
Stable Meadow
The Alders
Playing Field
Rutland Shaw
Sidcup Cemy.
7
18
F G H J K
1 2 3 4 5 6 7
48 49 70 71 72 73

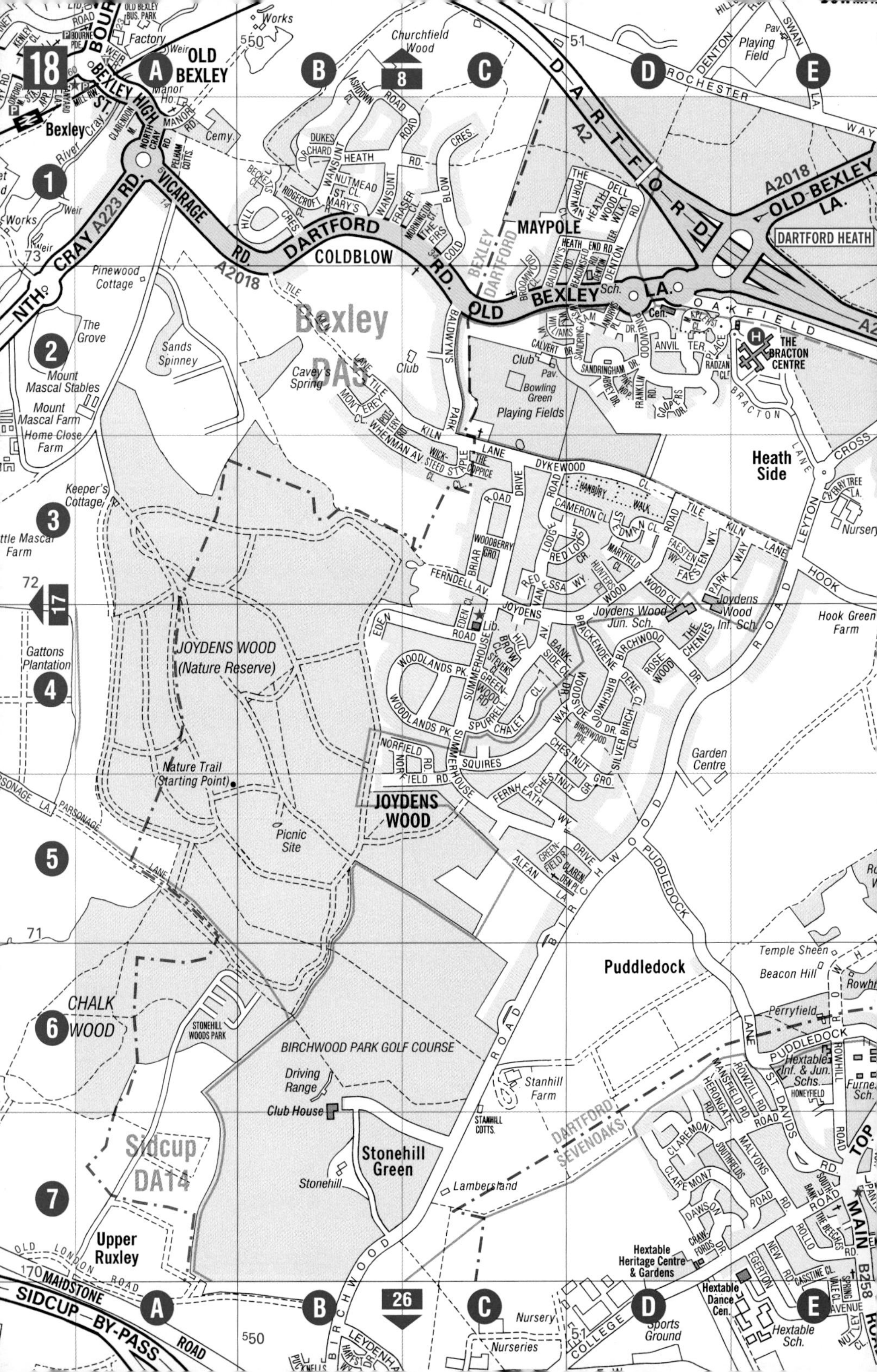

A
B
C
D
E
1
2
3
4
5
6
7
8
17
26
OLD BEXLEY
Bexley
Works
Factory
OLD BEXLEY BUS. PARK
Weir
Manor Ho.
Cemy.
River Cray
BOURNE
BEXLEY HIGH ST.
NORTH CRAY RD.
MANOR RD.
PELHAM COTTS.
CLARENDON M.
NTH. CRAY RD. A223
VICARAGE RD.
DARTFORD RD.
A2018
COLDBLOW
Churchfield Wood
ASHDOWN CL.
ROAD
DUKES ORCHARD
HEATH RD.
WANSUNT RD.
NUTMEAD CL.
ST. MARY'S
RIDGECROFT CL.
BECKETS CL.
HILL CRES.
FRASER CL.
MORNINGTON
THE FIRS
BLOW CRES.
COLD BLOW
DARTFORD
A2
MAYPOLE
BEXLEY
THE PORTMAN
HEATH WOOD
DELL WLK.
HEATH END RD.
DENTON TER.
OLD BEXLEY LA.
A2018
OLD BEXLEY LA.
DARTFORD HEATH
ROCHESTER WAY
DENTON
Playing Field
Pav.
SWAN LA.
HILL
OAKFIELD
THE BRACTON CENTRE
BRACTON
Heath Side
CROSS
CHERRY TREE LA.
Nursery
LEYTON
HOOK LANE
Hook Green Farm
Pinewood Cottage
The Grove
Sands Spinney
Mount Mascal Stables
Mount Mascal Farm
Home Close Farm
Keeper's Cottage
Little Mascal Farm
Gattons Plantation
Bexley DA5
Cavey's Spring
Club
TILE KILN LANE
MONTEREY CL.
WHENMAN AV.
WICKSTEED CL.
STAPLE CL.
THE COPPICE
BALDWYN'S PARK
Pav.
Bowling Green
Playing Fields
Club
CALVERT DR.
WILLIAMS
SANDRINGHAM DR.
PINEWOOD DR.
ANVIL TER.
PLACE
RADZAN CL.
FRANKLIN RD.
COOPERS DR.
Sch.
Cen.
DYKEWOOD CL.
HANBURY WALK
CAMERON CL.
STEDMAN CL.
TILE KILN LANE
FAESTEN WY.
PARK WAY
LODGE
RED LODGE CR.
MARYFIELD CL.
HUNTERS
WOOD CL.
WOODBERRY GRO.
BRIAR RD.
DRIVE
ROAD
FERNDELL AV.
VANESSA WY.
JOYDENS AV.
EDEN RD.
EDEN CL.
Lib.
Joydens Wood Jun. Sch.
Joydens Wood Inf. Sch.
THE CHENIES
BRACKENDENE
BIRCHWOOD DR.
ROSEWOOD
ROAD
BROW CL.
HILL
STEVENS CL.
BANKSIDE CL.
WOODLANDS PK.
SUMMERHOUSE DR.
GREENWOOD RD.
SPURRELL AV.
CHALET CL.
WOODSIDE WAY
BIRCHWOOD DR.
DENE CL.
SILVER BIRCH CL.
CHESTNUT GRO.
NORFIELD RD.
SQUIRES
FERNHEATH WY.
JOYDENS WOOD
JOYDENS WOOD (Nature Reserve)
Nature Trail (Starting Point)
Picnic Site
PARSONAGE LA.
PARSONAGE LANE
ALFAN LA.
GREENFIELD DR.
CLARENDEN PL.
Garden Centre
BIRCHWOOD ROAD
PUDDLEDOCK
Puddledock
Temple Sheen
Beacon Hill
Rowhill
Perryfield
PUDDLEDOCK LANE
Hextable Inf. & Jun. Schs.
HONEYFIELD
ROWHILL ROAD
Furner Sch.
CHALK WOOD
STONEHILL WOODS PARK
BIRCHWOOD PARK GOLF COURSE
Driving Range
Club House
Stonehill Green
Stonehill
Stanhill Farm
STANHILL COTTS.
Lambersland
DARTFORD SEVENOAKS
Sidcup DA14
Upper Ruxley
OLD LONDON ROAD
MAIDSTONE ROAD
SIDCUP BY-PASS
LEYDENHATCH
HARVEST
Nursery
Nurseries
MANSFIELD RD.
ROWZILL RD.
HERONGATE RD.
ST. DAVIDS RD.
CLAREMONT
SOUTHFIELDS
MALYONS ROAD
DAWSON
CRAWFORDS DR.
ROLLO RD.
THE BEECHES
SOUTH BANK ROAD
TOP
MAIN ROAD
B258
Hextable Heritage Centre & Gardens
COLLEGE
Sports Ground
Hextable Dance Cen.
EGERTON
NEW RD.
CASSTINE CL.
SPRING VALE CL.
AVENUE
NUTLEY CL.
Hextable Sch.
550
51
72
73
71
170

19
DARTFORD
9
Dartford Tech. Coll.
Youth Cen.
School for Girls
Tennis Courts
Playing Field
Playing Field
53
54
SHEPHERD'S
LA.
PRINCES
HEATHVIEW
HEATHCLOSE
ORCHARD AV.
COWDREY CL.
DERWENT
EGERTON
LINKS VW.
WINDERMERE CL.
CONISTON CL.
HEATH LANE
BLACKMANS CL.
WILLOW
LAUREL CL.
OLIVE
SYCAMORE RD.
HOLLY RD.
CHESTNUT RD.
LARCH RD.
HIGHFIELD
PHOENIX PLACE
GORDON RD.
THATCHER RD.
VAUXHALL PL.
CENTRAL PARK
Fairfield Pool & Leisure Cent.
Central Park Arena
CRANFORD RD.
INGRAM RD.
Sports
LOWFIELD STREET
B2174 ROAD
PRINCES A225 RD.
Superstores
Superstore
LABURNUM AVENUE
LINDEN AV.
ROWAN CR.
DA1
ASH ROAD
MEAD RD.
MEAD CR.
MEADOWSIDE
LOAM CT.
NORMAN RD.
BROOKLANDS RD.
Brooklands Lake
DARTFORD HEATH
DARTFORD GOLF COURSE
Brickhill Wood
Club Ho.
MAPLE RD.
ELM CL.
ELM RD.
ACACIA RD.
HAWTHORN RD.
HAZEL RD.
CEDAR RD.
BEECH RD.
MYRTLE RD.
Comm. Cen.
GREENACRE
WALNUT TREE AV.
MILL LANE
FAWKES
BUTTERLY
PEARSON
POWDER
APPLEGARTH DR.
QUESTOR
DARTFORD TRADE PARK
HAWLEY
A225
ROAD
73
Playing Field
Miskin Theatre
North West Kent College
Oakfield Schs.
OAKFIELD PK.
THE SPIRES
CARSINGTON GDS.
Pav. Oakfield Park
MONKS ORCHARD
SHEARS CL.
CHURCH HILL
HILL RD.
SACKVILLE RD.
CHURCHILL COPSE
MITCHELL CL.
CHAVE RD.
CHURCH FLD.
CHURCH WLK.
WARREN RD.
WARREN
GOTHIC CL.
CURATES WLK.
Hall
HEATH LANE
COMMON LANE
CLAYTON CFT. RD.
WILMINGTON CT. RD.
MANOR CL.
Rec. Grd.
Grammar Sch. for Girls
PARSONS LA.
HULSEWOOD CL.
OAKFIELD LANE
Dartford
A2
BY PASS
B258
ROAD
Leyton Cross
Turnagain Farm
Wilmington Common Prim. Sch.
Wilmington Hall Sch.
Wilmington Grammar Sch. for Boys
APPLETON DR.
TAYLOR ROW
MARTIN RD.
ALBERT RD.
HURLFIELD
THE CLOSE
EDWIN
LANE
HIGH
GARDEN PL.
LANGWORTH CL.
Day's Farm
Holland's Far.
72
20
Turnagain Croft
Playing Field
LANE
BROAD LANE
Hook Green
ROAD
HIGH
Cen.
WHITEHEAD CL.
BARNEND DR.
GERDVIEW DR.
STOCK LANE
THE LAURELS
STH. VIEW RD.
ORCHARD WY.
Rowhill School
Bybow Farm
DA2
WILMINGTON
MEADOW WLK.
BURR BANK TER.
CAPEL PL.
The Mount
Stanley Morgan House
Lower Barnend
Upper Barnend
Shirehall Farm Cottage
SHIREHALL
BURNT HOUSE LANE
ALFRED RD.
SAXON RD.
ETHELBERT RD.
HAROLD
ASH
MILL
ROAD
Hazelwood
Rowhill Wood
Paxwood
Hotel
71
BARN END
B258 ROAD
HIGHFIELD COTTAGES
DARTFORD
MAUDE RD.
MABEL RD.
HERBERT RD.
NUFFIELD RD.
FENS WAY
MIDFIELD AV.
DURANT
PLANTATION RD.
BOWER
Swanley
ROAD
Bottom
LANE
Wiffen's Farm
GILDENHILL
CLEMENT STREET
Clement Street
Clement Ho.
Sutton's Cotts.
Nursery
Old Mill Equestrian Centre
North View Cotts.
Nursery
M25
M25 MOTORWAY
HEXTABLE
Swanley BR8
Hextable Park
CHURCH
RD.
170
Holt's Farm
Gildenhill Farm
27
ROAD
RD.
St. Paul's C of E Prim. Sch.
SCHOOL
HILL RD.
Highlands Farm
SWANLEY
53
54
F
G
H
J
K
1
2
3
4
5
6
7

20
A
B
C
D
E
1
2
3
4
5
6
7
10
19
28
Junc.1b
PRINCES RD. INTERCHANGE
WATLING STREET
B2500
PRINCES ROAD
A225
A296
A282
B260
DA1
DA4
Dartford
FLEET DOWNS
DARENTH COUNTRY PARK
DARENTH INTERCHANGE
Junction 2
A2
DARTFORD ROAD
HAWLEY ROAD
M25
M25 MOTORWAY
HAWLEY
DARENTH
Lane End
SUTTON AT HONE
MAIN ROAD
Princes Golf & Leisure Club
Next Generation Club
The Leigh City Technology College
Playing Field
Brooklands Lake
Sports Ground
Central Park Arena
DARTFORD TRADE PARK
Claremont Cotts.
Holland's Farm
Hawley Manor
Blackdale Farm Cottages
Blackdale Farm
Trolling Down Hill
Downs Farm
Fleetdown Jun. & Inf. Schs.
Waller Park
Nursing Home
Darenth Grange
DARENTH HILL TRADING EST.
King George's Field
Works
Hawley Garden Centre
Yewtree Farm Nursery
Old Mill Farm
Darenth Court Farm
Depot
The Alders
Summit Farm
Broad Oak
Portway Nursery
Rec. Ground
Cemy.
Sutton at Hone C of E Prim. Sch.
Lib.
St. John's Jerusalem Garden
RIVER DARENT
DARTFORD
SEVENOAKS
ROMAN VILLA ROAD
GORE ROAD
DARENTH ROAD
PARSONAGE LANE
CLEMENT STREET
CHURCH ROAD
HOLMESDALE
555
56
73
72
71
70

Grid references (top): F, G, H, J, K with page number **21**

Major place names:
- Greenhithe DA9
- CHALK PIT
- DA10
- Bluewater
- Bluewater Shopping Centre
- Showcase Cinema
- Western Village
- Eastern Village
- Southern Village
- Water Circus
- Upper Thames Walk, Lower Thames Walk
- Upper Guild Hall, Lower Guild Hall
- Bus Sta.
- DARENT VALLEY HOSPITAL
- Arrow Riding Centre
- DARENTH WOOD
- DA2
- Badgers Mount
- JJ's Gun Club
- BEAN
- Nurseries
- Ightham Cotts.
- Nursery
- Hope Cotts.
- Bean House
- Bean Farm
- The Thrift
- Stonewood
- BLUE HILL COT.
- Beacon Wood Country Park
- Bean Prim. Sch.
- Bean Hill Cotts.
- Shellbank
- LADIES WOOD
- LORDS WOOD
- Darenth Hall
- Darenth Prim. Sch.
- Playing Field
- Stanley Cotts.
- GREEN STREET GREEN
- WOODVIEW
- Manor Farm
- Warrigal Farm
- SANDBANKS
- Westwood
- Malt House Farm
- St. Margarets
- St. Margaret's Farm
- Walnut Tree Farm
- Grubb Street
- Ryecrofts Farm
- Ryecrofts Wood
- Gill's Farm
- Works

Roads:
- WATLING STREET
- ST. JAMES
- ST. CLEMENTS RD.
- BEAN ST.
- B255
- A296
- A2
- BY-PASS
- BEAN LANE
- HIGH ST.
- SOUTHFLEET ROAD
- B255
- SANDY LA.
- PAGE CLOSE
- STONEWOOD
- BRAMBLE AV.
- BEACON RD.
- TURNER RD.
- SCHOOL
- DRIVE
- DARENTH WOOD ROAD
- DARENTH LANE
- GREEN STREET
- B260 ROAD
- SHELLBANK
- B262
- HILL
- BETSHAM
- HIGHCROSS RD.
- GREEN ROAD
- B260
- ST. MARGARETS
- GILLS
- MAPLE CT.
- OAK TREE AV.
- LIME TREE AV.
- THE WILLOWS
- LANGLANDS
- RIDGEWAY

Grid numbers (right): 1, 2, 3, 4, 5, 6, 7 and 59, 73, 72, 71, 70, 58

Continuation markers: 11, 22, 29, 58, 59

Grid references (bottom): F, G, H, J, K

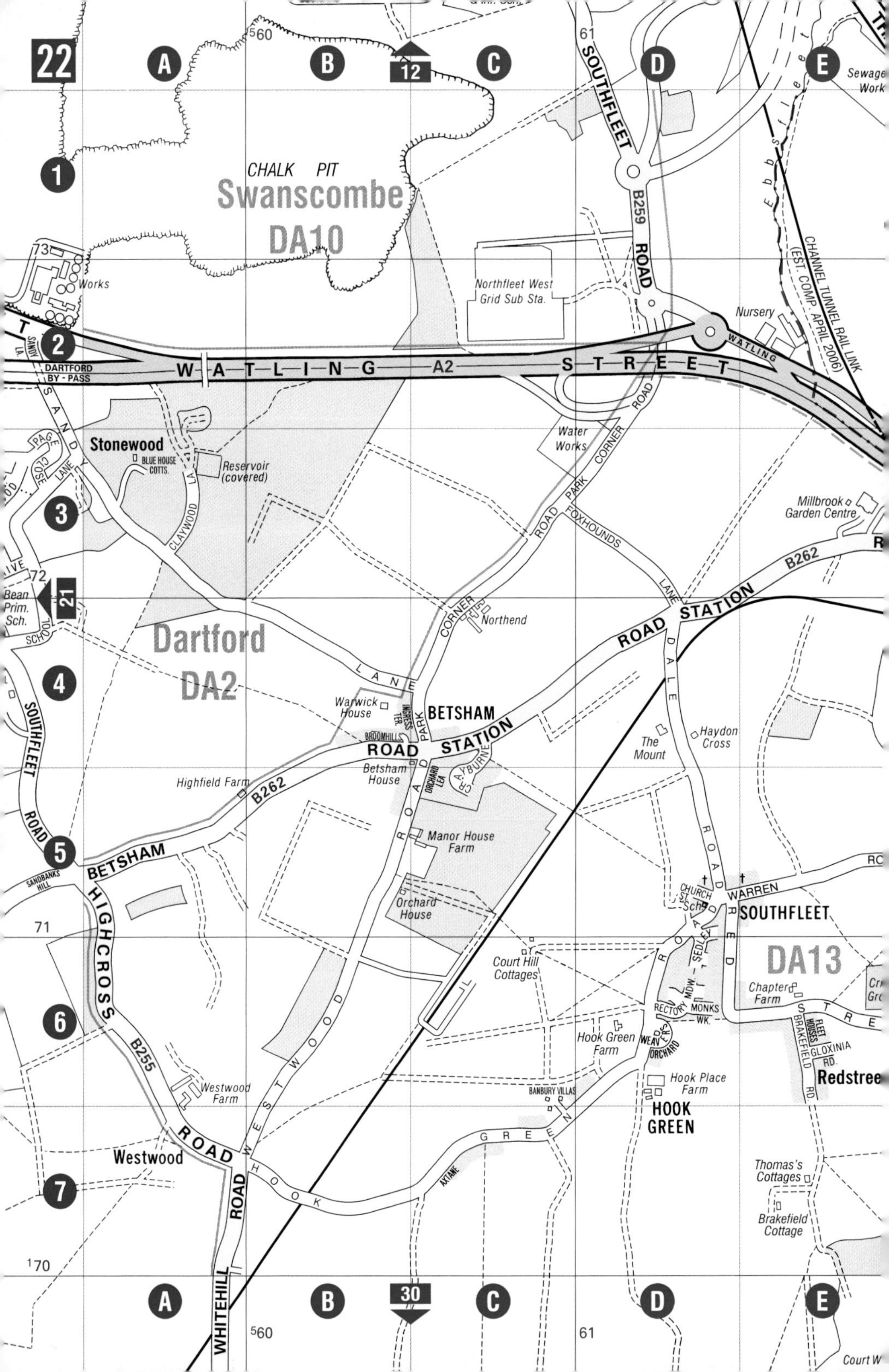

A
B
C
D
E
12
CHALK PIT
Swanscombe
DA10
Works
SANDY LA.
DARTFORD BY-PASS
WATLING STREET
A2
SOUTHFLEET
B259 ROAD
Northfleet West Grid Sub Sta.
Nursery
WATLING
CHANNEL TUNNEL RAIL LINK (EST. COMP. APRIL 2006)
Sewage Work
Ebbsfleet
Stonewood
BLUE HOUSE COTTS.
Reservoir (covered)
CLAYWOOD LA.
PAGE CLOSE
SANDY LANE
Water Works
PARK CORNER ROAD
FOXHOUNDS LANE
Millbrook Garden Centre
B262
STATION ROAD
Bean Prim. Sch.
SCHOOL
21
Dartford
DA2
Northend
CORNER LANE
Warwick House
INGRESS TER.
BETSHAM
BROOMHILLS
ROAD
STATION
PARK ROAD
Betsham House
ORCHARD LEA
CRAYBURNE
DALE ROAD
The Mount
Haydon Cross
Highfield Farm
B262
Manor House Farm
SOUTHFLEET ROAD
BETSHAM
SANDBANKS HILL
HIGHCROSS
Orchard House
CHURCH ST.
Sch.
WARREN
SOUTHFLEET
DA13
RED STREET
Court Hill Cottages
SEDLEY
RECTORY MDW.
MONKS WK.
Chapter Farm
FLEET HOUSES
BRAKEFIELD RD.
GLOXINIA RD.
Redstree
Hook Green Farm
WEAVERS ORCHARD
WESTWOOD
B255
Westwood Farm
BANBURY VILLAS
Hook Place Farm
HOOK GREEN
GREEN
ROAD
Westwood
HOOK
AXTANE
WHITEHILL ROAD
Thomas's Cottages
Brakefield Cottage
30
Court W
560
61
73
72
71
170
1
2
3
4
5
6
7

23
13
24
31
F
G
H
J
K
1
2
3
4
5
6
7
DA11
Gravesend
PERRY STREET
NEW HOUSE
Pepper Hill
Northfleet Green
ISTEAD RISE
DOVER RD.
THAMES WAY A226
SPRINGHEAD ROAD A2260
EAST OLD ROAD B261 WEST
WROTHAM ROAD A227
WATLING STREET A2
CHANNEL TUNNEL RAIL LINK
COLDHARBOUR ROAD
Wombwell Park
Northfleet Technology College
Cygnet Leisure Centre
Northfleet Sch. for Girls
Woodlands Park
St. George's C of E Sch.
MID KENT GOLF COURSE
Lions Hospice
Superstore
Madam Wood
Manor Farm
Northfleet Green Farm
Willerby Farm
Huntdown Wood
Chalk Hole Shaw
Marlboro Boarding Kennels
DARTFORD
GRAVESHAM

24
14
23
A
B
C
D
E
1
2
3
4
5
6
7
GRAVESEND
Sports Ground
Playing Field
St. John's RC Sch.
St. John's RC Prim. Sch.
WESTCOURT
KINGS FARM
Parrock Farm
Christian Fields
SINGLEWELL
RIVERVIEW PARK
MID KENT GOLF COURSE
Club House
DA11
DA13
Ifield
Ifield Court
Hever Court Farm
New Cottages
Chalk Hole Shaw
Cricket Ground
Claylane Wood
Feeder Station
Henhurst Dale
Twenty Acre Wood
CHANNEL TUNNEL RAIL LINK
WATLING STREET
A2
A226
A227
B261
ROCHESTER ROAD
OLD ROAD EAST
EAST ROAD
WROTHAM ROAD
VALLEY DRIVE
WHITEHILL ROAD
SINGLEWELL ROAD
Convent
Convent Prep. Sch.
Thamesview Sch.
Raynehurst Schs.
Riverview Jun. & Inf. Schs.
Kings Farm Prim. Sch.
Ifield Sch.
Springfield Lodge Day Nursery
Sports & Social Club
Playing Field
Reservoir (Covered)
Comm. Cen.
Recreation Ground
Singlewell Prim. Sch.
Subway
Windmill Hill
71
72
73
170
565
66

25
15
Great Clane Lane Marshes
FILBOROUGH MARSHES
Fish Pond
Queen's Farm
Queen's Farm Cotts.
Eastcourt Cotts.
Filborough Farm
Piggery
East Court Manor
HIGHAM
LOWER ROAD
QUEEN'S FARM ROAD
CHALK
ROCHESTER ROAD
Polperro
CHURCH LANE
The Cottage
Longten's Cotts.
Chalkpit Cotts.
Green Farm
New Cotts.
GREEN FARM
Homelea Farm
Golden Knob
Gravesend
Thames View Golf Course
Driving Range
Club Ho.
Ten. Cts.
Cascades
Club House
SOUTHERN VALLEY GOLF COURSE
DA12
MUGGINS LANE
GRAVESEND ROAD
A226
Lower Shorne
Robinson's Cotts.
BURDETT AV.
COUTTS AV.
CROWN LANE
MALTHOUSE LA.
CROWN GN.
Smith's Farm
The Warren
SHORNE
Prim. Sch.
Shorne Hill
HOLLANDS CL.
SWILLER'S LA.
WARREN VIEW
Harts Hill
Cats Wood
Ifield Farm
SHORNE IFIELD ROAD
Orchard Lea Farm
Brummelhill Wood
Westwood Farm
THONG
Cheneys Farm
Randall Bottom
Randall Heath
Thong Lodge
RANDALL WOOD
Fenn Wood
SHORNE RIDGEWAY
Starmore Wood
RIDGEWAY BUNGALOWS
PEARTREE LANE
BOWESDEN LA.
Furze Bank
THE RIDGEWAY
WOODLANDS ROAD
Rec. Grd.
Furzy Leas Wood
Gravelhill Wood
New Fish Pond
Old Fish Pond
SHORNE WOOD COUNTRY PARK
Shorne Wood Country Park Visitors Centre
Puckle Hill
BREWERS WOOD
Motel
The Square
Scalers Hill
BREWERS RD.
PARK PALE LA.
F
G
H
J
K
68
69
73
72
71
170
1
2
3
4
5
6
7

A
B
C
D
E
550
51
18
1
2
3
4
5
6
7
68
67
170
69
DA14
MAIDSTONE RD.
A20
SWANLEY BY PASS
LONDON ROAD
B2173
Hextable Heritage Cen. & Gdns.
Hextable Dance Cen.
Hextable Sch.
Sports Ground
COLLEGE
Nursery
Nurseries
LEYDENHATCH LANE
NEW BARN ROAD
Miniature Railway
Newbarn Cotts.
SWANLEY PARK
Birchwood Prim. Sch.
Birchwood Corner
COOKHAM ROAD
Burnt House Farm
Quoyne Cotts.
Hockenden Lodge
Lwr. Hockenden Farm
Vinsons Cotts.
TRUNKS ALLEY
HOCKENDEN
Hockenden House
Hogspring Cotts.
Milewood
BOURNE WOOD
Windmill Hill Wood
Play. Fld.
Playing Field
White Oak Leis. Cen.
White Oak Prim. Sch.
NORTHVIEW
Convent Prim. Sch.
Swanley Sch.
Coun. Offs.
Rec. Grd.
St. Mary's C of E Prim. Sch.
Superstore
Lib.
BARTHOLOMEW WY.
HIGH STREET
Swanley
SWANLEY
Works
High Firs Prim. Sch.
B258
BROMLEY
SEVENOAKS
Hook Spring
Tile Kilns Wood
Subway
Football Ground
Club Ho.
Nursery
War Mem.
Rec. Grd.
Pav.
GOLDSEL RD.
Swanley BR8
Petham Court
Fleetfoot Fm.
Prim. Sch.
Peartrees
CROCKENHILL
Cemetery
Crouch Farm
Nursery
The Mount Hall
CROCKENHILL ROAD
CRAY ROAD
EYNSFORD ROAD
Gosenhill Farm
Cherry Orchard
Cemy.
Felma House
Crouch Farm Cottages
Football Ground
Wested Farm Cotts.
Middle Farm Nursery
Willow Farm
Cacketshill Wood
Wested Farm
DALTONS ROAD
Highcroft Hall

Hextable Park
HEXTABLE
SWANLEY VILLAGE
St. Paul's C of E Prim. Sch.
Highlands Farm
HIGHLANDS FARM BUS. PARK
Holt's Farm
Gildenhill Farm
GILDENHILL ROAD
CHURCH RD.
The Orchard
Coldharbour Farm
Nursery
SHIP STREET
SHIP LANE
HIGHLANDS HILL
SWANLEY VILLAGE RD.
WOOD
BUTTON STREET BUS. CENTRE
Keston
The Beeches
Old Place Farm Nurseries
Playing Field
Tweed Hill
Rams Wood
Homefield Cotts.
The Old Bungalow
M25
Franks Park
Dartford DA4
Canada Heights
DARTFORD
SEVENOAKS
M25-MOTORWAY
New Cotts.
Parkwood Hall Sch.
Downsview Inf. & Jun. Schs.
The Olympic Golf & Leisure Centre
FARNINGHAM WOOD
Broom Hill
Junction 3 (M25)
Works
MORETON IND. ESTATE
B2173
Junction 1 (M20)
Hill Farm
Wildacres
Hill House
Hill Farm House
Industrial Estate
TEARDROP CENTRE
PEDHAM PLACE IND. EST.
SWANLEY INTERCHANGE
LONDON ROAD
FARNINGHAM HILL RD.
M20-MOTORWAY
M20
A20
Club House
Covered Reservoir
ROAD MAIN
Coldharbour Farm
The Beacon
Mill House
The Manor Ho.
FARNINGHAM
Little Wested House
Fort Cotts.
PEDHAM PLACE GOLF CENTRE
CROCKENHILL
WESTED
M25 MOTORWAY
SPAREPENNY LANE
Fountain Hoy
Polly Shaw
The Little House
EYNSFORD ROAD
F G H J K
1 2 3 4 5 6 7
53 54
170 69 68 67
19
28

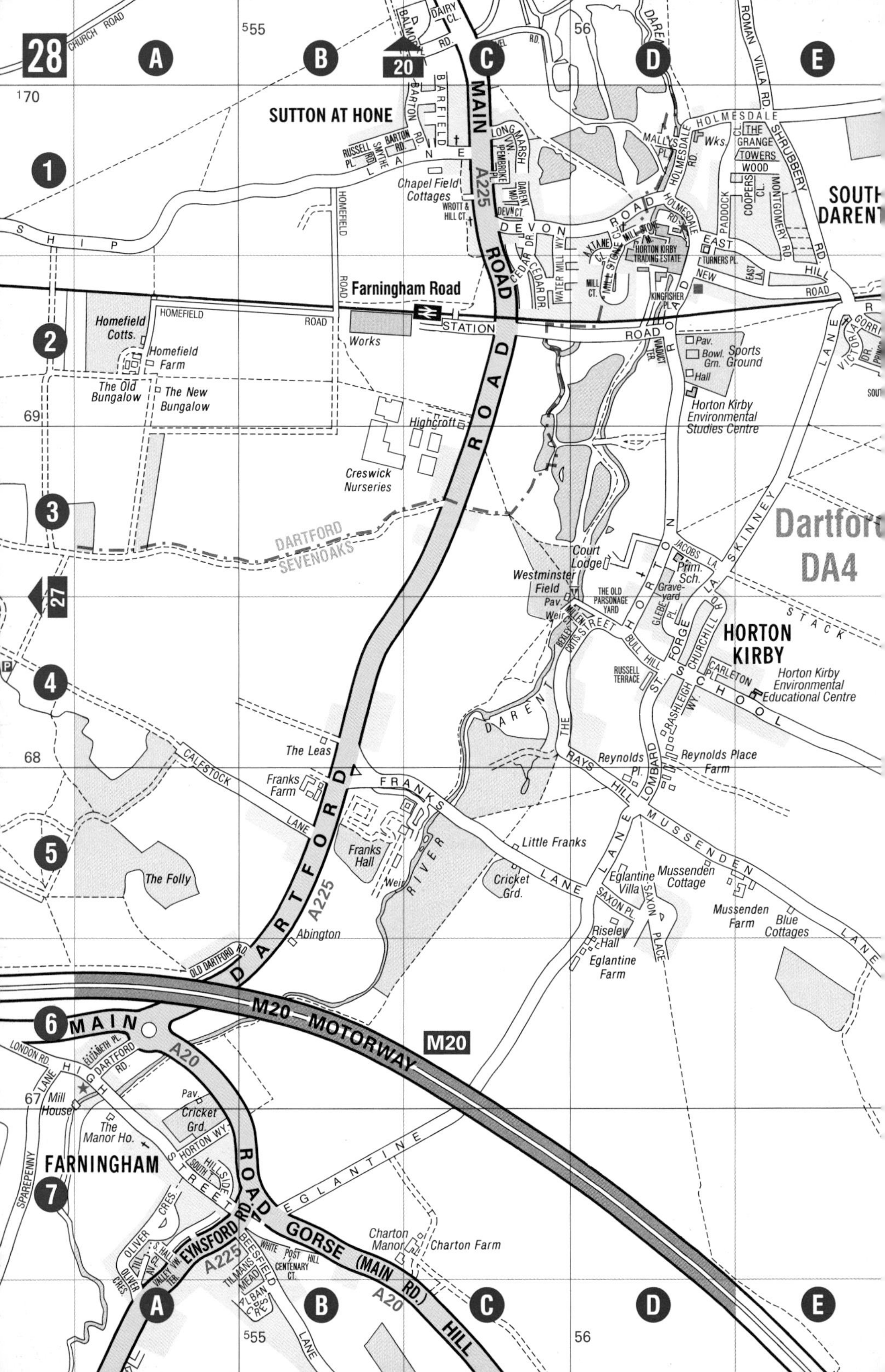

28
A
B
C
D
E
1
2
3
4
5
6
7
555
56
170
69
68
67
20
27
SUTTON AT HONE
SOUTH DARENTH
HORTON KIRBY
FARNINGHAM
Dartford DA4
DARTFORD
SEVENOAKS
Farningham Road
MAIN ROAD
A225
DARTFORD ROAD
M20 MOTORWAY
M20
A20
GORSE (MAIN RD.) HILL
EYNSFORD RD.
EGLANTINE LANE
FRANKS LANE
CALFSTOCK LANE
SHIP LANE
HOMEFIELD ROAD
STATION ROAD
DEVON ROAD
NEW ROAD
HOLMESDALE RD.
ROMAN VILLA RD.
SHRUBBERY RD.
HILL
SKINNEY LA.
STACK LANE
SCHOOL LANE
HORTON ROAD
STREET
BULL HILL
FORGE
MUSSENDEN LANE
LOMBARD
RAYS HILL
SAXON PLACE
RIVER DARENT
CHURCH ROAD
Homefield Cotts.
Homefield Farm
The Old Bungalow
The New Bungalow
Works
Highcroft
Creswick Nurseries
Chapel Field Cottages
Horton Kirby Trading Estate
Sports Ground
Horton Kirby Environmental Studies Centre
Court Lodge
Westminster Field
Prim. Sch.
Grave-yard
Horton Kirby Environmental Educational Centre
Reynolds Place Farm
The Leas
Franks Farm
Franks Hall
Little Franks
Cricket Grd.
Eglantine Villa
Mussenden Cottage
Mussenden Farm
Blue Cottages
Riseley Hall
Eglantine Farm
Abington
The Folly
Mill House
The Manor Ho.
Charton Manor
Charton Farm

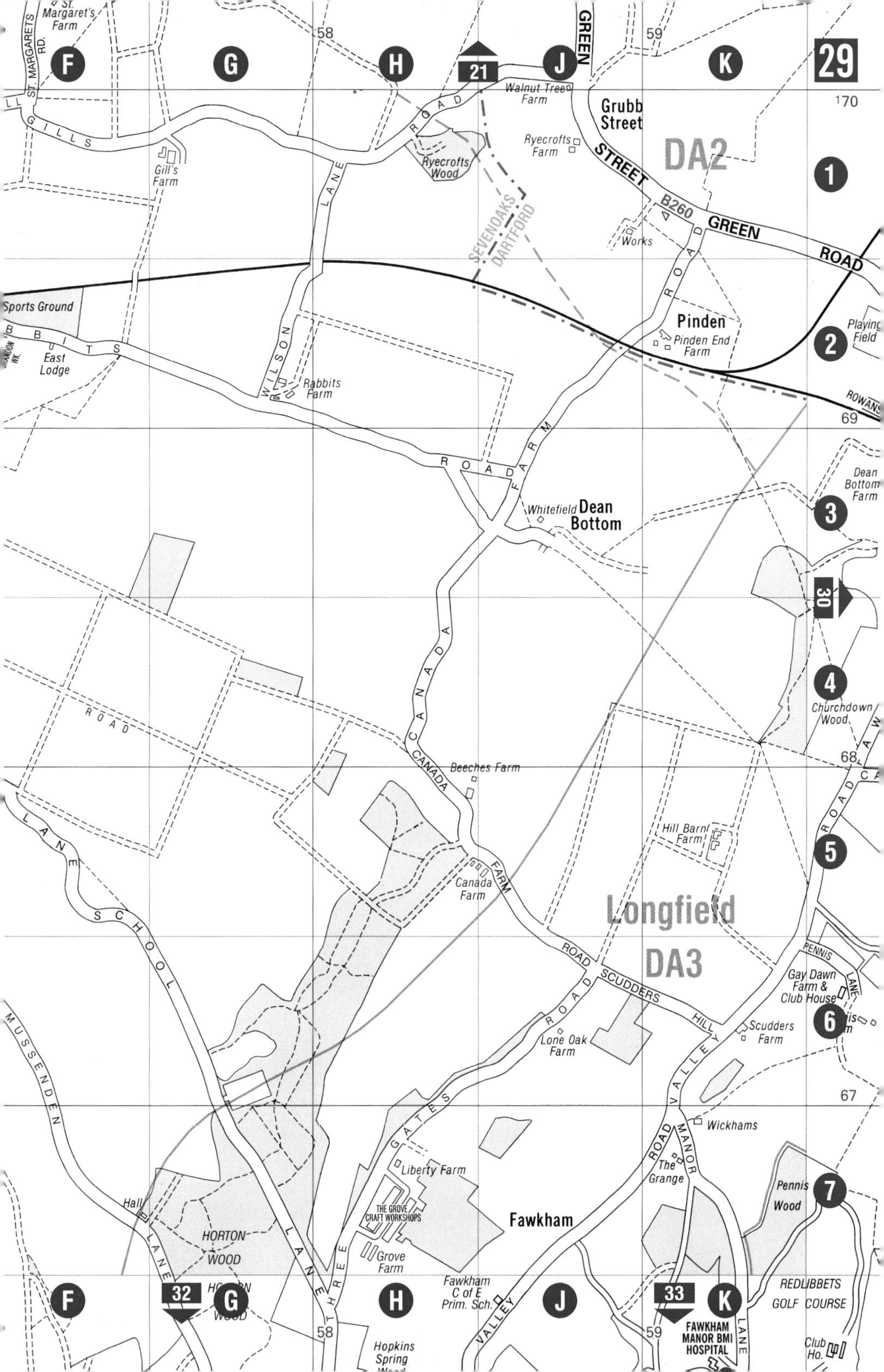
St. Margaret's Farm
ST. MARGARETS RD.
F
G
H
J
K
58
59
21
GREEN
Walnut Tree Farm
Grubb Street
170
GILLS
ROAD
Ryecrofts Farm
DA2
Gill's Farm
LANE
Ryecrofts Wood
STREET
1
SEVENOAKS
DARTFORD
B260
GREEN
ROAD
Works
ROAD
Sports Ground
RABBITS
WILSON
Pinden
Playing Field
2
Pinden End Farm
East Lodge
Rabbits Farm
ROWANS
69
FARM
ROAD
Dean Bottom Farm
Whitefield
Dean Bottom
3
30
CANADA
4
Churchdown Wood
ROAD
68
CANADA
Beeches Farm
ROAD
LANE
Hill Barn Farm
5
SCHOOL
Canada Farm
FARM
Longfield
DA3
PENNIS LANE
ROAD
SCUDDERS
Gay Dawn Farm & Club House
6
MUSSENDEN
ROAD
HILL
Scudders Farm
Lone Oak Farm
VALLEY
67
GATES
Wickhams
ROAD
MANOR
The Grange
Liberty Farm
Pennis Wood
7
Hall
THE GROVE CRAFT WORKSHOPS
Fawkham
LANE
HORTON WOOD
LANE
Grove Farm
THREE
REDLIBBETS GOLF COURSE
Fawkham C of E Prim. Sch.
32
33
VALLEY
LANE
58
59
FAWKHAM MANOR BMI HOSPITAL
Hopkins Spring
Club Ho.

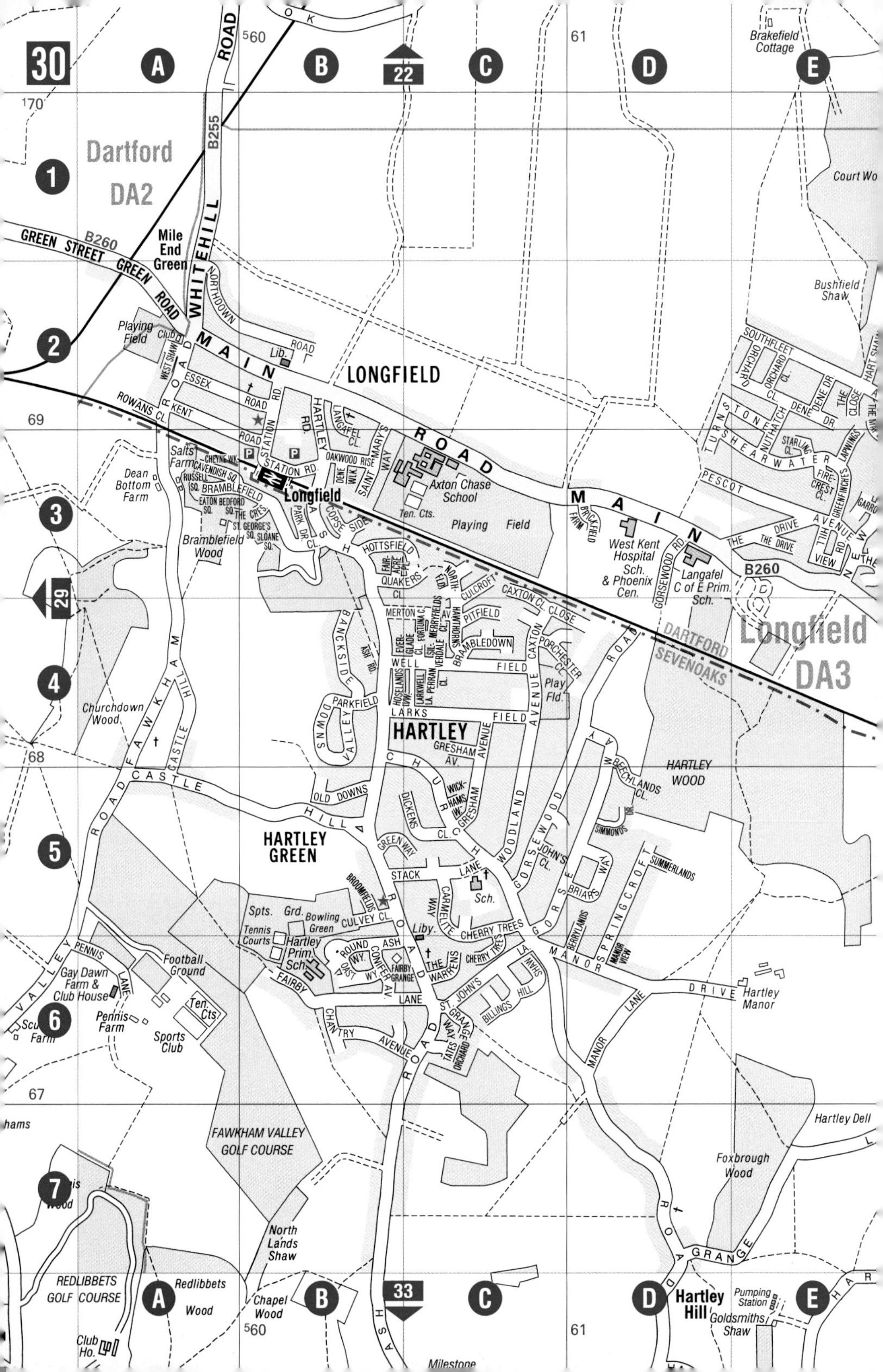

A
B
C
D
E
22
560
61
170
Brakefield Cottage
Dartford
DA2
Court Wo
B255
WHITEHILL ROAD
GREEN STREET GREEN ROAD
B260
Mile End Green
NORTHDOWN ROAD
Bushfield Shaw
Playing Field
Club
Lib.
MAIN ROAD
LONGFIELD
ESSEX ROAD
KENT ROAD
ROWANS CL.
WEST SHAW
STATION RD.
HARTLEY RD.
LANGAFEL CL.
SAINT MARY'S WAY
OAKWOOD RISE
DENE WLK.
Axton Chase School
Playing Field
Ten. Cts.
Salts Farm
CHEYNE WK.
CAVENDISH SQ.
RUSSELL SQ.
BRAMBLEFIELD
EATON SQ.
BEDFORD SQ.
THE CRES.
ST. GEORGE'S SQ.
SLOANE SQ.
Longfield
Dean Bottom Farm
Bramblefield Wood
PARK DR.
COPSE SIDE
ASH CL.
HOTTSFIELD
FAIRACRE
QUAKERS CL.
NORTH FLD.
CULCROFT
CAXTON CL.
CLOSE
MERTON
EVERGLADE CL.
FORTUNA CL.
MERRYFIELDS CL.
HAWTHORNS
VERDALE
PITFIELD
BRAMBLEDOWN
WELL FIELD
HOSELANDS VW.
LARKWELL
LA. PERRAN CL.
PORCHESTER CL.
CAXTON AVENUE
Play Fld.
BANCKSIDE
ASH RD.
PARKFIELD
DOWNS VALLEY
LARKS FIELD
HARTLEY
GRESHAM AV.
GRESHAM AVENUE
CHURCH
WICKHAMS W.
DICKENS CL.
OLD DOWNS
29
FAWKHAM ROAD
CASTLE HILL
Churchdown Wood
HARTLEY GREEN
GREEN WAY
STACK LANE
CARMELITE WAY
Sch.
WOODLAND
GORSEWOOD
GORSE WAY
JOHN'S CL.
BRIARS
SIMMONDS DR.
BEECHLANDS CL.
HARTLEY WOOD
SUMMERLANDS
SPRINGCROFT
BERRYLANDS
MANOR VIEW
CHERRY TREES
BROOMFIELDS
Spts. Grd.
Bowling Green
CULVEY CL.
Tennis Courts
Hartley Prim. Sch.
Liby.
ROUND ASH WY.
CONIFER AV.
FAIRBY GRANGE
OAST WY.
THE WARRENS
FAIRBY LANE
ST. JOHN'S
BILLINGS HILL
SHAW LA.
MANOR
MANOR LANE
DRIVE
Hartley Manor
Football Ground
Gay Dawn Farm & Club House
PENNIS LANE
VALLEY
Pennis Farm
Sports Club
Ten. Cts.
CHANTRY AVENUE
GRANGE WAY
ORCHARD
TATES
1
2
3
4
5
6
7
69
68
67
hams
FAWKHAM VALLEY GOLF COURSE
Hartley Dell
Foxbrough Wood
ROAD
GRANGE
North Lands Shaw
REDLIBBETS GOLF COURSE
Redlibbets Wood
Chapel Wood
33
Club Ho.
Hartley Hill
Pumping Station
Goldsmiths Shaw
Milestone
SOUTHFLEET
ORCHARD CL.
DENE DR.
THE CLOSE
HART SHAW
TURNSTONE
NUTHATCH
STARLING CL.
LAPWINGS
SHEARWATER
PESCOT
FIRECREST CL.
GREENFINCHES
GARRO
THE DRIVE
AVENUE
VIEW
B260
FARM
BROCKFIELD
GORSEWOOD RD.
West Kent Hospital Sch. & Phoenix Cen.
Langafel C of E Prim. Sch.
Longfield
DA3
DARTFORD
SEVENOAKS

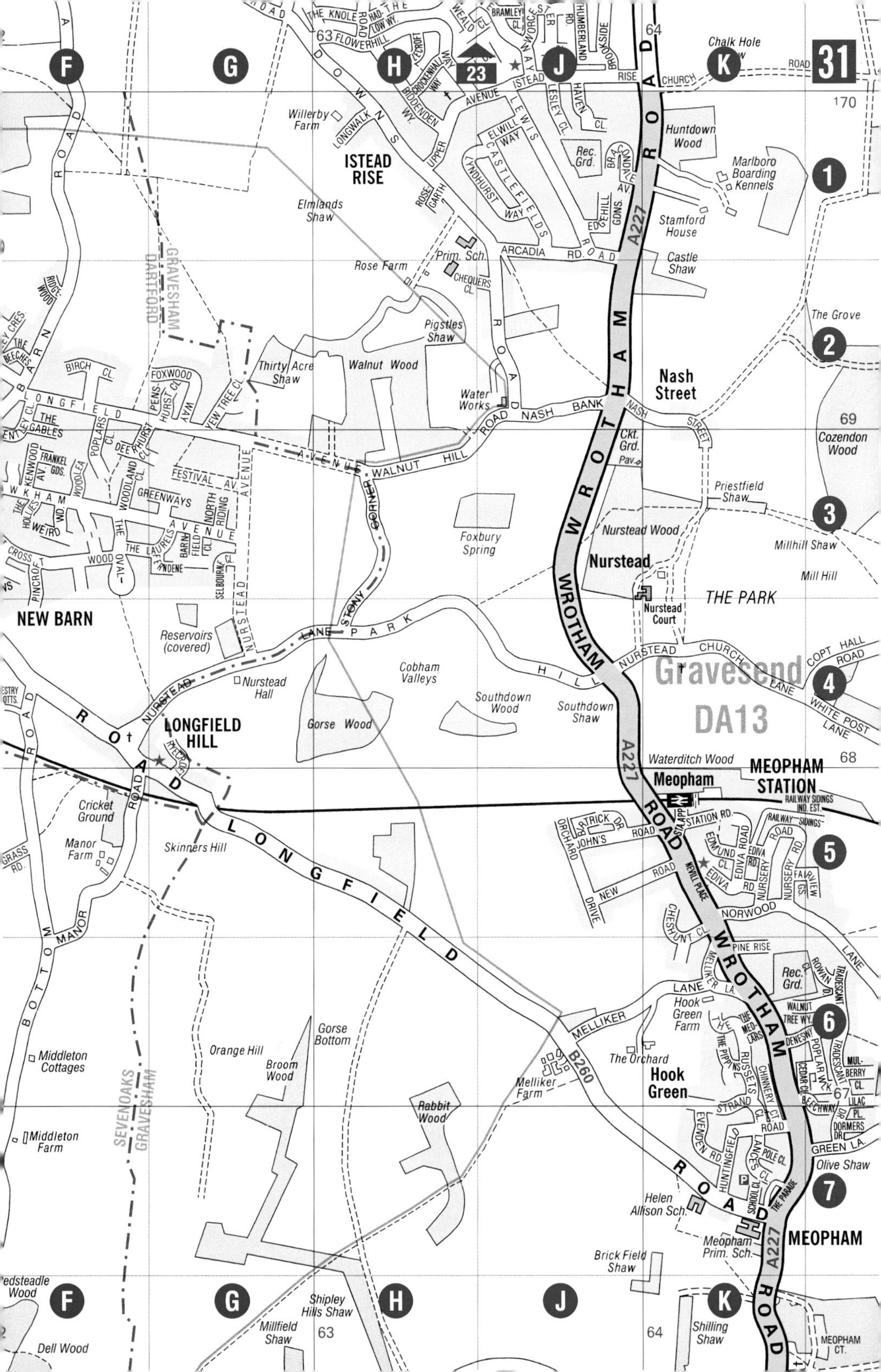
F
G
H
J
K
23
63
64
170
69
68
67
1
2
3
4
5
6
7
ISTEAD RISE
Willerby Farm
Elmlands Shaw
Rose Farm
Prim. Sch.
Pigstles Shaw
Walnut Wood
Thirty Acre Shaw
Water Works
Huntdown Wood
Marlboro Boarding Kennels
Rec. Grd.
Stamford House
Castle Shaw
The Grove
Chalk Hole
Nash Street
Cozendon Wood
Ckt. Grd.
Pav.
Priestfield Shaw
Millhill Shaw
Mill Hill
Nurstead Wood
Nurstead
Nurstead Court
THE PARK
Foxbury Spring
Gravesend
DA13
Cobham Valleys
Southdown Wood
Southdown Shaw
Waterditch Wood
Meopham
MEOPHAM STATION
RAILWAY SIDINGS IND. EST.
NEW BARN
LONGFIELD HILL
Reservoirs (covered)
Nurstead Hall
Gorse Wood
Cricket Ground
Manor Farm
Skinners Hill
GRAVESHAM
DARTFORD
SEVENOAKS
GRAVESHAM
Orange Hill
Broom Wood
Gorse Bottom
Rabbit Wood
Melliker Farm
Hook Green Farm
The Orchard
Hook Green
Middleton Cottages
Middleton Farm
Helen Allison Sch.
Meopham Prim. Sch.
MEOPHAM
Olive Shaw
Brick Field Shaw
Shipley Hills Shaw
Millfield Shaw
Shilling Shaw
Dell Wood
Bedsteadle Wood
WROTHAM ROAD
A227
B260
LONGFIELD ROAD
NURSTEAD ROAD
NURSTEAD CHURCH LANE
HILL
PARK LANE
STONY CORNER
WALNUT HILL ROAD
NASH BANK
NASH STREET
ARCADIA RD.
ISTEAD RISE
UPPER AVENUE
DOWNS ROAD
MELLIKER LANE
BOTTOM MANOR ROAD
NEW BARN ROAD
COPT HALL ROAD
WHITE POST LANE
CHURCH ROAD
NORWOOD LANE
STATION RD.
JOHN'S ROAD
ORCHARD DRIVE
NEW ROAD
BARTRICK DR.
CHESHUNT CL.
PINE RISE
MELLIKER LA.
NEVILL PLACE
EDMUND CL.
EDIVA ROAD
EDIVA RD.
NURSERY RD.
FAIRVIEW GS.
RAILWAY SIDINGS
ROWAN CL.
TRADESCANT DR.
WALNUT TREE WY.
DENESWY
POPLAR WK.
CEDAR CL.
BEECHWAY
MULBERRY CL.
LILAC PL.
DORMERS DR.
GREEN LA.
STRAND CL.
CHINNERY CT.
RUSSETS
THE PIPPINS
THE MEDLARS
EVENDEN RD.
HUNTINGFIELD ROAD
LANCES CL.
POLE CL.
SCHOOL CL.
THE PARADE
MEOPHAM CT.
LONGFIELD AVENUE
NURSTEAD AVENUE
FESTIVAL AV.
GREENWAYS
NORTH RIDING
BIRCH CL.
FOXWOOD WAY
PENSHURST CL.
YEW TREE CL.
THE GABLES
POPLARS CL.
DEERHURST CL.
WOODLAND CL.
WOODLEA
KENWOOD AV.
FRANKEL GDS.
WICKHAM AV.
THE HOLLIES
WEIRD WD.
THE OVAL
THE LAURELS
BARNFIELD CL.
SELBOURNE CL.
WOOD AVENUE
PINCROFT WOOD
CROSS
RIDGEWOOD
THE BEECHES
RYECROFT
LONGWALK
BIDDENDEN WY.
CROCKENHALL WAY
FLOWERHILL
THE KNOLE
WEALD CL.
BRAMLEY CL.
WORCESTER RD.
HUMBERLAND
BROOKSIDE
LESLEY CL.
HAVEN CL.
LEWIS ROAD
ELWILL WAY
CASTLEFIELDS
LYNDHURST WAY
BRACONDALE AV.
EDGEHILL GDNS.
ROSE GARTH
CHEQUERS CL.
GRASS RD.
VESTRY COTTS.

A
28
B
C
29
D
E
57
58
Dartford
DA4
M20
M20-MOTORWAY
Fawkham
Fawkham C of E Prim. Sch.
HORTON WOOD
Hopkins Spring Wood
Hatchfield Wood
THE GROVE CRAFT WORKSHOPS
Farm
Hall
MUSSENDEN LANE
SCHOOL LANE
THREE GATES ROAD
VALLEY ROAD
66
165
64
63
Speedgate Farm
Speedgate House
White House Farm
SPEEDGATE HILL
Choaks Farm
Choaks Wood
GABRIELSPRING ROAD
Gabrielspring Wood
CRATCHERS
EAST
SUN
Wilmay Copse Nature Reserve
Hazlewood
Birchgrove
Longfield
DA3
FAWKHAM GREEN
MICHAELS
SMALL GRAINS
WOODMAN VILLAS
FAIRVIEW
Greenlands
Cherrywood
The Haven
BRANDS HATCH RD.
FAWKHAM GREEN
GORSE HILL
A20 (MAIN ROAD)
Gorse Hill Farm
Ashen Grove
BRANDS HATCH PK.
Brands Hatch Place
Saxten's Wood
Cage's Wood
ROGERS WOOD LANE
GALLOWS WOOD
Eastwood
Woodlands
Rogers Wood
Gallows Wood
Shetley Shaws
Grand Stand
Stand
Hotel
Offices
Vineyard Shaw
BRANDS HATCH MOTOR RACING CIRCUIT
Grove Wood
FAWKHAM ROAD
LONDON
Kingsdown Farm
Cowless Shaw
HEVER AV.
HEVER ROAD
SYMONDS CL.
AVENUE
GILLIES RD
VIKING WAY
BLUE CHALET INDUSTRIAL PARK
Maplebank Nursery
PHELPS CL.
STACKLANDS CL.
BRAKES PL.
OAKLANDS
OAKLANDS CL.
LOVELACE CL.
REGENCY CL.
SHERBOURNE CL.
NEAL
MILLFIELD
MILLFIELD ROAD
KNATTS VALLEY ROAD
BOTSOM LANE
FLORENCE FARM MOBILE HOME PARK
THE BRIARS
MULTON RD.
PENSHURST CL.
WOOD RD.
ASTOR RD.
HOWELLS CL.
WHITEGATES AV.
TURNERS CT.
WOODVIEW CL.
MITCHEM CL.
GAPP CL.
Rec. Grd.
Westfield Cotts.
THE LONDON
Broomfield Wood
CHURCH WOOD
Kingsdown House
Springham's Cotts.
Crowhurst Farm
CROWHURST LANE
CLEARWAYS BUS. EST.
JASMINE CT.
SURREY CT.
KENT CT.
CARTER AV.
RUSSETT CL.
CLEARWAYS CARAVAN PK.
Sidehilly Wood
RUSHETTS RD.
KAYSLAND CARAVAN PARK
KINGSFISHER CT.
KINGSINGFIELD CL.
KINGSINGFIELD RD.
KINGSWOOD CT.
CHURCH AV.
CHANCEL CL.
CHURCH RD.
WEST KINGSDOWN
SOUTHFIELDS
WINDMILL GRANGE
BAKERS AV.
ASH TREE DR.
BIRCHWAY
WARLAND RD.
Lib.
Pav.
Ten. Cts.
Sports Gnd.
MEADOW BNK CL.
POUND BANK CL.
BLACKTHORN CL.
ASH TREE CT.
THE GRANGE
VERNON CL.
PORTOBELLO PDE.
Sch.
WEST KINGSDOWN INDUSTRIAL EST.
Richardson's Farm
Ashen Shaw
Inges Shaw

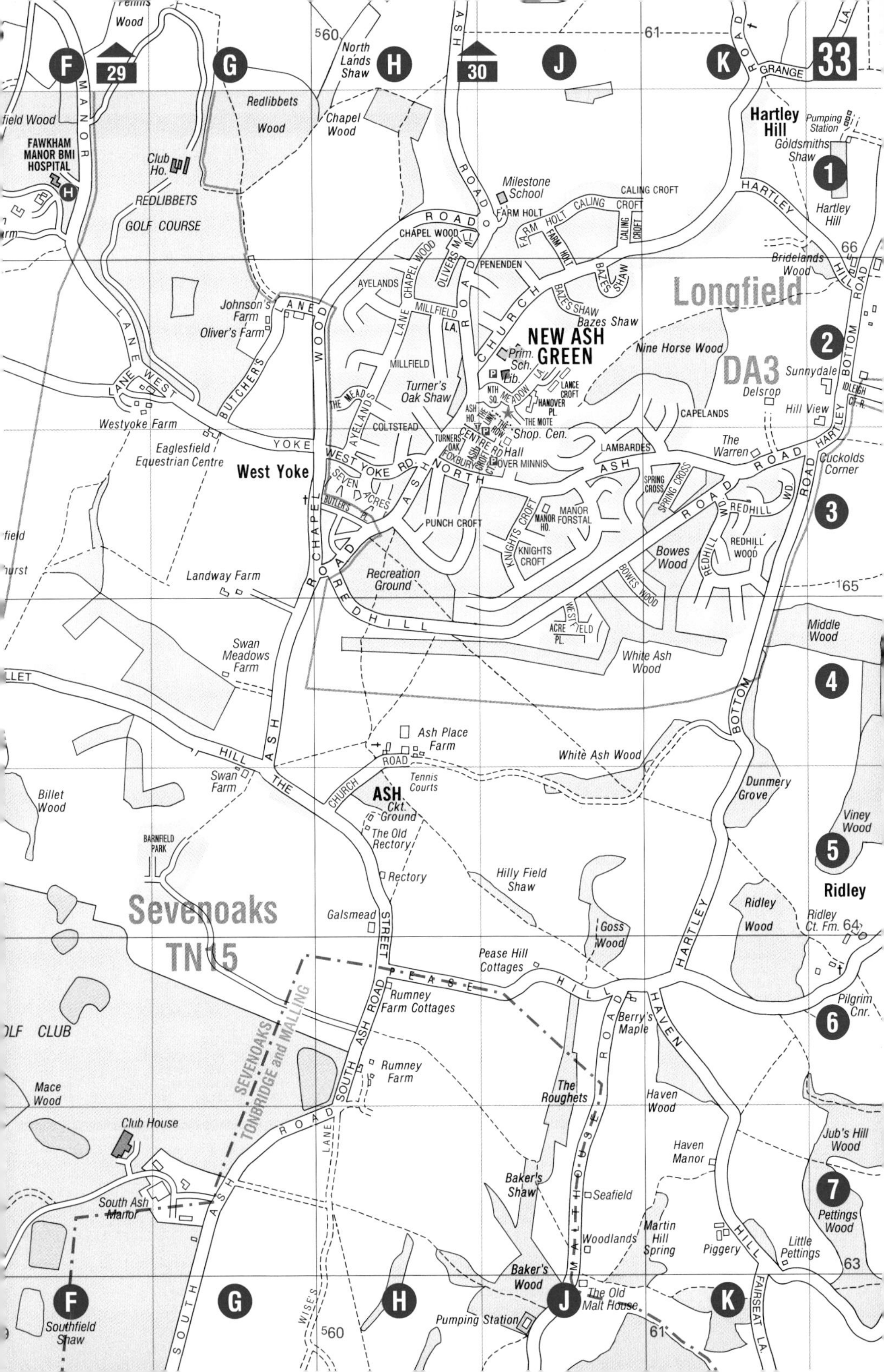
33
29
30
F
G
H
J
K
Wood
North Lands Shaw
Redlibbets Wood
Chapel Wood
field Wood
FAWKHAM MANOR BMI HOSPITAL
Club Ho.
REDLIBBETS GOLF COURSE
Hartley Hill
Pumping Station
Goldsmiths Shaw
Milestone School
FARM HOLT
CALING CROFT
Hartley Hill
Bridelands Wood
Longfield
CHAPEL WOOD
AYELANDS
MILLFIELD
PENENDEN
Bazes Shaw
NEW ASH GREEN
Nine Horse Wood
DA3
Sunnydale
Delsrop
Hill View
Johnson's Farm
Oliver's Farm
Turner's Oak Shaw
Prim. Sch.
Lib.
LANCE CROFT
HANOVER PL.
CAPELANDS
THE MOTE
Shop. Cen.
Hall
Westyoke Farm
Eaglesfield Equestrian Centre
West Yoke
COLTSTEAD
LAMBARDES
The Warren
Cuckolds Corner
PUNCH CROFT
MANOR FORSTAL
KNIGHTS CROFT
SPRING CROSS
REDHILL WOOD
Bowes Wood
Landway Farm
Recreation Ground
Middle Wood
Swan Meadows Farm
White Ash Wood
Ash Place Farm
White Ash Wood
Swan Farm
Tennis Courts
ASH
Ckt. Ground
Dunmery Grove
Billet Wood
The Old Rectory
Viney Wood
BARNFIELD PARK
Rectory
Hilly Field Shaw
Ridley
Sevenoaks TN15
Galsmead
Ridley Wood
Goss Wood
Ridley Ct. Fm.
Pease Hill Cottages
Rumney Farm Cottages
Berry's Maple
Pilgrim Cnr.
OLF CLUB
SEVENOAKS TONBRIDGE and MALLING
Rumney Farm
The Roughets
Mace Wood
Haven Wood
Club House
Haven Manor
Jub's Hill Wood
Baker's Shaw
Seafield
South Ash Manor
Martin Hill Spring
Pettings Wood
Woodlands
Piggery
Little Pettings
Baker's Wood
The Old Malt House
Southfield Shaw
Pumping Station
560
61
1
2
3
4
5
6
7
63
64
65
66

INDEX

Including Streets, Places & Areas, Hospitals & Hospices, Industrial Estates,
Selected Flats & Walkways, Junction Names, Stations and Selected Places of Interest.

HOW TO USE THIS INDEX

1. Each street name is followed by its Postcode District (or, if outside the London Postcodes, by its Locality Abbreviation(s)), and then by its map reference; e.g. **Abbey Cres.** DA17: Belv . . . **4E 4** is in the DA17 Postcode District and is to be found in square 4E on page **4**. The page number being shown in bold type.

2. A strict alphabetical order is followed in which Av., Rd., St., etc. (though abbreviated) are read in full and as part of the street name; e.g. **Abbeyhill Rd.** appears after **Abbey Gro.** but before **Abbey Mt.**

3. Streets and a selection of flats and walkways too small to be shown on the maps, appear in the index with the thoroughfare to which it is connected shown in brackets; e.g. **Alnwick Ct.** DA2: Dart . . . .6C **10** (off Osbourne Rd.)

4. Addresses that are in more than one part are referred to as not continuous.

5. Places and areas are shown in the index in BLUE TYPE and the map reference is to the actual map square in which the town centre or area is located and not to the place name shown on the map; e.g. ABBEY WOOD 4A 4

6. An example of a selected place of interest is Bexley Mus. 6B 8

7. An example of a station is Abbey Wood Station (Rail) 3A 4

8. Junction names are shown in the index in BOLD CAPITAL TYPE; e.g. BLACK PRINCE INTERCHANGE 6A 8

9. An example of a hospital is ERITH & DISTRICT HOSPITAL 6H 5

GENERAL ABBREVIATIONS

All. : Alley	**Est.** : Estate	**Mus.** : Museum
App. : Approach	**Fld.** : Field	**Nth.** : North
Av. : Avenue	**Flds.** : Fields	**Pde.** : Parade
Blvd. : Boulevard	**Gdns.** : Gardens	**Pk.** : Park
Bri. : Bridge	**Ga.** : Gate	**Pl.** : Place
Bungs. : Bungalows	**Gt.** : Great	**Prom.** : Promenade
Bus. : Business	**Grn.** : Green	**Ri.** : Rise
Cvn. : Caravan	**Gro.** : Grove	**Rd.** : Road
C'way. : Causeway	**Hgts.** : Heights	**Shop.** : Shopping
Cen. : Centre	**Ho.** : House	**Sth.** : South
Chu. : Church	**Ho's.** : Houses	**Sq.** : Square
Circ. : Circle	**Ind.** : Industrial	**St.** : Street
Cir. : Circus	**Info.** : Information	**Ter.** : Terrace
Cl. : Close	**Intl.** : International	**Trad.** : Trading
Cnr. : Corner	**La.** : Lane	**Up.** : Upper
Cotts. : Cottages	**Lit.** : Little	**Va.** : Vale
Ct. : Court	**Lwr.** : Lower	**Vw.** : View
Cres. : Crescent	**Mnr.** : Manor	**Vs.** : Villas
Cft. : Croft	**Mkt.** : Market	**Vis.** : Visitors
Dr. : Drive	**Mdw.** : Meadow	**Wlk.** : Walk
E. : East	**M.** : Mews	**W.** : West
Ent. : Enterprise	**Mt.** : Mount	**Yd.** : Yard

LOCALITY ABBREVIATIONS

Ash : **Ash**	Fawk : **Fawkham**	St P : **St Pauls Cray**
Bean : **Bean**	Grav'nd : **Gravesend**	Shorne : **Shorne**
Belv : **Belvedere**	Grays : **Grays**	Sidc : **Sidcup**
Bexl : **Bexley**	Ghithe : **Greenhithe**	Sole S : **Sole Street**
Bex : **Bexleyheath**	Hart : **Hartley**	S Dar : **South Darenth**
Bluew : **Bluewater**	High'm : **Higham**	Sflt : **Southfleet**
Bor G : **Borough Green**	Hort K : **Horton Kirby**	Stans : **Stansted**
Chst : **Chislehurst**	Ist R : **Istead Rise**	Sutt H : **Sutton At Hone**
Cobh : **Cobham**	Knat : **Knatts Valley**	Swan : **Swanley**
Cray : **Crayford**	Knock : **Knockholt**	Swans : **Swanscombe**
Crock : **Crockenhill**	Lfield : **Longfield**	Tilb : **Tilbury**
Dart : **Dartford**	Long H : **Longfield Hill**	Well : **Welling**
E Til : **East Tilbury**	Meop : **Meopham**	W King : **West Kingsdown**
Erith : **Erith**	New A : **New Ash Green**	W Thur : **West Thurrock**
Eyns : **Eynsford**	Nflt : **Northfleet**	W Til : **West Tilbury**
Farn : **Farningham**	Nflt G : **Northfleet Green**	Wro : **Wrotham**

A

Abbey Cres. DA17: Belv 4E **4**	**Abbey Rd.** DA12: Grav'nd 1D **24**
Abbey Dr. DA2: Bexl 2D **18**	DA17: Belv 4B **4**
Abbey Gro. SE2 . . . . .4A **4**	SE2 . . . . .4A **4**
Abbeyhill Rd. DA15: Sidc 2F **17**	**Abbey Ter.** SE2 . . . . .4A **4**
Abbey Mt. DA17: Belv 5D **4**	ABBEY WOOD 4A **4**
Abbey Pl. DA1: Dart 5J **9**	**Abbey Wood Camping & Cvn. Site**
Abbey Rd. DA7: Bex 4H **7**	SE2 . . . . .4A **4**
DA9: Ghithe 5K **11**	**Abbey Wood Rd.** SE2 . . . . .4A **4**
	Abbey Wood Station (Rail) 3A **4**
	Abbots Fld. DA12: Grav'nd 6B **24**
	Abbotswood Cl. DA17: Belv 3C **4**

Abbotts Cl. BR8: Swan 4F **27**
SE28 . . . . .1A **4**
Abbott's Wlk. DA7: Bex 7B **4**
Acacia Ct. DA11: Grav'nd 7K **13**
Acacia Rd. DA1: Dart 1J **19**
DA9: Ghithe 6F **11**
Acacia Wlk. BR8: Swan 2C **26**
Acacia Way DA15: Sidc 1C **16**
Acorn Cl. BR7: Chst 5A **16**
Acorn Ind. Pk. DA1: Cray 5F **9**
Acorn Rd. DA1: Cray 5E **8**

Acworth Pl. DA1: Dart 6H **9**
Adams Sq. DA6: Bex 3H **7**
Adelaide Rd. RM18: Tilb 1J **13**
Admirals Wlk. DA9: Ghithe 5J **11**
Agaton Rd. SE9 2A **16**
Aintree Cl. DA12: Grav'nd 3A **24**
Airedale Cl. DA2: Dart 1D **20**
Alamein Gdns. DA2: Dart 7E **10**
Alamein Rd. DA10: Swans 6A **12**
Alanbrooke DA12: Grav'nd 7B **14**
Alan Cl. DA1: Dart 4H **9**
Alban Cres. DA4: Farn 7B **28**
Albany Cl. DA5: Bexl 7F **7**
Albany Park Station (Rail) 2G **17**
Albany Rd. DA5: Bexl 7F **7**
DA17: Belv 6D **4**
RM18: Tilb 1K **13**
Alberta Rd. DA8: Erith 1B **8**
Albert Murray Cl. DA12: Grav'nd 7B **14**
Albert Rd. DA2: Dart 3H **19**
DA5: Bexl 6K **7**
DA10: Swans 6C **12**
DA17: Belv 5D **4**
Albert Rd. Est. DA17: Belv 5D **4**
Albion Pde. DA12: Grav'nd 6C **14**
Albion Rd. DA6: Bex 4J **7**
DA12: Grav'nd 7B **14**
Albion Ter. DA12: Grav'nd 6B **14**
Albury Av. DA7: Bex 2H **7**
Alconbury DA6: Bex 5A **8**
Alderman Cl. DA1: Cray 7D **8**
Alderney Rd. DA8: Erith 2J **5**
Alder Rd. DA14: Sidc 3C **16**
Alder Way BR8: Swan 2C **26**
Alderwood Rd. SE9 6A **6**
Aldwick Cl. SE9 3A **16**
Alers Rd. DA6: Bex 5G **7**
Alexander Cl. DA15: Sidc 5B **6**
Alexander Rd. DA7: Bex 2G **7**
DA9: Ghithe 5K **11**
Alexandra Cl. BR8: Swan 2D **26**
Alexandra Rd. DA8: Erith 6K **5**
DA12: Grav'nd 7D **14**
RM18: Tilb 2J **13**
Alexandra Wlk. DA4: S Dar 2F **29**
Alfan La. DA2: Dart 5C **18**
Alford Rd. DA8: Erith 5G **5**
Alfred Ho. DA11: Nflt 1J **23**
Alfred Pl. DA11: Nflt 1J **23**
Alfred Rd. DA2: Dart 4K **19**
DA11: Grav'nd 2A **24**
DA17: Belv 5D **4**
Alfriston Cl. DA1: Cray 6D **8**
Alicia Ho. DA16: Well 1E **6**
Alkerden La. DA9: Ghithe, Swans 6K **11**
DA10: Ghithe, Swans 6K **11**
Allendale Cl. DA2: Dart 1E **20**
Allens Mead DA12: Grav'nd 1E **24**
Allington Cl. DA12: Grav'nd 1E **24**
All Saints Cl. DA10: Swans 5C **12**
All Saints Rd. DA11: Nflt 1J **23**
Alma, The DA12: Grav'nd 5E **24**
Alma Rd. DA10: Swans 5C **12**
DA14: Sidc 3D **16**
Almond Dr. BR8: Swan 2C **26**
Almond Rd. DA2: Dart 7D **10**
Alnwick Ct. *DA2: Dart* *6C* ***10***
(off Osbourne Rd.)
Alsike Rd. DA18: Erith 3B **4**
SE2 3B **4**
Alton Cl. DA5: Bexl 1H **17**
Amberley Ct. DA14: Sidc 5F **17**
Amberley Rd. SE2 6B **4**
Ambleside Rd. DA7: Bex 2K **7**
Ambrooke Rd. DA17: Belv 3E **4**
Ambrose Cl. DA1: Cray 4E **8**
Ames Rd. DA10: Swans 6B **12**
AMF Bowling
Gravesend 6K **13**
Ampleforth Rd. SE2 2A **4**
Ancaster St. SE18 1B **6**
Anchor Bay Ind. Est. DA8: Erith 1J **5**
Anchor Blvd. DA2: Dart 4D **10**
Anchor Ct. DA8: Erith 7K **5**
Anderson Way DA17: Belv 2F **5**
Andrew Cl. DA1: Cray 5C **8**
Andrews Pl. DA2: Bexl 2D **18**
Anglesea Cen. DA11: Grav'nd 6A **14**
Anglesea Pl. *DA11: Grav'nd* *6A* ***14***
(off New Rd.)
Annandale Rd. DA15: Sidc 7B **6**
Anne Boleyn Ct. SE9 6A **6**
Anne of Cleeves Ct. SE9 6A **6**
Anne of Cleves Rd. DA1: Dart 5J **9**
Anstridge Path SE9 6A **6**
Anstridge Rd. SE9 6A **6**
Anthony La. BR8: Swan 1F **27**
Anthony Rd. DA16: Well 1D **6**
Anvil Ter. DA2: Bexl 2D **18**
Aperfield Rd. DA8: Erith 6K **5**
Apollo Way DA8: Erith 4H **5**
Appledore Av. DA7: Bex 1B **8**
Appledore Cres. DA14: Sidc 3B **16**
Applegarth Dr. DA1: Dart 2K **19**
Applegarth Ho. DA8: Erith 2E **8**
Applegarth Rd. SE28 1A **4**
Apple Orchard BR8: Swan 4C **26**
Appleshaw Cl. DA11: Grav'nd 5K **23**
Appleton Cl. DA7: Bex 2B **8**
Appleton Dr. DA2: Dart 3G **19**
Appold St. DA8: Erith 6K **5**
Apsledene DA12: Grav'nd 6C **24**
Arbuthnot La. DA5: Bexl 6H **7**
Arcadian Av. DA5: Bexl 6H **7**
Arcadian Cl. DA5: Bexl 6H **7**
Arcadian Rd. DA5: Bexl 6H **7**
Arcadia Rd. DA13: Ist R 1J **31**
Archer Way BR8: Swan 2E **26**
ARCHERY HOUSE 6C **10**
Arethusa Pl. DA9: Ghithe 4J **11**
Argali Ho. *DA18: Erith* *3C* ***4***
(off Kale Rd.)
Argles Cl. DA9: Ghithe 5H **11**
Ariel Cl. DA12: Grav'nd 4E **24**
Arkwright Rd. RM18: Tilb 2K **13**
Arlington Cl. DA15: Sidc 7B **6**
Armoury Dr. DA12: Grav'nd 7B **14**
Arnold Pl. RM18: Tilb 1B **14**
Arnold Rd. DA12: Grav'nd 2C **24**
Arnold's La. DA4: Sutt H 6A **20**
Arnott Cl. SE28 1A **4**
Arnsberg Way DA6: Bex 4J **7**
DA7: Bex 4J **7**
Arnside Rd. DA7: Bex 1K **7**
Arran Cl. DA8: Erith 6H **5**
Artemis Cl. DA12: Grav'nd 7D **14**
Arthur St. DA8: Erith 7K **5**
DA11: Grav'nd 7K **13**
Arthur St. W. DA11: Grav'nd 7K **13**
Artillery Row DA12: Grav'nd 7B **14**
Arundel Cl. DA5: Bexl 6J **7**
Arundel Rd. DA1: Dart 4H **9**
Ascot Ct. DA5: Bexl 7J **7**
Ascot Rd. DA12: Grav'nd 3A **24**
ASH 5H **33**
Ashbourne Av. DA7: Bex 7C **4**
Ashburnham Rd. DA17: Belv 4G **5**
Ash Cl. BR8: Swan 2B **26**
DA14: Sidc 3E **16**
Ashcroft Av. DA15: Sidc 6D **6**
Ash Cft. Ct. DA3: New A 3J **33**
Ashcroft Ct. DA1: Dart 7B **10**
Ashcroft Cres. DA15: Sidc 6D **6**
Ashdown Cl. DA5: Bexl 7B **8**
Ashen Dr. DA1: Dart 6F **9**
Ashfield La. BR7: Chst 7A **16**
(not continuous)
Ash Ho. DA3: New A 2H **33**
Ashmore Gdns. DA11: Nflt 3G **23**
Ashmore Gro. DA16: Well 3A **6**
Ash Rd. DA1: Dart 1J **19**
DA2: Dart 4A **20**
DA3: Hart, New A, Lfield 3B **30**
DA12: Grav'nd 4B **24**
TN15: Ash, New A 4G **33**
Ash Tree Cl. TN15: W King 7C **32**
Ash Tree Ct. TN15: W King 7C **32**
Ash Tree Dr. TN15: W King 7C **32**
Ashurst Cl. DA1: Cray 3E **8**
Ashwood Pl. DA2: Bean 3J **21**
Ashworth Av. *TN15: W King* *7A* ***32***
(off London Rd.)
Askern Cl. DA6: Bex 4G **7**
Aspdin Rd. DA11: Nflt 3G **23**
Aspen Cl. BR8: Swan 1C **26**
Aspen Ct. DA1: Dart 6B **10**
Aspen Grn. DA18: Erith 3D **4**
Aspen Ho. DA15: Sidc 3D **16**
Aston Cl. DA14: Sidc 3D **16**
Astor Rd. TN15: W King 6B **32**
Astra Dr. DA12: Grav'nd 5D **24**
Athol Rd. DA8: Erith 5G **5**
Atlantic Cl. DA10: Swans 5B **12**
Atlas Rd. DA1: Dart 3A **10**
Attlee Dr. DA1: Dart 5B **10**
Attlee Rd. SE28 1A **4**
Auckland Cl. RM18: Tilb 2K **13**
Augustine Rd. DA12: Grav'nd 7B **14**
(not continuous)
Austen Cl. DA9: Ghithe 6K **11**
RM18: Tilb 2B **14**
SE28 1A **4**
Austen Gdns. DA1: Dart 4A **10**
Austen Rd. DA8: Erith 7F **5**
Austin Rd. DA11: Nflt 1J **23**
Austral Cl. DA15: Sidc 3C **16**
Aveley Cl. DA8: Erith 6K **5**
Avenue, The BR5: St P 7E **16**
DA5: Bexl 7G **7**
DA9: Ghithe 4J **11**
DA11: Grav'nd 1K **23**
Avenue Rd. DA7: Bex 3H **7**
DA8: Erith 7G **5**
DA17: Belv, Erith 4G **5**
AVERY HILL 6A **6**
Avery Hill Rd. SE9 6A **6**
Avery Way DA1: Dart 2A **20**
Avon Cl. DA12: Grav'nd 2C **24**
Avondale Rd. DA16: Well 2F **7**
Avonmouth Rd. DA1: Dart 5J **9**
Awliscombe Rd. DA16: Well 2C **6**
Axminster Cres. DA16: Well 1F **7**
Axtane DA13: Sflt 7C **22**
Axtane Cl. DA4: S Dar 1D **28**
Ayelands DA3: New A 2H **33**
Ayelands La. DA3: New A 3H **33**
Azalea Dr. BR8: Swan 4C **26**

B

Back La. DA5: Bexl 7K **7**
Back Rd. DA14: Sidc 4D **16**
Baden Powell Ho. *DA17: Belv* *3E* ***4***
(off Ambrooke Rd.)
Bader Wlk. DA11: Nflt 3J **23**
Badlow Cl. DA8: Erith 7J **5**
Baker Beal Ct. DA7: Bex 3A **8**
Bakerhill Cl. DA11: Nflt 4J **23**
Bakers Av. TN15: W King 7B **32**
Balcombe Cl. DA6: Bex 4G **7**
Baldwyn's Pk. DA5: Bexl 2C **18**
Baldwyn's Rd. DA5: Bexl 2C **18**
Balliol Rd. DA16: Well 2E **6**
Balmoral Gdns. DA5: Bexl 7J **7**
Balmoral Rd. DA4: Sutt H 7C **20**
Baltimore Pl. DA16: Well 2C **6**
Banbury Vs. DA13: Sflt 6C **22**
Banckside DA3: Hart 4B **30**
Bank Ct. DA1: Dart 6K **9**
Bankside DA11: Nflt 6F **13**
Bankside Cl. DA5: Bexl 4C **18**
Banks La. DA6: Bex 4J **7**
Bank St. DA12: Grav'nd 6A **14**
Banwell Rd. DA5: Bexl 6G **7**
Barfield DA4: Sutt H 7C **20**
Barham Cl. DA12: Grav'nd 1E **24**
Barham Rd. DA1: Dart 7B **10**
Barnard Cl. BR7: Chst 7A **16**
Barnard Ct. *DA2: Dart* *6C* ***10***
(off Clifton Wlk.)
Barndale Ct. DA12: Shorne 5K **25**
BARNEHURST 3B **8**
Barnehurst Av. DA7: Bex 1B **8**
DA8: Erith 1B **8**
Barnehurst Cl. DA8: Erith 1B **8**
Barnehurst Rd. DA7: Bex 2B **8**
Barnehurst Station (Rail) 2B **8**
Barn End Dr. DA2: Dart 4H **19**
Barn End La. DA2: Dart, Swan 5H **19**
BARNES CRAY 4F **9**

Barnes Cray Rd. DA1: Cray 4F **9**
Barnett Cl. DA8: Erith 2E **8**
Barnfield DA11: Grav'nd 2K **23**
Barnfield Cl. BR8: Crock 7B **26**
  DA3: Lfield 3G **31**
  DA9: Ghithe 6G **11**
Barnfield Pk. TN15: Ash 5G **33**
Barnfield Rd. DA17: Belv 6D **4**
Barnock Cl. DA1: Cray 7D **8**
Barn Theatre, The
  Bexley 1D **16**
Barnwell Rd. DA1: Dart 3A **10**
Barrack Row DA11: Grav'nd 6A **14**
Barrington Rd. DA7: Bex 2G **7**
Barr Rd. DA12: Grav'nd 2E **24**
Barry Av. DA7: Bex 7C **4**
Bartholomew Way BR8: Swan 3D **26**
Bartlett Rd. DA11: Grav'nd 1K **23**
Barton Cl. DA6: Bex 5H **7**
Barton Rd. DA4: Sutt H 1C **28**
  DA14: Sidc 6H **17**
Bascombe Gro. DA1: Bexl, Cray 7D **8**
Basilon Rd. DA7: Bex 2H **7**
Basing Dr. DA5: Bexl 6J **7**
Bath Rd. DA1: Dart 7G **9**
Bath St. DA11: Grav'nd 6A **14**
Battle Rd. DA8: Erith 4G **5**
  DA17: Belv, Erith 4G **5**
Baugh Rd. DA14: Sidc 5F **17**
Bayard Ct. DA6: Bex 4A **8**
Bayley Wlk. SE2 . . . . .6C **4**
Bayly Rd. DA1: Dart 6B **10**
Baynham Cl. DA5: Bexl 6J **7**
Baytree Cl. DA15: Sidc 1C **16**
Bazes Shaw DA3: New A 2J **33**
          (not continuous)
Beacon Dr. DA2: Bean 3J **21**
Beacon Rd. DA8: Erith 2K **5**
Beaconsfield Rd. DA5: Bexl 2D **18**
Beacon Wood Country Pk. 4J **21**
Beal Cl. DA16: Well 1D **6**
BEAN 3K **21**
Beane Cft. DA12: Grav'nd 1E **24**
Bean Hill Cotts. DA2: Bean 4K **21**
          (not continuous)
Bean La. DA2: Bean 2J **21**
Bean Rd. DA6: Bex 4G **7**
  DA9: Ghithe 5J **11**
Beaton Cl. DA9: Ghithe 5J **11**
Beatrice Gdns. DA11: Nflt 2H **23**
Beaumont Dr. DA11: Nflt 7H **13**
Beaverbank Rd. SE9 . . . . .1A **16**
Beavers Lodge DA14: Sidc 4C **16**
Beaverwood Rd. BR7: Chst 5B **16**
Beckets Sports Cen. 6H **9**
Beckett Cl. DA17: Belv 3D **4**
Becketts Cl. DA5: Bexl 1B **18**
Beckley Cl. DA12: Grav'nd 2G **25**
Becks Rd. DA14: Sidc 3D **16**
Becton Pl. DA8: Erith 7F **5**
Bedale Wlk. DA2: Dart 1C **20**
Bedens Rd. DA14: Sidc 6H **17**
Bedford Rd. DA1: Dart 7B **10**
  DA11: Nflt 2J **23**
  DA15: Sidc 3B **16**
Bedford Sq. DA3: Lfield 3A **30**
Bedonwell Rd. DA7: Belv, Erith, Bex 6C **4**
  DA17: Belv 6C **4**
  SE2 . . . . .6C **4**
Bedwell Rd. DA17: Belv 5E **4**
Beech Av. BR8: Swan 4E **26**
  DA15: Sidc 7D **6**
Beech Ct. DA1: Dart 6B **10**
Beechcroft Av. DA7: Bex 1C **8**
Beechenlea La. BR8: Swan 4F **27**
Beeches, The BR8: Swan 7E **18**
  DA3: Lfield 2F **31**
  RM18: Tilb 2A **14**
Beechfield Rd. DA8: Erith 7J **5**
Beech Haven Ct. DA1: Cray 5C **8**
       (off London Rd.)
Beechlands Cl. DA3: Hart 5D **30**
Beech Rd. DA1: Dart 1J **19**
Beech Wlk. DA1: Cray 4F **9**
Beechway DA5: Bexl 6G **7**
  DA13: Meop 6K **31**
Beechwood Cres. DA7: Bex 3G **7**

Beesfield La. DA4: Farn 7B **28**
Beeston Ct. DA2: Dart 6C **10**
      (off Hardwick Cres.)
Bell Cl. DA9: Ghithe 5G **11**
Bellegrove Cl. DA16: Well 2C **6**
Bellegrove Pde. DA16: Well 3C **6**
Bellegrove Rd. DA16: Well 2A **6**
Bellevue Rd. DA6: Bex 5J **7**
Bellman Av. DA12: Grav'nd 1D **24**
Bellring Cl. DA17: Belv 6E **4**
Belmont Av. DA16: Well 2B **6**
Belmont La. BR7: Chst 5A **16**
       (not continuous)
Belmont Rd. DA8: Erith 7E **4**
Beltana Dr. DA12: Grav'nd 4D **24**
Belton Rd. DA14: Sidc 4D **16**
Belvedere Rd. DA17: Belv 4G **5**
BELVEDERE 3E **4**
Belvedere Cl. DA12: Grav'nd 1B **24**
Belvedere Ct. DA17: Belv 3D **4**
Belvedere Ind. Est. DA17: Belv 1G **5**
Belvedere Link Bus. Pk. DA8: Erith 3G **5**
BELVEDERE PRIVATE CLINIC 5A **4**
Belvedere Rd. DA7: Bex 3J **7**
  SE2 . . . . .1A **4**
Belvedere Station (Rail) 3F **5**
Benedict Cl. DA17: Belv 3C **4**
Benjamin Ct. DA17: Belv 6D **4**
Bennett Cl. DA16: Well 2D **6**
Bennett Ho. DA11: Nflt 3J **23**
Bennett Way DA2: Dart 4E **20**
Bentham Rd. SE28 . . . . .1A **4**
Bentley Cl. DA3: Lfield 3F **31**
Bentley St. DA12: Grav'nd 6B **14**
Bentley St. Ind. Est. DA12: Grav'nd . . .6B **14**
Bere Cl. DA9: Ghithe 5K **11**
Berens Ct. DA14: Sidc 4C **16**
Beresford Rd. DA11: Nflt 7H **13**
Berkeley Av. DA7: Bex 1G **7**
Berkeley Ct. BR8: Swan 3D **26**
Berkeley Cres. DA1: Dart 1A **20**
Berkeley Ter. RM18: Tilb 1K **13**
Berkhampstead Rd. DA17: Belv 5E **4**
Berkley Cres. DA12: Grav'nd 6B **14**
Berkley Rd. DA12: Grav'nd 6A **14**
Bermuda Rd. RM18: Tilb 2K **13**
Bernard St. DA12: Grav'nd 6A **14**
Berrylands DA3: Hart 6D **30**
Bertha Hollamby Ct. DA14: Sidc 5F **17**
      (off Sidcup Hill)
Berwick Cres. DA15: Sidc 7B **6**
Berwick Rd. DA16: Well 1E **6**
Besant Ct. SE28 . . . . .1A **4**
      (off Titmuss Av.)
Best Ter. BR8: Crock 6B **26**
Bethel Rd. DA16: Well 3F **7**
BETSHAM 4C **22**
Betsham Rd. DA8: Erith 7K **5**
  DA10: Swans 7B **12**
  DA13: Sflt 5A **22**
Betterton Dr. DA14: Sidc 2H **17**
Beult Rd. DA1: Cray 4F **9**
Bevan Pl. BR8: Swan 4E **26**
Bevans Cl. DA9: Ghithe 6K **11**
Bevercote Wlk. DA17: Belv 6D **4**
      (off Osborne Rd.)
Beverley Av. DA15: Sidc 7C **6**
Beverley Rd. DA7: Bex 2B **8**
Bevis Cl. DA2: Dart 7D **10**
BEXLEY 7K **7**
Bexley Cl. DA1: Cray 5D **8**
Bexley Cotts. DA4: Hort K 4C **28**
BEXLEYHEATH 4J **7**
Bexleyheath Sports Club 3F **7**
Bexleyheath Station (Rail) 2H **7**
Bexley High St. DA5: Bexl 7K **7**
Bexley La. DA1: Cray 5D **8**
  DA14: Sidc 4F **17**
Bexley Lawn Tennis & Squash Club 7K **7**
Bexley Mus. 6B **8**
Bexley Music & Dance Cen. 4D **16**
      (off Station Rd.)
Bexley Rd. DA8: Erith 7G **5**
  SE9 . . . . .5A **6**
Bexley Station (Rail) 1K **17**
Biddenden Way DA13: Ist R 7H **23**
Bideford Rd. DA16: Well 7A **4**

Billet Hill TN15: Ash 4F **33**
Billings Hill Shaw DA3: Hart 6C **30**
Bilton Rd. DA8: Erith 2J **5**
Binsey Wlk. SE2 . . . . .2A **4**
      (not continuous)
Birch Cl. DA3: Lfield 2F **31**
Birches, The BR8: Swan 2D **26**
Birch Gro. DA16: Well 4D **6**
Birchington Cl. DA7: Bex 1A **8**
Birch Pl. DA9: Ghithe 6F **11**
Birch Wlk. DA8: Erith 6G **5**
Birchway TN15: W King 7C **32**
Birchwood Av. DA14: Sidc 2E **16**
Birchwood Dr. DA2: Dart 4D **18**
Birchwood Pde. DA2: Dart 4D **18**
Birchwood Pk. Av. BR8: Swan 3D **26**
Birchwood Rd. BR8: Swan 1B **26**
  DA2: Dart 5C **18**
Birkbeck Rd. DA14: Sidc 3D **16**
Birling Rd. DA8: Erith 7H **5**
Birtrick Dr. DA13: Meop 5J **31**
Bishops Ct. DA9: Ghithe 5G **11**
Blackberry Fld. BR5: St P 7D **16**
BLACKFEN 7D **6**
Blackfen Pde. DA15: Sidc 6D **6**
Blackfen Rd. DA15: Sidc 5B **6**
Blackhorse Rd. DA14: Sidc 4D **16**
Blackmans Cl. DA1: Dart 1H **19**
BLACK PRINCE INTERCHANGE 6A **8**
Blackthorn Cl. TN15: W King 7C **32**
Blackthorn Gro. DA7: Bex 3H **7**
Bladindon Dr. DA5: Bexl 7F **7**
Blair Cl. DA15: Sidc 5B **6**
Blake Cl. DA16: Well 1B **6**
Blake Gdns. DA1: Dart 4A **10**
Blakemore Way DA17: Belv 3C **4**
Blake Way RM18: Tilb 2B **14**
Bledlow Cl. SE28 . . . . .1A **4**
BLENDON 6G **7**
Blendon Dr. DA5: Bexl 6G **7**
Blendon Rd. DA5: Bexl 6G **7**
Blenheim Cl. DA1: Dart 6H **9**
Blenheim Ct. DA14: Sidc 3A **16**
Blenheim Dr. DA16: Well 1C **6**
Blenheim Gro. DA12: Grav'nd 7B **14**
Blenheim Rd. DA1: Dart 6H **9**
  DA15: Sidc 1F **17**
Blewbury Ho. SE2 . . . . .2A **4**
      (Tavy Bri.)
  SE2 . . . . .2B **4**
      (Tilehurst Point)
Bligh Rd. DA11: Grav'nd 6K **13**
Blue Chalet Ind. Pk. TN15: W King 5A **32**
Blue Ho. Cotts. DA2: Bean 3A **22**
BLUEWATER .1G **21**
Bluewater Parkway DA9: Bluew, Ghithe . .7G **11**
Bluewater Shop. Cen. DA9: Bluew 7G **11**
Blyth Rd. SE28 . . . . .1A **4**
Bob Dunn Way DA1: Dart 4H **9**
Bodle Av. DA10: Swans 7B **12**
Boevey Path DA17: Belv 5D **4**
Bognor Rd. DA16: Well 1G **7**
Boleyn Way DA10: Swans 7B **12**
Bonaventure Ct. DA12: Grav'nd 4E **24**
Bondfield Wlk. DA1: Dart 4A **10**
Bonney Way BR8: Swan 2D **26**
Booth Cl. SE28 . . . . .1A **4**
Borland Cl. DA9: Ghithe 5H **11**
Bostall Hill SE2 . . . . .6A **4**
Bostall La. SE2 . . . . .4A **4**
Bostall Mnr. Way SE2 . . . . .4A **4**
Bostall Pk. Av. DA7: Bex 7C **4**
Bostall Rd. BR5: St P 7E **16**
Bosworth Ho. DA8: Erith 5J **5**
      (off Saltford Cl.)
Botany Rd. DA11: Nflt 4D **13**
Botsom La. TN15: W King 6A **32**
Bott Rd. DA2: Dart 4A **20**
Boucher Dr. DA11: Nflt 3J **23**
Boulevard, The DA9: Ghithe 4K **11**
Boundary Ho. DA11: Nflt 1J **23**
      (off Victoria Rd.)
Boundary Rd. DA15: Sidc 5B **6**
Boundary St. DA8: Erith 7K **5**
Bourne Ind. Pk., The DA1: Cray 5D **8**
Bourne Mead DA5: Bexl 5B **8**
Bourne Pde. DA5: Bexl 7A **8**

Bourne Rd.—Camden Ct.

Bourne Rd. DA1: Cray 5C 8
DA5: Bexl, Dart 7A 8
DA12: Grav'nd 2E 24
Bourne Way BR8: Swan 3B 26
Bow Arrow La. DA1: Dart 6B 10
DA2: Dart 6C 10
Bower Rd. BR8: Swan 7F 19
Bowers Av. DA11: Nflt 4J 23
Bowes Cl. DA15: Sidc 6E 6
Bowes Ct. *DA2: Dart 6C 10*
(off Osbourne Rd.)
Bowesden La. DA12: Shorne 7K 25
Bowes Wood DA3: New A 3J 33
Bowford Av. DA7: Bex 1H 7
BOWMANS 7F 9
Bowman's Rd. DA1: Dart 7E 8
Bown Cl. RM18: Tilb 3A 14
Bowness Rd. DA7: Bex 2A 8
Boxgrove Rd. SE2 3A 4
Brabourne Cres. DA7: Bex 6D 4
Brackendene DA2: Dart 4D 18
Bracondale Av. DA13: Ist R 1J 31
BRACTON CENTRE, THE 2E 18
Bracton La. DA2: Bexl 2E 18
Bradbourne Rd. DA5: Bexl 7K 7
Bradbury Ct. DA11: Nflt 1J 23
Bradenham Av. DA16: Well 4D 6
Braemar Av. DA7: Bex 4B 8
Braemar Gdns. DA15: Sidc 3A 16
Braeside Cres. DA7: Bex 4B 8
Braesyde Cl. DA17: Belv 4D 4
Brakefield Rd. DA13: Sflt 6E 22
Brakes Pl. TN15: W King 6B 32
Bramber Ct. *DA2: Dart 6C 10*
(off Bow Arrow La.)
Bramble Av. DA2: Bean 3K 21
Bramble Cft. DA8: Erith 4G 5
Brambledown DA3: Hart 4C 30
Bramblefield Cl. DA3: Lfield 3A 30
Bramley Cl. BR8: Swan 4D 26
DA13: Ist R 7J 23
Bramley Ct. DA16: Well 1E 6
Bramley Pl. DA1: Cray 4F 9
Brampton Rd. DA7: Bex 3G 7
SE2 6A 4
Brandon Rd. DA1: Dart 7B 10
Brandon St. DA11: Grav'nd 7A 14
Brands Hatch Motor Racing Circuit 5B 32
Brands Hatch Pk. DA3: Fawk 3C 32
Brands Hatch Rd. DA3: Fawk 4D 32
Bransell Cl. BR8: Crock 6B 26
Branton Rd. DA9: Ghithe 6G 11
Brantwood Av. DA8: Erith 7G 5
Brantwood Rd. DA7: Bex 2A 8
Brasted Cl. DA6: Bex 5G 7
Brasted Rd. DA8: Erith 7J 5
Braundton Av. DA15: Sidc 1C 16
Braywood Rd. SE9 4A 6
Breakneck Hill DA9: Ghithe 5J 11
Bremner Cl. BR8: Swan 4F 27
Brenchley Av. DA11: Grav'nd 5A 24
Brenda Ter. DA10: Swans 7B 12
Brendon Cl. DA8: Erith 1D 8
Brendon Rd. SE9 2A 16
Brennan Rd. RM18: Tilb 2A 14
Brent, The DA1: Dart 7B 10
Brent Cl. DA2: Dart 6C 10
DA5: Bexl 1H 17
Brentfield Rd. DA1: Dart 6B 10
Brentlands Dr. DA1: Dart 1B 20
Brent La. DA1: Dart 7A 10
Brent Way DA2: Dart 6C 10
Brewer's Fld. DA2: Dart 4H 19
Brewers Rd. DA12: Shorne 7H 25
Brewhouse Yd. DA12: Grav'nd 6A 14
Briarfield Cl. DA7: Bex 2K 7
Briar Rd. DA5: Bexl 3C 18
Briars, The TN15: W King 6A 32
Briars Way DA3: Hart 5D 30
Briary Ct. DA14: Sidc 5E 16
Brickfield Farm DA3: Lfield 3D 30
Bridge Cl. DA2: Dart 3E 10
Bridge Ho. DA1: Dart 7K 9
BRIDGEN 7H 7
Bridgen Rd. DA5: Bexl 7H 7
Bridge Rd. DA7: Bex 2H 7
DA8: Erith 2E 8
Bridges Dr. DA1: Dart 5C 10
Bridge Vw. DA9: Ghithe 4J 11
Bright Cl. DA17: Belv 4B 4
Brightlands DA11: Nflt 4H 23
Brigstock Rd. DA17: Belv 4F 5
Brindle Ga. DA15: Sidc 1B 16
Brindley Cl. DA7: Bex 3A 8
Brisbane Ho. RM18: Tilb 1K 13
Bristol Rd. DA12: Grav'nd 3C 24
Bristow Rd. DA7: Bex 1H 7
Britannia Cl. DA8: Erith 6K 5
Britannia Dr. DA12: Grav'nd 5E 24
Brixham Rd. DA16: Well 1G 7
Broad Ditch Rd.
DA13: Ist R, Nflt G 7F 23
Broad La. DA2: Dart 4F 19
Broadoak Cl. DA4: Sutt H 6B 20
Broadoak Rd. DA8: Erith 7H 5
Broad Rd. DA10: Swans 6B 12
Broadway BR8: Crock 6B 26
DA6: Bex 4H 7
(not continuous)
RM18: Tilb 2J 13
Broadway Shop. Cen. DA6: Bex 4K 7
Broadway Sq. DA6: Bex 4K 7
Broadwood DA11: Grav'nd 5A 24
Bromley La. BR7: Chst 7A 16
Bromley Ski Cen. 7H 17
Brompton Dr. DA8: Erith 2K 5
Bronte Cl. DA8: Erith 7F 5
RM18: Tilb 2B 14
Bronte Gro. DA1: Dart 4A 10
Bronte Vw. DA12: Grav'nd 1B 24
Bronze Age Way DA8: Erith 4H 5
DA17: Belv 2F 5
Brookdale Rd. DA5: Bexl 6H 7
Brooke Dr. DA12: Grav'nd 1G 25
Brookend Rd. DA15: Sidc 1B 16
Brooklands DA1: Dart 1K 19
Brooklands Av. DA15: Sidc 2A 16
Brook La. DA5: Bexl, Bex 6G 7
Brook Pk. DA1: Dart 2B 20
Brook Rd. BR8: Swan 3C 26
DA11: Nflt 1H 23
Brookside Rd. DA13: Ist R 7J 23
Brook St. DA8: Erith 5F 5
DA17: Belv, Erith 5F 5
Brookvale DA8: Erith 1A 8
Broomfield Rd. DA6: Bex 5K 7
DA10: Swans 6B 12
Broomfields DA3: Hart 5B 30
Broom Hill Ri. DA6: Bex 5K 7
Broomhill Rd. DA1: Dart 6G 9
Broomhills DA13: Sflt 4B 22
Broom Mead DA6: Bex 6K 7
Broomwood Cl. DA5: Bexl 2C 18
Brougham Ct. *DA2: Dart 6C 10*
(off Hardwick Cres.)
Browning Cl. DA16: Well 1B 6
Browning Rd. DA1: Dart 4A 10
Browning Wlk. RM18: Tilb 2B 14
Brown Rd. DA12: Grav'nd 1D 24
Bruce Cl. DA16: Well 1E 6
Bruce Ct. DA15: Sidc 4C 16
Brummel Cl. DA7: Bex 3B 8
Brunel Cl. RM18: Tilb 3A 14
Brunswick Cl. DA6: Bex 4G 7
Brunswick Rd. DA6: Bex 4G 7
Brunswick Wlk. DA12: Grav'nd 7C 14
(not continuous)
Bryanston Rd. RM18: Tilb 2B 14
Buckingham Av. DA16: Well 4B 6
Buckingham Rd. DA11: Nflt 7G 13
Buckles Ct. DA17: Belv 4B 4
Buckley Cl. DA1: Cray 2E 8
Bucks Cross Rd. DA11: Nflt 3J 23
Buckthorn Ho. *DA15: Sidc 3C 16*
(off Longlands Rd.)
Buckwheat Ct. DA18: Erith 3B 4
Budleigh Cres. DA16: Well 1F 7
Bullace La. DA1: Dart 6K 9
Bull All. DA16: Well 3E 6
Bullbanks Rd. DA17: Belv 4G 5
Bullers Cl. DA14: Sidc 5H 17
Bull Hill DA4: Hort K 4D 28
Bullivant Cl. DA9: Ghithe 5H 11
Bull La. BR7: Chst 7A 16
Bulls Head Yd. *DA1: Dart 6K 9*
(off High St.)
Bull Yd. *DA12: Grav'nd 6A 14*
(off Crooked La.)
Bunkers Hill DA14: Sidc 3J 17
DA17: Belv 4E 4
Bunny Hill DA12: Shorne 6K 25
Burcharbro Rd. SE2 6B 4
Burch Rd. DA11: Nflt 6J 13
Burdett Av. DA12: Shorne 4K 25
Burdett Cl. DA14: Sidc 5H 17
Burgate Cl. DA1: Cray 3E 8
Burghfield Rd. DA13: Ist R 7J 23
Burleigh Av. DA15: Sidc 5C 6
Burman Cl. DA2: Dart 7D 10
Burnaby Rd. DA11: Nflt 7H 13
Burnell Av. DA16: Well 2D 6
Burnham Cres. DA1: Dart 4H 9
Burnham Rd. DA1: Dart 4H 9
DA14: Sidc 2H 17
Burnham Ter. DA1: Dart 5J 9
Burnham Trad. Est. DA1: Dart 4J 9
Burnley Rd. RM20: W Thur 1G 11
Burns Av. DA15: Sidc 6E 6
Burns Cl. DA8: Erith 1E 8
DA16: Well 1C 6
Burns Pl. RM18: Tilb 1A 14
Burnt Ho. La. DA1: Dart 3A 20
DA2: Dart 4K 19
Burnt Oak La. DA15: Sidc 6D 6
Burr Bank Ter. DA2: Dart 4H 19
Burr Cl. DA7: Bex 3J 7
Bursdon Cl. DA15: Sidc 2C 16
Bushey Ct. *DA8: Erith 1F 9*
(off Hazel Rd.)
Bushfield Wlk. DA10: Swans 6B 12
Bushy Lees DA15: Sidc 6C 6
Butchers Hill DA12: Shorne 5K 25
Butcher's La. TN15: Ash, Hart 2G 33
Butcher Wlk. DA10: Swans 7B 12
Butler's Pl. TN15: New A 3H 33
Butterly Av. DA1: Dart 2A 20
Button St. BR8: Swan 2H 27
Button St. Bus. Cen. BR8: Swan 2H 27
Buxton Rd. DA8: Erith 7H 5
Bycliffe Ter. DA11: Grav'nd 7J 13
Bynon Av. DA7: Bex 3J 7
Byron Cl. SE28 1A 4
Byron Dr. DA8: Erith 7F 5
Byron Gdns. RM18: Tilb 1B 14
Byron Ho. DA1: Cray 5D 8
Byron Rd. DA1: Dart 4C 10

C

Cables Cl. DA17: Erith 3G 5
Cadogan Av. DA2: Dart 7E 10
Caerleon Cl. DA14: Sidc 5F 17
Cairns Cl. DA1: Dart 5J 9
Caithness Gdns. DA15: Sidc 6C 6
Calais Cotts. DA3: Fawk 2D 32
Calcroft Av. DA9: Ghithe 5K 11
Calcutta Rd. RM18: Tilb 2J 13
Calderwood DA12: Grav'nd 5D 24
Caldy Rd. DA17: Belv 3F 5
Calfstock La. DA4: Farn 4A 28
Caling Cft. DA3: New A 1J 33
Caliph Cl. DA12: Grav'nd 3E 24
Callenders Cotts. DA17: Erith 2H 5
Calshot Ct. *DA2: Dart 6C 10*
(off Osbourne Rd.)
Calvert Cl. DA14: Sidc 6H 17
DA17: Belv 4E 4
Calvert Dr. DA2: Bexl 2C 18
Camborne Rd. DA14: Sidc 3F 17
DA16: Well 2B 6
Cambria Cl. DA15: Sidc 1A 16
Cambria Cres. DA12: Grav'nd 4D 24
Cambria Ho. *DA8: Erith 7J 5*
(off Larner Rd.)
Cambrian Gro. DA11: Grav'nd 7K 13
Cambridge Av. DA16: Well 4C 6
Cambridge Rd. DA14: Sidc 4B 16
Camdale Rd. SE18 1C 6
Camden Cl. DA11: Nflt 1F 23
Camden Ct. DA17: Belv 5E 4

Camden Rd.—Church Vw.

Camden Rd. DA5: Bexl 1H **17**
Cameron Cl. DA5: Bexl 3D **18**
Campbell Rd. DA11: Grav'nd 1J **23**
Campion Cl. DA11: Nflt 4H **23**
Camrose Av. DA8: Erith 6F **5**
Canada Farm Rd.
DA2: Dart, S Dar 4H **29**
DA3: Fawk 4H **29**
DA4: S Dar 4H **29**
Canada Heights 3J **27**
Canada Rd. DA8: Erith 2K **5**
Canal Basin DA12: Grav'nd 6C **14**
Canal Ind. Pk. DA12: Grav'nd 6C **14**
Canal Rd. DA12: Grav'nd 6B **14**
Canberra Rd. DA7: Bex 6B **4**
Canberra Sq. RM18: Tilb 2K **13**
Cannon Rd. DA7: Bex 1H **7**
Cannon Wlk. *DA12: Grav'nd 7B **14***
(off Albert Murray Cl.)
Canterbury Av. DA15: Sidc 2E **16**
Canterbury Cl. DA1: Dart 7B **10**
Canterbury Ho. DA8: Erith 7K **5**
Canterbury Rd. DA12: Grav'nd 2B **24**
Canterbury Way RM20: W Thur 1F **11**
Capability Way DA9: Ghithe 4K **11**
Capelands DA3: New A 2K **33**
Capel Pl. DA2: Dart 4H **19**
Capital Ind. Est. DA17: Belv 3F **5**
Capstan Cen. RM18: Tilb 1G **13**
Capstan Ct. DA2: Dart 4D **10**
Capstan M. DA11: Nflt 7H **13**
Cardinal Cl. BR7: Chst 7A **16**
Carey Ct. DA6: Bex 5A **8**
Carisbrooke Av. DA5: Bexl 1G **17**
Carisbrooke Ct. *DA2: Dart 6C **10***
(off Osbourne Rd.)
Carl Ekman Ho. DA11: Nflt 7G **13**
Carleton Pl. DA4: Hort K 4D **28**
Carleton Rd. DA1: Dart 7B **10**
Carlisle Rd. DA1: Dart 6B **10**
Carlton Av. DA9: Ghithe 6F **11**
Carlton Grn. DA14: Sidc 4C **16**
Carlton Rd. DA8: Erith 6F **5**
DA14: Sidc 5C **16**
DA16: Well 3E **6**
Carlyle Rd. SE28 1A **4**
Carmelite Way DA3: Hart 5C **30**
Carnet Cl. DA1: Cray 7D **8**
Carrack Ho. *DA8: Erith 5J **5***
(off Saltford Cl.)
Carr Ho. DA1: Cray 5D **8**
Carrill Way DA17: Belv 3B **4**
Carrington Rd. DA1: Dart 6A **10**
Carsington Gdns. DA1: Dart 2J **19**
Carter Av. TN15: W King 7A **32**
Carters Row DA11: Nflt 1J **23**
Cartmel Rd. DA7: Bex 1K **7**
Cascades Leisure Cen. 4F **25**
Caspian Way DA10: Swans 5B **12**
Casstine Cl. BR8: Swan 7E **18**
Castalia Ct. DA1: Dart 3A **10**
Castlefields DA13: Ist R 1J **31**
Castle Hill DA3: Fawk, Hart 5A **30**
Castle La. DA12: Grav'nd 2G **25**
Castle Rd. DA10: Swans 6C **12**
Castle St. DA9: Ghithe 5H **11**
DA10: Swans 6C **12**
Castleton Av. DA7: Bex 1C **8**
Catherine Howard Ct. SE9 6A **6**
Catherine of Aragon Ct. SE9 6A **6**
Catherine Parr Ct. SE9 6A **6**
Cavell Cres. DA1: Dart 4B **10**
Cavendish Av. DA8: Erith 6G **5**
DA15: Sidc 7D **6**
DA16: Well 3C **6**
Cavendish Sq. DA3: Lfield 3A **30**
Caxton Cl. DA3: Hart 4C **30**
Cecil Rd. DA11: Grav'nd 1J **23**
Cedar Av. DA12: Grav'nd 4B **24**
DA15: Sidc 7D **6**
Cedar Cl. BR8: Swan 2B **26**
DA13: Meop 6K **31**
Cedar Dr. DA4: Sutt H 2C **28**
Cedar Gro. DA5: Bexl 6G **7**
Cedarhurst Cotts. DA5: Bexl 7K **7**
Cedar Rd. DA1: Dart 1J **19**
DA8: Erith 1F **9**
Celia Av. *TN15: W King 7B **32***
(off London Rd.)
Centenary Ct. DA4: Farn 7B **28**
Central Av. DA12: Grav'nd 2A **24**
DA16: Well 2C **6**
RM18: Tilb 1K **13**
Central Pde. DA15: Sidc 3D **16**
Central Pk. Arena 1K **19**
Central Rd. DA1: Dart 4K **9**
Centre Rd. DA3: New A 3H **33**
Centurion Way DA18: Erith 3D **4**
Centuryan Pl. DA1: Cray 4G **9**
Cerne Rd. DA12: Grav'nd 4D **24**
Cervia Way DA12: Grav'nd 3E **24**
Chadfields RM18: Tilb 1K **13**
Chadwick Cl. DA11: Nflt 2H **23**
Chalet Cl. DA5: Bexl 4C **18**
Chalice Way DA9: Ghithe 5F **11**
CHALK 1F **25**
Chalk Rd. DA12: Grav'nd 1F **25**
Chalkstone Cl. DA16: Well 1D **6**
Chalky Bank DA11: Grav'nd 4K **23**
Challenge Cl. DA12: Grav'nd 4E **24**
Chambers Cl. DA9: Ghithe 5H **11**
Chancel Cl. TN15: W King 7B **32**
Chancelot Rd. SE2 4A **4**
Chancery Ct. DA1: Dart 7B **10**
Chandlers Dr. DA8: Erith 4H **5**
Chandlers M. DA9: Ghithe 4K **11**
Chantry Av. DA3: Hart 6B **30**
Chantry Cl. DA14: Sidc 5H **17**
SE2 3A **4**
Chantry Ct. DA12: Grav'nd 6B **14**
Chantry Heritage Cen. 6B **14**
Chapel Cl. DA1: Cray 5D **8**
Chapel Ct. DA10: Swans 6B **12**
Chapel Hill DA1: Cray 5D **8**
Chapel Rd. DA7: Bex 4K **7**
Chapel Wlk. *DA2: Bexl 2D **18***
(off Maplehurst Cl.)
Chapel Wood DA3: New A 1H **33**
Chapel Wood Rd. DA3: Hart 3H **33**
TN15: Ash, Hart 3H **33**
Chapman Rd. DA17: Belv 5E **4**
Chapman's La. SE2 4A **4**
Charles Cl. DA14: Sidc 4E **16**
Charles Ct. DA8: Erith 6J **5**
Charles St. DA9: Ghithe 5F **11**
Charlieville Rd. DA8: Erith 7G **5**
Charlotte Cl. DA6: Bex 5H **7**
Charmouth Rd. DA16: Well 1F **7**
Charnock BR8: Swan 4D **26**
(not continuous)
Charter Dr. DA5: Bexl 7H **7**
Charton Cl. DA17: Belv 6D **4**
Chartwell Cl. SE9 2A **16**
Chase, The DA7: Bex 3A **8**
Chase Sq. DA11: Grav'nd 6A **14**
Chastilian Rd. DA1: Dart 7E **8**
Chatsworth Av. DA15: Sidc 1D **16**
Chatsworth Rd. DA1: Dart 5H **9**
Chaucer Cl. RM18: Tilb 2B **14**
Chaucer Pk. DA1: Dart 7A **10**
Chaucer Rd. DA11: Nflt 3G **23**
DA15: Sidc 1F **17**
DA16: Well 1B **6**
Chaucer Way DA1: Dart 4B **10**
(not continuous)
Chave Rd. DA2: Dart 3K **19**
Chelsiter Ct. DA14: Sidc 4C **16**
Cheltenham Cl.
DA12: Grav'nd 5B **24**
Chenies, The DA2: Dart 4D **18**
Chequers Cl. DA13: Ist R 2H **31**
Cherry Av. BR8: Swan 4C **26**
Cherrydown Rd. DA14: Sidc 2G **17**
Cherry Tree La. DA2: Dart 3E **18**
Cherry Trees DA3: Hart 5C **30**
Cherrywood Dr. DA11: Nflt 4H **23**
Cheshunt Cl. DA13: Meop 5K **31**
Cheshunt Rd. DA17: Belv 5E **4**
Chessington Av. DA7: Bex 7C **4**
Chesterfield Dr. DA1: Dart 5G **9**
Chester Rd. DA15: Sidc 5B **6**
(not continuous)
Chesterton Way RM18: Tilb 2B **14**
Chestnut Av. DA9: Bluew 7G **11**
Chestnut Cl. DA11: Nflt 6J **13**
DA15: Sidc 1D **16**
Chestnut Dr. DA7: Bex 3G **7**
Chestnut Gro. DA2: Dart 4C **18**
Chestnut Rd. DA1: Dart 1J **19**
Cheswick Cl. DA1: Cray 4E **8**
Chesworth Cl. DA8: Erith 2D **8**
Chevenings, The DA14: Sidc 3F **17**
Cheviot Cl. DA7: Bex 2D **8**
Cheviot Ho. *DA11: Nflt 6G **13***
(off Laburnum Gro.)
Cheyne Wlk. DA3: Lfield 3A **30**
Chichester Ri. DA12: Grav'nd 4C **24**
Chichester Rd. DA9: Ghithe 6G **11**
Chichester Wharf DA8: Erith 5J **5**
Chiddingstone Av. DA7: Bex 7D **4**
Chieveley Pde. *DA7: Bex 4A **8***
(off Chieveley Rd.)
DA7: Bex 3A **8**
(Mayplace Rd. E.)
Chieveley Rd. DA7: Bex 4A **8**
Chiffinch Gdns. DA11: Nflt 3H **23**
Childs Cres. DA10: Swans 6A **12**
Chilham Cl. DA5: Bexl 7J **7**
Chiltern Cl. DA7: Bex 1D **8**
Chiltern Rd. DA11: Nflt 3H **23**
Chinnery Ct. DA13: Meop 6K **31**
Chipperfield Rd. BR5: St P 7D **16**
(not continuous)
Chipstead Rd. DA8: Erith 7J **5**
Chislehurst Rd. DA14: Sidc 5D **16**
Christchurch Av. DA8: Erith 6H **5**
Christ Chu. Cres.
DA12: Grav'nd 7B **14**
Christchurch Rd. DA1: Dart 7H **9**
DA12: Grav'nd 1B **24**
DA15: Sidc 4C **16**
RM18: Tilb 1K **13**
CHRISTIAN FIELDS 4C **24**
Christian Flds. Av.
DA12: Grav'nd 4B **24**
Christopher Cl. DA15: Sidc 5C **6**
Christopher Ho. *DA15: Sidc 2D **16***
(off Station Rd.)
Chudleigh DA14: Sidc 4E **16**
Church All. *DA11: Grav'nd 6A **14***
(off Princes St.)
Church Av. DA14: Sidc 5D **16**
Church Farm Cl. BR8: Crock 6B **26**
Church Fld. DA2: Dart 2J **19**
Churchfield Rd. DA16: Well 3D **6**
Church Hill DA1: Cray 4D **8**
DA2: Dart 2J **19**
DA9: Ghithe 5F **11**
Churchill Cl. DA1: Dart 1C **20**
Churchill Pk. DA1: Dart 5B **10**
Churchill Rd. DA4: Hort K 4D **28**
DA11: Grav'nd 1J **23**
Church La. BR7: Chst 7A **16**
DA12: Grav'nd 3H **25**
Church Manorway DA8: Erith 4H **5**
Church Path BR8: Swan 1G **27**
DA9: Ghithe 5G **11**
(not continuous)
DA11: Nflt 6F **13**
Church Rd. BR8: Crock 7C **26**
BR8: Swan 1J **27**
DA3: Hart, New A 5C **30**
DA4: Sutt H 6A **20**
(not continuous)
DA7: Bex 2J **7**
DA8: Erith 5H **5**
DA9: Ghithe 5G **11**
DA10: Swans 6C **12**
DA12: Grav'nd 6B **24**
DA13: Cobh, Grav'nd 7K **23**
DA14: Sidc 4D **16**
DA16: Well 2E **6**
RM18: Tilb 1J **13**
TN15: Ash 5H **33**
TN15: W King 7B **32**
Church Row BR7: Chst 7A **16**
Church Row M. BR7: Chst 7A **16**
Church St. DA11: Grav'nd 6A **14**
DA13: Sflt 5D **22**
Church Trad. Est. DA8: Erith 7K **5**
Church Vw. BR8: Swan 3C **26**

Church Wlk. DA2: Dart 3J 19
  DA12: Grav'nd 1C 24
    (not continuous)
Chyngton Cl. DA15: Sidc 3C 16
Cimba Wood DA12: Grav'nd 4D 24
Cineworld Cinema
  Bexleyheath .4K 7
Circle, The RM18: Tilb 1K 13
Cirrus Cres. DA12: Grav'nd 5D 24
Civic Sq. RM18: Tilb 2K 13
Claire C'way. DA2: Dart 4F 11
Claremont Cres. DA1: Cray 4D 8
Claremont Pl. DA11: Grav'nd 7A 14
    (off Arthur St.)
Claremont Rd. BR8: Swan 7D 18
Clarence Cres. DA14: Sidc 3E 16
Clarence Pl. DA12: Grav'nd 7A 14
Clarence Rd. DA6: Bex 4H 7
  DA14: Sidc .3E 16
Clarence Row DA12: Grav'nd 7A 14
Clarenden Pl. DA2: Dart 5D 18
Clarendon Gdns. DA2: Dart 7E 10
Clarendon M. DA5: Bexl 1A 18
Clarendon Rd. DA12: Grav'nd 6B 14
Clare Way DA7: Bex 1H 7
Clark Cl. DA8: Erith 1F 9
Claston Cl. DA1: Cray 4D 8
Clay Farm Rd. SE9 . . . . .2A 16
Clayton Cft. Rd. DA2: Dart 2F 19
Claytonville Ter. DA17: Belv 2G 5
Claywood La. DA2: Bean 3A 22
Clayworth Cl. DA15: Sidc 6E 6
Clearways Bus. Est. TN15: W King 7B 32
Clearways Cvn. Pk. TN15: W King 7A 32
Cleeve Pk. Gdns. DA14: Sidc 2E 16
Cleeves Vw. DA1: Dart 6J 9
    (off Priory Pl.)
CLEMENT STREET 6J 19
Clement St. BR8: Swan, Dart 6J 19
  DA4: Sutt H, Swan 6J 19
Cleveland Ho. DA11: Nflt 6G 13
Cleveland Rd. DA16: Well 2C 6
Cleve Rd. DA14: Sidc 3G 17
Cleves Ct. DA1: Dart 7K 9
Clewer Ho. SE2 . . . . .2B 4
    (off Wolvercote Rd.)
Cliff Reach DA9: Bluew 6G 11
Clifton Gro. DA11: Grav'nd 7A 14
Clifton Marine Pde.
  DA11: Nflt, Grav'nd 6J 13
    (not continuous)
Clifton Rd. DA11: Grav'nd 6K 13
  DA14: Sidc .4B 16
  DA16: Well 3F 7
Clifton Wlk. DA2: Dart 6C 10
Clinton Av. DA16: Well 4D 6
Clipper Blvd. DA2: Dart 3F 11
Clipper Blvd. W. DA2: Dart 3E 10
Clipper Cres. DA12: Grav'nd 4E 24
Clive Av. DA1: Cray 6E 8
Clive Rd. DA11: Grav'nd 6A 14
  DA17: Belv 4E 4
Cloisters, The DA1: Dart 6K 9
    (off Orchard St.)
Cloisters Ct. DA7: Bex 3A 8
Close, The DA2: Dart 3H 19
  DA3: Lfield .2E 30
  DA5: Bexl 6K 7
  DA14: Sidc 4E 16
Cloudesley Rd. DA7: Bex 1J 7
  DA8: Erith 1E 8
Clovelly Rd. DA7: Bex 6C 4
Cloverdale Gdns. DA15: Sidc 6C 6
Clovers, The DA11: Nflt 4H 23
Clydesdale Ho. DA18: Erith 2C 4
    (off Kale Rd.)
Clydon Cl. DA8: Erith 6J 5
Coalhouse Fort 1J 15
Cob Dr. DA12: Shorne 5K 25
Cobham Cl. DA9: Ghithe 6J 11
  DA15: Sidc .6E 6
Cobham Ho. DA8: Erith 7K 5
Cobham Pl. DA6: Bex 5G 7
Cobham St. DA11: Grav'nd 7K 13
Cobham Ter. DA9: Ghithe 5J 11
  DA11: Nflt 1J 23
    (off Southfleet Rd.)

Cobsdene DA12: Grav'nd 6C 24
Cocksure La. DA14: Sidc 3K 17
Codrington Cres. DA12: Grav'nd 5B 24
Codrington Gdns. DA12: Grav'nd 5C 24
    (not continuous)
Coldart Bus. Cen. DA1: Dart 6J 9
COLDBLOW 1B 18
Cold Blow Cres. DA5: Bexl 1C 18
Coldharbour Rd. DA11: Nflt 2H 23
Colebeck St. DA8: Erith 6K 5
Colebrooke Ct. DA14: Sidc 3E 16
Cole Cl. SE28 .1A 4
Coleman Rd. DA17: Belv 4E 4
Colepits Wood Rd. SE9 . . . . .5A 6
Coleridge Rd. DA1: Dart 4C 10
  RM18: Tilb .2B 14
Colin Cl. DA2: Dart 6C 10
College Pl. DA9: Ghithe 4K 11
College Rd. BR8: Swan 1D 26
  DA11: Nflt 5E 12
Coller Cres. DA2: Dart 5F 21
Collindale Av. DA8: Erith 7F 5
  DA15: Sidc .1D 16
Collington Cl. DA11: Nflt 7H 13
Collingwood Ho. DA9: Ghithe 5K 11
Colney Rd. DA1: Dart 6A 10
Coltstead DA3: New A 2H 33
Columbus Ct. DA8: Erith 7K 5
Columbus Sq. DA8: Erith 6K 5
Colyer Cl. DA8: Erith 1C 8
Colyers Cl. DA8: Erith 1B 8
Colyers La. DA8: Erith 1B 8
Colyers Wlk. DA8: Erith 1D 8
Colyton Cl. DA16: Well 1G 7
Combeside SE18 . . . . .1C 6
Commercial Pl. DA12: Grav'nd 6B 14
Common La. DA2: Dart 2F 19
Commonwealth Way SE2 . . . . .5A 4
Compton Pl. DA8: Erith 6K 5
Conference Rd. SE2 . . . . .4A 4
Congress Rd. SE2 . . . . .4A 4
Conifer Av. DA3: Hart 6B 30
Conifer Way BR8: Swan 1B 26
Conisborough Ct. DA2: Dart 6C 10
    (off Osbourne Rd.)
Coniston Av. DA16: Well 3B 6
Coniston Cl. DA1: Dart 1G 19
  DA7: Bex 1B 8
  DA8: Erith 7J 5
Coniston Rd. DA7: Bex 1B 8
Constable Rd. DA11: Nflt 3H 23
Constitution Cres. DA12: Grav'nd 1B 24
    (off Constitution Hill)
Constitution Hill DA12: Grav'nd 1B 24
Consul Gdns. BR8: Swan 7E 18
Cookham Rd. BR8: Swan 2A 26
Cookson Gro. DA8: Erith 7J 5
Cook Sq. DA8: Erith 7K 5
Coombe Rd. DA12: Grav'nd 2B 24
Coombfield Dr. DA2: Dart 4E 20
Cooper Cl. DA9: Ghithe 5G 11
Coopers Cl. DA4: S Dar 1E 28
Coopers Dr. DA2: Bexl 2D 18
Coopers Rd. DA10: Swans 7C 12
  DA11: Nflt 1J 23
Coote Rd. DA7: Bex 1J 7
Copper Beech Cl. DA12: Grav'nd 7C 14
Copperfield Cl. DA12: Grav'nd 1F 25
Copperfields Shop. Cen. DA1: Dart 6K 9
    (off Spital St.)
Copperfield Way BR7: Chst 6A 16
Coppice, The DA5: Bexl 3C 18
Copse Side DA3: Hart 3B 30
Copsewood Cl. DA15: Sidc 6B 6
Coptefield Dr. DA17: Belv 3B 4
Copt Hall Rd. DA13: Meop, Sole S 4K 31
Coralline Wlk. SE2 . . . . .3A 4
Corbylands Rd. DA15: Sidc 7B 6
Corhaven Ho. DA8: Erith 7J 5
Corinthian Manorway DA8: Erith 4H 5
Corinthian Rd. DA8: Erith 4H 5
Cornel Ho. DA15: Sidc 3D 16
Cornelia Pl. DA8: Erith 6J 5
Cornell Cl. DA14: Sidc 6H 17
Cornwall Av. DA16: Well 3B 6
Cornwall Dr. BR5: St P 7F 17

Cornwallis Av. SE9 . . . . .2A 16
Cornwallis Cl. DA8: Erith . . . . . .6K 5 & 1J 5
Cornwall Rd. DA1: Dart 3A 10
Cornwell Av. DA12: Grav'nd 3B 24
Coronation Cl. DA5: Bexl 6G 7
Coronation Ct. DA8: Erith 7H 5
Cortland Cl. DA1: Cray 6D 8
Cotleigh Av. DA5: Bexl 2G 17
Coton Rd. DA16: Well 3D 6
Cotswold Cl. DA7: Bex 2D 8
Cotswold Rd. DA11: Nflt 3H 23
Cottage Fld. Cl. DA14: Sidc 1F 17
Cotton La. DA2: Dart, Ghithe 5D 10
  DA9: Ghithe 5D 10
Coulter Ho. DA9: Ghithe 5K 11
Coulton Av. DA11: Nflt 7H 13
Council Av. DA11: Nflt 6F 13
County Ga. SE9 . . . . .3A 16
Court Av. DA17: Belv 5D 4
Court Cres. BR8: Swan 4D 26
Courtleet Dr. DA8: Erith 1A 8
Court Lodge DA12: Shorne 6K 25
  DA17: Belv 5E 4
Court Rd. DA2: Dart 5F 21
Coutts Av. DA12: Shorne 4K 25
Cowdrey Cl. DA1: Dart 7G 9
Cowley Av. DA9: Ghithe 5G 11
Cowper Av. RM18: Tilb 1A 14
Cowper Cl. DA16: Well 5D 6
Cowper Rd. DA17: Belv 4E 4
Crabtree Manorway Nth.
  DA17: Belv, Erith 2G 5
Crabtree Manorway Sth.
  DA17: Belv 3G 5
Cradley Rd. SE9 . . . . .1A 16
Cramonde Ct. DA16: Well 2D 6
Cranbrook Ho. DA8: Erith 7K 5
    (off Boundary St.)
Cranbrook Rd. DA7: Bex 1J 7
Crandon Wlk. DA4: S Dar 2F 29
Cranford Rd. DA1: Dart 1K 19
Cranleigh Cl. DA5: Bex 6A 8
Cranleigh Dr. BR8: Swan 4D 26
Crawfords BR8: Swan 7D 18
Crawley Ct. DA11: Grav'nd 6K 13
Craybrooke Rd. DA14: Sidc 4E 16
Crayburne DA13: Sflt 5C 22
Cray Cl. DA1: Cray 4F 9
Craydene Rd. DA8: Erith 1E 8
CRAYFORD 5E 8
Crayford High St. DA1: Cray 4D 8
Crayford Ind. Est. DA1: Cray 5E 8
Crayford Rd. DA1: Cray 5E 8
Crayford Stadium (Greyhound) 6D 8
Crayford Station (Rail) 6D 8
Crayford Way DA1: Cray 5E 8
Craylands La. DA10: Ghithe, Swans . . .5A 12
Craylands Sq. DA10: Swans 5A 12
Crayleigh Ter. DA14: Sidc 6F 17
Craymill Sq. DA1: Cray 2E 8
Cray Rd. BR8: Crock 6A 26
  DA14: Sidc .6F 17
  DA17: Belv 6E 4
Crayside Ind. Est. DA1: Cray 4G 9
Crayside Leisure Cen. 6D 8
Creek, The DA11: Nflt 5E 12
Cremorne Rd. DA11: Nflt 7J 13
Crescent, The DA3: Lfield 3B 30
  DA5: Bexl 7F 7
  DA9: Ghithe 5K 11
  DA11: Nflt 2J 23
  DA14: Sidc .4C 16
Crescent Gdns. BR8: Swan 2B 26
Crescent Rd. DA8: Erith 6K 5
  DA15: Sidc .3C 16
Crest Vw. DA9: Ghithe 4H 11
Crete Hall Rd. DA11: Nflt 6G 13
Crichton Ho. DA14: Sidc 6G 17
Cricketers Cl. DA8: Erith 5J 5
CRITTALLS CORNER 7F 17
Crockenhall Way DA13: Ist R 7H 23
CROCKENHILL 6C 26
Crockenhill La. BR8: Crock 7F 27
  DA4: Eyns, Farn 7F 27
Crockenhill Rd. BR8: Crock 6A 26
Croft, The BR8: Swan 3B 26
Croft Cl. DA17: Belv 5D 4

Crofton Av.—Dunkirk Cl.

Crofton Av. DA5: Bexl 7G **7**
Croft Way DA15: Sidc 3B **16**
Crombie Rd. DA15: Sidc 1A **16**
Cromwell Lodge DA6: Bex 5H **7**
Crooked La. DA12: Grav'nd 6A **14**
Crook Lodge Sports Cen. 3G 7
Crook Log DA6: Bex 3G **7**
Cross La. DA5: Bexl 7J **7**
Cross La. E. DA12: Grav'nd 2A **24**
Cross La. W. DA11: Grav'nd 2A **24**
Crossness Footpath DA18: Erith 1D **4**
Cross Rd. DA1: Dart 6H **9**
DA2: Dart 4A **20**
DA11: Nflt 6J **13**
DA14: Sidc 4E **16**
Cross St. DA8: Erith 6J **5**
DA12: Grav'nd 6A ***14***
(off Terrace St.)
Crossways DA2: Dart 4D **10**
Crossways 25 Bus. Pk.
DA2: Dart 4D **10**
Crossways Blvd. DA2: Dart 4D **10**
DA9: Dart, Ghithe 4E **10**
Crowden Way SE28 1A **4**
Crowhurst La. TN15: Ash, W King 7D **32**
Crown Ct. RM18: Tilb 2K **13**
Crown Grn. DA12: Shorne 5K **25**
Crown La. DA12: Shorne 5K **25**
Crown Woods Way SE9 5A **6**
Croxley Grn. BR5: St P 7E **16**
Croyde Cl. DA15: Sidc 7A **6**
Cruden Rd. DA12: Grav'nd 3E **24**
Crumpsall St. SE2 4A **4**
Crusader Ct. DA1: Dart 5A **10**
Crusoe Rd. DA8: Erith 5H **5**
Cugley Rd. DA2: Dart 7D **10**
Culcroft DA3: Hart 3C **30**
Culvers Ct. DA12: Grav'nd 7E **14**
Culvey Cl. DA3: Hart 5B **30**
Cumberland Av. DA12: Grav'nd 7B **14**
DA16: Well 3B **6**
Cumberland Ct. DA16: Well 2B **6**
Cumberland Dr. DA1: Dart 7A **10**
DA7: Bex 7C **4**
Cumbrian Av. DA7: Bex 2D **8**
Curates Wlk. DA2: Dart 3J **19**
Curlews, The DA12: Grav'nd 2C **24**
Curran Av. DA15: Sidc 5C **6**
Cutmore St. DA11: Grav'nd 7A **14**
Cuxton Cl. DA6: Bex 5H **7**
Cyclamen Rd. BR8: Swan 4C **26**
Cygnet Gdns. DA11: Nflt 2J **23**
Cygnet Leisure Cen. 2H 23
Cypress Tree Cl. DA15: Sidc 1C **16**
Cyril Lodge DA14: Sidc 4D **16**
Cyril Rd. DA7: Bex 2H **7**

D

Dabbling Cl. DA8: Erith 1K **5**
Dahlia Dr. BR8: Swan 2E **26**
Dairy Cl. DA4: Sutt H 7C **20**
Dalberg Way SE2 3B **4**
Dale Cl. DA1: Cray 6E **8**
Dale End DA1: Cray 6E **8**
Dalefield Way DA12: Grav'nd 7E **14**
Dale Rd. BR8: Swan 2B **26**
DA1: Cray 6E **8**
DA13: Sflt 4D **22**
Dale Vw. DA8: Erith 2E **8**
Dale Wlk. DA2: Dart 1D **20**
Dallin Rd. DA6: Bex 4G **7**
Dalmeny Rd. DA8: Erith 1A **8**
Daltons Rd. BR8: Crock 7B **26**
Damigos Rd. DA12: Grav'nd 1E **24**
Damon Cl. DA14: Sidc 3E **16**
Damson Ct. BR8: Swan 4C **26**
Dane Cl. DA5: Bexl 7K **7**
Danehill Wlk. DA14: Sidc 3D **16**
Danes Cl. DA11: Nflt 3F **23**
Dansington Rd. DA16: Well 4D **6**
Danson Cres. DA16: Well 3E **6**
DANSON INTERCHANGE 5G **7**
Danson La. DA16: Well 4E **6**
Danson Mead DA16: Well 3F **7**
Danson Pk. 5F 7
Danson Rd. DA5: Bexl, Bex 6F **7**
DA6: Bex 5G **7**
Danson Underpass DA15: Sidc 6F **7**
Danson Water Sports Cen. 4F 7
DARENTH 5D **20**
Darenth Country Pk. 2E 20
Darenth Dr. DA12: Grav'nd 1G **25**
Darenth Hill DA2: Dart 5D **20**
Darenth Hill Trad. Est. DA2: Dart 5C **20**
DARENTH INTERCHANGE 3C **20**
Darenth Park Av. DA2: Dart 2E **20**
Darenth Pl. DA2: Dart 5E **20**
Darenth Rd. DA1: Dart 7A **10**
DA16: Well 1D **6**
Darenth Rd. Sth. DA2: Dart 4C **20**
Darenth Wood Rd. DA2: Dart 1F **21**
(not continuous)
Darent Mead DA4: Sutt H 1C **28**
DARENT VALLEY HOSPITAL 1F 21
Darlton Cl. DA1: Cray 3E **8**
Darnley Ct. *DA11: Grav'nd 7K* ***13***
(off Darnley Rd.)
Darnley Rd. DA11: Grav'nd 1K **23**
(not continuous)
Darnley St. DA11: Grav'nd 7K **13**
Darns Hill BR8: Crock 7B **26**
DARTFORD 6K **9**
Dartford Borough Mus. 7K 9
Dartford By-Pass DA1: Bexl, Dart 7C **8**
DA2: Bean, Dart, Bexl 4A **20**
DA5: Bexl, Dart 7C **8**
Dartford Crossing RM20: Dart 2F **11**
DARTFORD HEATH 1E **18**
Dartford Rd. DA1: Dart 6F **9**
DA4: Farn, Hort K, Knock, S Dar 6B **28**
DA5: Bexl 1B **18**
Dartford Station (Rail) 6K **9**
Dartford Trade Pk. DA1: Dart 2K **19**
Dartford Tunnel DA1: Dart 3E **10**
Dartford Tunnel App. Rd. DA1: Dart 7C **10**
Darwin Rd. DA16: Well 3C **6**
RM18: Tilb 1J **13**
Dashwood Cl. DA6: Bex 5K **7**
Dashwood Rd. DA11: Grav'nd 1K **23**
Davenport Rd. DA14: Sidc 2H **17**
David Coffer Ct. DA17: Belv 4F **5**
David Ho. DA15: Sidc 3D **16**
David Lloyd Leisure
Sidcup 5F 17
Davis Av. DA11: Nflt 1H **23**
Davy's Pl. DA12: Grav'nd 6D **24**
Dawes Cl. DA9: Ghithe 5G **11**
Dawson Dr. BR8: Swan 7D **18**
Days La. DA15: Sidc 7B **6**
DEAN BOTTOM 3J **29**
Debrabant Cl. DA8: Erith 6H **5**
Deepdene Rd. DA16: Well 3D **6**
Deerhurst Cl. DA3: Lfield 3F **31**
Defoe Cl. DA8: Erith 1D **8**
Deirdre Chapman Ho. *DA10: Swans 6B* ***12***
(off Craylands La.)
Dell, The DA5: Bexl 1D **18**
DA9: Ghithe 5J **11**
De Luci Rd. DA8: Erith 5G **5**
De Lucy St. SE2 4A **4**
Denberry Dr. DA14: Sidc 3E **16**
Dene Av. DA15: Sidc 7E **6**
Dene Cl. DA2: Dart 4D **18**
Dene Dr. DA3: Lfield 2E **30**
Dene Holm Rd. DA11: Nflt 3G **23**
Dene Rd. DA1: Dart 7A **10**
Denesway DA13: Meop 6K **31**
Dene Wlk. DA3: Lfield 3B **30**
Denham Cl. DA16: Well 3F **7**
Deniston Av. DA5: Bexl 1H **17**
Dennis Rd. DA11: Grav'nd 3K **23**
Denny Ct. *DA2: Dart 6C* ***10***
(off Bow Arrow La.)
DENTON 7D **14**
Denton Ct. Rd. DA12: Grav'nd 7D **14**
Denton Rd. DA1: Dart 7D **8**
DA5: Bexl 2D **18**
DA16: Well 7A **4**
Denton St. DA12: Grav'nd 7D **14**
Denton Ter. DA5: Bexl 2D **18**
Denver Rd. DA1: Dart 7F **9**
Dering Way DA12: Grav'nd 1E **24**
Derwent Cl. DA1: Dart 1G **19**
Derwent Cres. DA7: Bex 2K **7**
Detling Rd. DA8: Erith 7H **5**
DA11: Nflt 1G **23**
Devon Ct. DA4: Sutt H 1C **28**
Devon Rd. DA4: S Dar, Sutt H 1C **28**
Devonshire Av. DA1: Dart 6G **9**
Devonshire Rd. DA6: Bex 4H **7**
DA12: Grav'nd 1A **24**
Dewlands Av. DA2: Dart 7C **10**
Dexter Ho. *DA18: Erith 3C* ***4***
(off Kale Rd.)
Dial Cl. DA9: Ghithe 5K **11**
Diana Cl. DA14: Sidc 2H **17**
Diana Ct. DA8: Erith 6J **5**
Dickens Av. DA1: Dart 4B **10**
RM18: Tilb 1A **14**
Dickens Cl. DA3: Hart 5C **30**
DA8: Erith 7F **5**
Dickens Dr. BR7: Chst 6A **16**
Dickens Rd. DA12: Grav'nd 1D **24**
Disraeli Cl. SE28 1A **4**
Ditton Rd. DA6: Bex 5G **7**
Dobson Rd. DA12: Grav'nd 5D **24**
Dock Rd. RM17: Grays 1H **13**
RM18: Tilb 1H **13**
Dogwood Cl. DA11: Nflt 4J **23**
Dolphin Yd., The *DA12: Grav'nd 6A* ***14***
(off Queen St.)
Donald Biggs Dr. DA12: Grav'nd 1B **24**
Donnington Ct. *DA2: Dart 6C* ***10***
(off Bow Arrow La.)
Dorchester Av. DA5: Bexl 1G **17**
Dorchester Cl. BR5: St P 7E **16**
DA1: Dart 7A **10**
Dorchester Rd. DA12: Grav'nd 3C **24**
Dorcis Av. DA7: Bex 2H **7**
Doria Dr. DA12: Grav'nd 3D **24**
Doris Av. DA8: Erith 1B **8**
Dormers Dr. DA13: Meop 7K **31**
Dorothy Evans Cl. DA7: Bex 4A **8**
Dorrit Way BR7: Chst 6A **16**
Dorset Av. DA16: Well 4C **6**
Dorset Cres. DA12: Grav'nd 4D **24**
Douglas Rd. DA16: Well 1E **6**
Dovedale Cl. DA16: Well 2D **6**
Dovedale Rd. DA2: Dart 1D **20**
Dover Rd. DA11: Nflt 7G **13**
Dover Rd. E. DA11: Grav'nd 7H **13**
Dowding Wlk. DA11: Nflt 3H **23**
Dowling Ho. DA17: Belv 3D **4**
Downage, The DA11: Grav'nd 2K **23**
Downbank Av. DA7: Bex 1C **8**
Downe Cl. DA16: Well 7A **4**
Downs Av. DA1: Dart 7B **10**
Downs Hill DA13: Ist R 7F **23**
Downs Rd. DA13: Nflt G, Ist R 4G **23**
Downs Valley DA3: Hart 4B **30**
Downsview Cl. BR8: Swan 3E **26**
Doyle Cl. DA8: Erith 1D **8**
Doyle Way RM18: Tilb 2B **14**
Dragons Health Club
St Paul's Cray 7G **17**
Drake Ct. *DA8: Erith 7K* ***5***
(off Frobisher Rd.)
Draper Cl. DA17: Belv 4D **4**
Drive, The DA3: Lfield 3E **30**
DA5: Bexl 6F **7**
DA8: Erith 7F **5**
DA12: Grav'nd 4C **24**
DA14: Sidc 3E **16**
Drove Way, The DA13: Ist R 7H **23**
Drudgeon Way DA2: Bean 3J **21**
Drummond Cl. DA8: Erith 1D **8**
Dryden Pl. RM18: Tilb 1A **14**
Dryden Rd. DA16: Well 1C **6**
Dryhill Rd. DA17: Belv 6D **4**
Ducketts Rd. DA1: Cray 5E **8**
Dudley Rd. DA11: Nflt 7H **13**
Dudsbury Rd. DA1: Dart 6G **9**
DA14: Sidc 6E **16**
Dukes Orchard DA5: Bexl 1B **18**
Dulverton Rd. SE9 2A **16**
Duncannon Pl. DA9: Ghithe 4K **11**
Duncroft SE18 1B **6**
Dunkin Rd. DA1: Dart 4B **10**
Dunkirk Cl. DA12: Grav'nd 5B **24**

40 A-Z Dartford

Dunlop Cl.—Fawkham Manor BMI Hospital

Dunlop Cl. DA1: Dart . . . 3K 9
Dunlop Rd. RM18: Tilb . . . 1J 13
Dunstall Welling Est. DA16: Well . . . 2E 6
Dunwich Rd. DA7: Bex . . . 1J 7
Durant Rd. BR8: Swan . . . 6F 19
Durham Rd. DA14: Sidc . . . 5E 16
Duriun Way DA8: Erith . . . 2K 5
Durndale La. DA11: Nflt . . . 4H 23
Durrant Way DA10: Swans . . . 7B 12
Duxford Ho. *SE2* . . . *2B 4*
(off Wolvercote Rd.)
Dykewood Cl. DA5: Bexl . . . 3C 18
Dylan Rd. DA17: Belv . . . 3E 4

E

Eagles Rd. DA9: Ghithe . . . 4J 11
Eagle Way DA11: Nflt . . . 5D 12
Eardemont Cl. DA1: Cray . . . 4E 8
Eardley Rd. DA17: Belv . . . 5E 4
Earl Rd. DA11: Nflt . . . 2H 23
Eastcote Rd. DA16: Well . . . 2A 6
East Cres. Rd. DA12: Grav'nd . . . 6B 14
Eastern Ind. Est. DA18: Erith . . . 2E 4
Eastern Way DA17: Belv . . . 2A 4
DA18: Belv, Erith . . . 2A 4
SE2 . . . 2A 4
SE28 . . . 2A 4
East Hill DA1: Dart . . . 7A 10
DA4: S Dar . . . 1D 28
E. Hill Dr. DA1: Dart . . . 7A 10
East Holme DA8: Erith . . . 1C 8
E. Kent Av. DA11: Nflt . . . 6F 13
East La. DA4: S Dar . . . 2E 28
Eastleigh Rd. DA7: Bex . . . 3B 8
East Mill DA11: Grav'nd . . . 6J 13
E. Milton Rd. DA12: Grav'nd . . . 7C 14
Eastnor Rd. SE9 . . . 1A 16
East Rd. DA16: Well . . . 2E 6
E. Rochester Way DA15: Bexl, Sidc . . . 4B 6
Eastry Rd. DA8: Erith . . . 7E 4
East St. DA7: Bex . . . 4K 7
East Ter. DA12: Grav'nd . . . 6B 14
DA15: Sidc . . . 1B 16
E. Thamesmead Bus. Pk. DA18: Erith . . . 2D 4
EAST WICKHAM . . . 1F 7
East Woodside DA5: Bexl . . . 7H 7
Eaton Rd. DA14: Sidc . . . 2G 17
Eaton Sq. DA3: Lfield . . . 3A 30
Ebbsfleet Ind. Est. DA11: Nflt . . . 5D 12
Ebbsfleet Station (Rail) . . . 7D 12
Ebbsfleet Wlk. DA11: Nflt . . . 6E 12
Echo Ct. DA12: Grav'nd . . . 2B 24
Echo Sq. DA12: Grav'nd . . . 2B 24
Edam Ct. DA15: Sidc . . . 3D 16
Eden Cl. DA5: Bexl . . . 4C 18
Edendale Rd. DA7: Bex . . . 1C 8
Eden Pl. DA12: Grav'nd . . . 7A 14
Eden Rd. DA5: Bexl . . . 4B 18
Edgar Cl. BR8: Swan . . . 3E 26
Edgefield Cl. DA1: Dart . . . 1C 20
Edge Hill Ct. DA14: Sidc . . . 4C 16
Edgehill Gdns. DA13: Ist R . . . 1J 31
Edgington Way DA14: Sidc . . . 7F 17
Edinburgh Ct. DA8: Erith . . . 7H 5
Edinburgh M. RM18: Tilb . . . 2A 14
Edington Rd. SE2 . . . 3A 4
Edison Gro. SE18 . . . 1C 6
Edison Rd. DA16: Well . . . 1C 6
Edison's Pk. DA2: Dart . . . 3E 10
Ediva Rd. DA13: Meop . . . 5K 31
Edmund Cl. DA13: Meop . . . 5K 31
Edmund Rd. DA16: Well . . . 3D 6
Edwards Gdns. BR8: Swan . . . 4C 26
Edwards Rd. DA17: Belv . . . 4E 4
Edwin Arnold Ct. DA14: Sidc . . . 4C 16
Edwin Cl. DA7: Bex . . . 6D 4
Edwin Petty Pl. DA2: Dart . . . 7D 10
Edwin Rd. DA2: Dart . . . 3G 19
Edwin St. DA12: Grav'nd . . . 7A 14
Egerton Av. BR8: Swan . . . 7E 18
Egerton Cl. DA1: Dart . . . 1G 19
Eglantine La. DA4: Farn, Hort K . . . 7B 28
Eglinton Rd. DA10: Swans . . . 6C 12
Elbourne Trad. Est. DA17: Belv . . . 3F 5
Elder Cl. DA15: Sidc . . . 1C 16
Elgar Gdns. RM18: Tilb . . . 1K 13
Eliot Rd. DA1: Dart . . . 5C 10
Elizabeth Cl. RM18: Tilb . . . 2A 14
Elizabeth Ct. DA11: Grav'nd . . . 6K 13
Elizabeth Garrett Anderson Ho.
DA17: Belv . . . 3E 4
(off Ambrook Rd.)
Elizabeth Huggins Cotts.
DA11: Grav'nd . . . 2A 24
Elizabeth Pl. DA4: Farn . . . 6A 28
Elizabeth St. DA9: Ghithe . . . 5F 11
Eliza Cook Cl. DA9: Ghithe . . . 4J 11
Ellenborough Rd. DA14: Sidc . . . 5G 17
ELLENOR FOUNDATION (HOSPICE) . . . 7A 10
(next to Livingstone Hopsital)
Ellerman Rd. RM18: Tilb . . . 1J 13
Ellerslie DA12: Grav'nd . . . 7C 14
Elliott St. DA12: Grav'nd . . . 7C 14
Ellis Cl. BR8: Swan . . . 4C 26
Ellison Rd. DA15: Sidc . . . 1A 16
Ellis Way DA1: Dart . . . 2A 20
Elmbourne Dr. DA17: Belv . . . 4F 5
Elm Cl. DA1: Dart . . . 1H 19
Elmcroft Av. DA15: Sidc . . . 7C 6
Elm Dr. BR8: Swan . . . 2C 26
Elmfield Cl. DA11: Grav'nd . . . 1A 24
Elmfield Ct. DA16: Well . . . 1E 6
Elm Gro. DA8: Erith . . . 7H 5
Elmhurst DA9: Ghithe . . . 6J 11
DA17: Belv . . . 6C 4
Elmington Cl. DA5: Bexl . . . 6A 8
Elm Pde. DA14: Sidc . . . 4D 16
Elm Rd. DA1: Dart . . . 1J 19
DA8: Erith . . . 1F 9
DA9: Ghithe . . . 6F 11
DA12: Grav'nd . . . 3B 24
DA14: Sidc . . . 4D 16
Elmstead Rd. DA8: Erith . . . 1D 8
Elmsted Cres. DA16: Well . . . 6A 4
Elmwood Dr. DA5: Bexl . . . 7H 7
Elrick Cl. DA8: Erith . . . 6J 5
Elsa Rd. DA16: Well . . . 2E 6
Elstree Gdns. DA17: Belv . . . 4C 4
Eltham Crematorium SE9 . . . 4A 6
Elwick Ct. DA1: Cray . . . 4F 9
Elwill Way DA13: Ist R . . . 1J 31
Ely Cl. DA8: Erith . . . 2E 8
Embassy Ct. DA14: Sidc . . . 3E 16
DA16: Well . . . 3E 6
EMD Cinema . . . 6A 14
Emersons Av. BR8: Swan . . . 7E 18
Emerton Cl. DA6: Bex . . . 4H 7
Emes Rd. DA8: Erith . . . 7G 5
Empire Wlk. DA9: Ghithe . . . 4K 11
Empress Rd. DA12: Grav'nd . . . 7D 14
Ennerdale Rd. DA7: Bex . . . 1K 7
Epsom Cl. DA7: Bex . . . 3A 8
Erica Ct. BR8: Swan . . . 4D 26
ERITH . . . 5K 5
ERITH & DISTRICT HOSPITAL . . . 6H 5
Erith High St. DA8: Erith . . . 5J 5
Erith Library & Mus. . . . 5J 5
Erith Playhouse . . . *5K 5*
(off Wharfside Cl.)
Erith Rd. DA7: Bex . . . 4A 8
DA8: Bex, Erith . . . 4A 8
DA8: Erith . . . 5E 4
DA17: Belv, Erith . . . 5E 4
Erith School Community Sports Cen. . . . 7H 5
Erith Small Bus. Cen. *DA8: Erith . . . 6K 5*
(off Erith High St.)
Erith Sports Cen. . . . 6J 5
Erith Stadium . . . 6J 5
Erith Station (Rail) . . . 5J 5
Erith Yacht Club . . . 1K 5
Ermington Rd. SE9 . . . 2A 16
Esher Cl. DA5: Bexl . . . 1H 17
Eskdale Cl. DA2: Dart . . . 2D 20
Eskdale Rd. DA7: Bex . . . 2K 7
Esporta Health & Fitness
Chislehurst . . . 5B 16
Essenden Rd. DA17: Belv . . . 5E 4
Essex Rd. DA1: Dart . . . 6J 9
(not continuous)
DA3: Lfield . . . 2A 30
DA11: Grav'nd . . . 1K 23
Etfield Gro. DA14: Sidc . . . 5E 16
Ethelbert Rd. DA2: Dart . . . 4K 19
DA8: Erith . . . 7G 5
Ethronvi Rd. DA7: Bex . . . 3H 7
Eton Way DA1: Dart . . . 4H 9
Europa Trad. Est. DA8: Erith . . . 5H 5
Euro Trade Cen. DA17: Belv . . . 2G 5
Evans Cl. DA9: Ghithe . . . 5H 11
Evenden Rd. DA13: Meop . . . 7K 31
Evenlode Ho. SE2 . . . 2A 4
Everest Cl. DA11: Nflt . . . 3H 23
Everest Pl. BR8: Swan . . . 4C 26
Everett Wlk. *DA17: Belv . . . 5D 4*
(off Osborne Rd.)
Everglade Cl. DA3: Hart . . . 4B 30
Eversley Av. DA7: Bex . . . 2C 8
Eversley Cross DA7: Bex . . . 2D 8
Evesham Rd. DA12: Grav'nd . . . 2C 24
Evry Rd. DA14: Sidc . . . 6F 17
Exeter Rd. DA12: Grav'nd . . . 3C 24
DA16: Well . . . 2B 6
Exmouth Rd. DA16: Well . . . 1F 7
Eynsford Cres. DA5: Bexl . . . 1F 17
Eynsford Rd. BR8: Crock . . . 6C 26
DA9: Ghithe . . . 5K 11
Eynsham Dr. SE2 . . . 3A 4
Eynswood Dr. DA14: Sidc . . . 5E 16

F

Factory Rd. DA11: Nflt . . . 6F 13
Faesten Way DA5: Bexl . . . 3D 18
Fairacre Pl. DA3: Hart . . . 3B 30
Fairby Grange DA3: Hart . . . 6B 30
Fairby La. DA3: Hart . . . 6B 30
Fairfax Rd. RM18: Tilb . . . 1J 13
Fairfield Cl. DA15: Sidc . . . 6C 6
Fairfield Pool & Leisure Cen. . . . 7K 9
Fairfield Rd. DA7: Bex . . . 2J 7
Fairfields DA12: Grav'nd . . . 5D 24
Fairford Av. DA7: Bex . . . 1C 8
Fairlawn Av. DA7: Bex . . . 2G 7
Fairlight Cross DA3: Lfield . . . 3E 30
Fairmont Cl. DA17: Belv . . . 5D 4
Fairoak Dr. SE9 . . . 5A 6
Fairseat La. TN15: Stans . . . 7K 33
Fairview DA3: Fawk . . . 3E 32
DA8: Erith . . . 7K 5
Fairview Gdns. DA13: Meop . . . 5K 31
Fairview Rd. DA13: Ist R . . . 7G 23
Fairwater Av. DA16: Well . . . 4D 6
Fairway DA6: Bex . . . 5H 7
Fairway, The DA11: Grav'nd . . . 2K 23
Fairway Dr. DA2: Dart . . . 7C 10
Falcon Cl. DA1: Dart . . . 5A 10
Falcon M. DA11: Nflt . . . 1H 23
FALCONWOOD . . . 4C 6
FALCONWOOD . . . 4A 6
Falconwood Av. DA16: Well . . . 2A 6
Falconwood Pde. DA16: Well . . . 4B 6
Falconwood Station (Rail) . . . 4A 6
Fallowfield DA2: Bean . . . 3J 21
Falstaff Cl. DA1: Cray . . . 7D 8
Faraday Av. DA14: Sidc . . . 2D 16
Faraday Rd. DA16: Well . . . 3D 6
Farley Rd. DA12: Grav'nd . . . 1E 24
Farlow Cl. DA11: Nflt . . . 3J 23
Farm Av. BR8: Swan . . . 3B 26
Farmcroft DA11: Grav'nd . . . 2K 23
Farm Holt DA3: New A . . . 1J 33
Farm Pl. DA1: Cray . . . 4F 9
Farm Va. DA5: Bexl . . . 6A 8
Farnham Rd. DA16: Well . . . 2F 7
FARNINGHAM . . . 7A 28
Farningham Hill Rd. DA4: Farn . . . 5H 27
Farningham Road Station (Rail) . . . 2C 28
Farnol Rd. DA1: Dart . . . 5B 10
Farriers Cl. DA12: Grav'nd . . . 1E 24
Farrington Pl. BR7: Chst . . . 7A 16
Farthing Cl. DA1: Dart . . . 4A 10
Farwell Rd. DA14: Sidc . . . 4E 16
Fawkes Av. DA1: Dart . . . 2A 20
FAWKHAM . . . 7J 29
Fawkham Av. DA3: Lfield . . . 3F 31
FAWKHAM GREEN . . . 3E 32
Fawkham Grn. Rd. DA3: Ash, Fawk . . . 3E 32
FAWKHAM MANOR BMI HOSPITAL . . . 1F 33

Fawkham Rd.—Graham Ter.

Fawkham Rd. DA3: Fawk .4C 32
DA3: Fawk, Lfield .4A 30
TN15: W King .7D 32
Faygate Cres. DA6: Bex .5K 7
Federation Rd. SE2 .4A 4
Feenan Highway RM18: Tilb .1A 14
Felix Mnr. BR7: Chst .6B 16
Felixstowe Rd. SE2 .3A 4
Felton Lea DA14: Sidc .5C 16
Fendyke Rd. DA17: Belv .4B 4
Fen Gro. DA15: Sidc .5C 6
Fenners Marsh DA12: Grav'nd .7E 14
Fens Way BR8: Swan .6F 19
Fenswood Cl. DA5: Bexl .6K 7
Ferby Ct. *DA14: Sidc .4C 16*
(off Main Rd.)
SE9 .3A 16
(off Main Rd.)
Ferguson Av. DA12: Grav'nd .4B 24
Fernbrook Av. DA15: Sidc .5B 6
Fern Cl. DA8: Erith .1G 9
Fern Ct. DA7: Bex .4K 7
Ferndale Cl. DA7: Bex .1H 7
Ferndale Rd. DA12: Grav'nd .2A 24
Ferndell Av. DA5: Bexl .3C 18
Ferndene DA3: Lfield .3G 31
Fernheath Way DA2: Dart .5C 18
Ferry Rd. RM18: Tilb .3K 13
Festival Av. DA3: Lfield .3G 31
Festival Cl. DA5: Bexl .1G 17
DA8: Erith .7K 5
Fiddler's Cl. DA9: Ghithe .4J 11
Fielding Av. RM18: Tilb .1A 14
Filborough Way DA12: Grav'nd .2G 25
Filston Rd. DA8: Erith .5G 5
Finch Ct. DA14: Sidc .3E 16
Finchley Cl. DA1: Dart .6B 10
Finsbury Way DA5: Bexl .6J 7
Firecrest Cl. DA3: Lfield .3E 30
Firmin Rd. DA1: Dart .5H 9
Firs, The DA5: Bexl .1C 18
DA15: Sidc .2C 16
Firside Gro. DA15: Sidc .1C 16
First Av. DA7: Bex .7A 4
DA11: Nflt .1H 23
Fishermens Hill DA11: Nflt .5E 12
Fishers Way DA17: Belv .1G 5
Fitzroy Ct. *DA1: Dart .1C 20*
(off Churchill Cl.)
Fiveash Rd. DA11: Grav'nd .7J 13
Five Wents BR8: Swan .2F 27
Flats, The DA9: Ghithe .5K 11
Flaxman Ct. *DA17: Belv .5E 4*
(off Hoddesdon Rd.)
Flaxton Rd. SE18 .1A 6
Fleet Av. DA2: Dart .1D 20
Fleetdale Pde. DA2: Dart .1D 20
FLEET DOWNS .1D 20
Fleet Ho's. DA13: Sflt .6E 22
Fleet Rd. DA2: Dart .1C 20
DA11: Nflt .3F 23
Fleming Gdns. RM18: Tilb .1B 14
Flora St. DA17: Belv .5D 4
Florence Farm Mobile Home Pk.
TN15: W King .6A 32
Florence Rd. SE2 .4B 4
Flowerhill Way DA13: Ist R .7H 23
Foley Ct. *DA1: Dart .1C 20*
(off Churchill Cl.)
Foord Cl. DA2: Dart .2F 21
FOOTS CRAY .6F 17
Foots Cray High St. DA14: Sidc .6F 17
Foots Cray La. DA14: Sidc .1F 17
Footscray Rd. SE9 .2A 16
Ford Rd. DA11: Nflt .5E 12
Foresters Cres. DA7: Bex .4A 8
Forest Rd. DA8: Erith .1F 9
Forest Way DA15: Sidc .7A 6
Forge La. DA4: Hort K .4D 28
DA12: Grav'nd .2E 24
DA12: Shorne .5K 25
Forge Pl. DA12: Grav'nd .1E 24
Fort Gardens .*6B 14*
(off Milton Pl.)
Fortress Distribution Pk. RM18: Tilb .4K 13
Fort Rd. RM18: Tilb, W Til .4A 14
Fortrye Cl. DA11: Nflt .2H 23
Fortuna Cl. DA3: Hart .4C 30
Forty Foot Way SE9 .7A 6
Fosset Lodge DA7: Bex .1B 8
Fossington Rd. DA17: Belv .4B 4
Fountain Ct. DA15: Sidc .6E 6
Fountain Wlk. DA11: Nflt .6H 13
Fourth Av. DA11: Nflt .1H 23
Fowlers Cl. DA14: Sidc .5H 17
Foxberry Wlk. DA11: Nflt .3G 23
Foxbury DA3: New A .3H 33
Foxbury Av. BR7: Chst .6A 16
Foxglove Cl. DA15: Sidc .6D 6
Fox Hollow Dr. DA7: Bex .3G 7
Foxhounds La. DA13: Sflt .3D 22
Fox Ho. Rd. DA17: Belv .5F 5
(not continuous)
Foxwood Gro. DA11: Nflt .1H 23
Foxwood Rd. DA2: Bean .3J 21
Foxwood Way DA3: Lfield .2G 31
Francis Av. DA7: Bex .2K 7
Francis Rd. DA1: Dart .5J 9
Frank Godley Ct. DA14: Sidc .5E 16
Franklin Rd. DA2: Bexl .2D 18
DA7: Bex .1H 7
DA12: Grav'nd .5C 24
Franks La. DA4: Hort K .5B 28
Fraser Cl. DA5: Bexl .1B 18
Fraser Rd. DA8: Erith .5H 5
Freeland Ct. DA15: Sidc .3D 16
Freeland Way DA8: Erith .1F 9
Freeman Rd. DA12: Grav'nd .3D 24
Fremantle Ho. RM18: Tilb .1J 13
Fremantle Rd. DA17: Belv .4E 4
Frensham Rd. SE9 .2A 16
Freta Rd. DA6: Bex .5J 7
Friars Wlk. SE2 .5B 4
Friday Rd. DA8: Erith .5H 5
Frimley Ct. DA14: Sidc .5F 17
Frinsted Rd. DA8: Erith .7H 5
Frinton Rd. DA14: Sidc .2H 17
Friswell Pl. DA6: Bex .4K 7
Frobisher Rd. DA8: Erith .7K 5 & 2J 5
Frobisher Way DA9: Ghithe .4J 11
DA12: Grav'nd .5D 24
Frognal Av. DA14: Sidc .5D 16
FROGNAL CORNER .6C 16
Frognal Pl. DA14: Sidc .6D 16
Fuchsia St. SE2 .5A 4
Fulwich Rd. DA1: Dart .6A 10
Furner Cl. DA1: Cray .3E 8

G

Gable Cl. DA1: Cray .5F 9
Gables, The DA3: Lfield .2F 31
Gabriel Gdns. DA12: Grav'nd .5D 24
Gabrielspring Rd. DA3: Fawk .2A 32
Gabrielspring Rd. E.
DA3: Fawk, Hort K .2B 32
Gainsborough Av. DA1: Dart .5H 9
RM18: Tilb .1K 13
Gainsborough Dr. DA11: Nflt .3G 23
Gainsborough Sq. DA6: Bex .3G 7
Gala Bingo
Bexleyheath .4A 8
Dartford .6J 9
Galleon Blvd. DA2: Dart .4E 10
Galleon Cl. DA8: Erith .4H 5
Galleon M. DA11: Nflt .7H 13
Galley Hill Ind. Est. DA10: Swans .5B 12
Galley Hill Rd. DA10: Nflt .5C 12
DA11: Nflt .5C 12
Galloway Dr. DA1: Cray .7D 8
Gallows Wood DA3: Fawk .4D 32
Galsworthy Rd. RM18: Tilb .1B 14
Gapp Cl. TN15: W King .7B 32
Garden Av. DA7: Bex .3J 7
Garden Pl. DA2: Dart .3J 19
Garden Row DA11: Nflt .3J 23
Gargery Cl. DA12: Grav'nd .1F 25
Garland Rd. SE18 .1A 6
Garrard Cl. DA7: Bex .3K 7
Garrick St. DA11: Grav'nd .6A 14
Garrolds Cl. BR8: Swan .2C 26
Garrow DA3: Lfield .3E 30
Gascoyne Dr. DA1: Cray .3E 8
Gasson Rd. DA10: Swans .6B 12
Gateacre Ct. DA14: Sidc .4E 16
Gateway Pde. DA12: Grav'nd .4E 24
Gattons Way DA14: Sidc .4J 17
Gatwick Rd. DA12: Grav'nd .3A 24
Gaylor Rd. RM18: Tilb .1J 13
Gayton Rd. SE2 .3A 4
Gazelle Glade DA12: Grav'nd .5E 24
Geddes Pl. *DA7: Bex .4K 7*
(off Arnsberga Way)
Genesta Glade DA12: Grav'nd .5F 25
Geoffrey Whitworth Theatre .4F 9
Gerald Rd. DA12: Grav'nd .7D 14
Gerdview Dr. DA2: Dart .4H 19
Gertrude Rd. DA17: Belv .4E 4
Gibson Cl. DA11: Nflt .3J 23
Gideon Cl. DA17: Belv .4F 5
Gilbert Cl. DA10: Swans .6A 12
Gilbert Rd. DA17: Belv .3E 4
Gilbert Row DA11: Nflt .2J 23
Gildenhill Rd. BR8: Swan .7H 19
Giles Fld. DA12: Grav'nd .1E 24
Gill Cres. DA11: Nflt .3J 23
Gillies Rd. TN15: W King .5B 32
Gills Rd. DA2: Dart .1F 29
DA4: S Dar .1F 29
Gipsy Rd. DA16: Well .7B 4
Glades, The DA12: Grav'nd .6C 24
Gladeswood Rd. DA17: Belv .4F 5
Gladstone Rd. DA1: Dart .6A 10
Glebelands DA1: Cray .4E 8
Glebe Pl. DA4: Hort K .4D 28
Glebe Rd. DA11: Grav'nd .1J 23
Glebe Way DA8: Erith .6J 5
Glen Ct. DA15: Sidc .4D 16
Glendale BR8: Swan .4E 26
Glendale Rd. DA8: Erith .4G 5
DA11: Nflt .4H 23
Glendale Way SE28 .1A 4
Glengall Rd. DA7: Bex .3H 7
Glenhurst Av. DA5: Bexl .1J 17
Glenmore Rd. DA16: Well .1C 6
Glenrosa Gdns. DA12: Grav'nd .5E 24
Glenrose Ct. DA14: Sidc .5E 16
Glen Vw. DA12: Grav'nd .1B 24
Glenview SE2 .6B 4
Glenwood Ct. DA14: Sidc .4D 16
Glimpsing Grn. DA18: Erith .3C 4
Gloucester Av. DA15: Sidc .2B 16
DA16: Well .4C 6
Gloucester Ct. RM18: Tilb .2J 13
Gloucester Pde. DA15: Sidc .5D 6
Gloucester Rd. DA1: Dart .7G 9
DA12: Grav'nd .4B 24
DA17: Belv .5D 4
Glover Cl. SE2 .4A 4
Gloxinia Rd. DA13: Sflt .6E 22
Glynde Rd. DA7: Bex .3G 7
Glyn Dr. DA14: Sidc .4E 16
Goals Football Training Cen. .3J 7
Godstow Rd. SE2 .2A 4
Goldsel Rd. BR8: Crock, Swan .5C 26
Golf Links Av. DA11: Grav'nd .5A 24
Goodwin Dr. DA14: Sidc .3G 17
Goodwood Cres. DA12: Grav'nd .5B 24
Gordon Cl. RM18: E Til .1J 15
Gordon Pl. DA12: Grav'nd .6B 14
Gordon Prom. DA12: Grav'nd .6B 14
Gordon Prom. E. DA12: Grav'nd .6B 14
Gordon Rd. DA1: Dart .7J 9
DA11: Nflt .7H 13
DA15: Sidc .5B 6
DA17: Belv .4G 5
Gore Cotts. DA2: Dart .3D 20
Gore Rd. DA2: Dart .2D 20
Gorringe Av. DA4: S Dar .2E 28
Gorse Hill DA4: Farn, Fawk .7B 28 & 2A 32
Gorse Way DA3: Hart .5C 30
Gorse Wood Rd. DA3: Lfield .3D 30
Gorsewood Rd. DA3: Hart .5C 30
Goss Hill BR8: Swan .6H 19
Gothic Cl. DA1: Dart .3J 19
Gouge Av. DA11: Nflt .1H 23
Grace Av. DA7: Bex .2J 7
Graham Rd. DA6: Bex .4J 7
Graham Ter. *DA15: Sidc .6E 6*
(off Westerham Dr.)

42 A-Z Dartford

Granby Rd. DA11: Nflt 6F 13
(not continuous)
Grange, The DA4: S Dar 1E 28
TN15: W King 7C 32
Grange Cl. DA15: Sidc 3D 16
Grange Cres. DA2: Dart 6C 10
Grange Ho. DA8: Erith 2F 9
DA11: Grav'nd 7K 13
Grange La. DA3: Hart 7D 30
Grange Rd. DA11: Grav'nd 7K 13
Grange Way DA3: Hart 6C 30
DA8: Erith 2K 5
Grangeways Cl. DA11: Nflt 4J 23
Grangewood DA5: Bexl 1J 17
Granton Rd. DA14: Sidc 6F 17
Granville M. DA14: Sidc 4D 16
Granville Rd. DA11: Grav'nd 7J 13
DA14: Sidc 4D 16
DA16: Well 3F 7
Grasmere Rd. DA7: Bex 2B 8
Grassington Rd. DA14: Sidc 4D 16
Grass Rd. DA3: Lfield 5F 31
Gravel Hill DA6: Bex 4A 8
Gravel Hill Cl. DA6: Bex 5A 8
Gravel Pit La. SE9 . . . . .5A 6
Gravel Rd. DA4: Sutt H 7C 20
GRAVESEND 6A 14
Gravesend & Northfleet FC 5D 12
GRAVESEND & NORTH KENT HOSPITAL
. . . . .6K 13
Gravesend Rd. DA12: Shorne 3J 25
Gravesend Sailing Club 6C 14
(off Gordon Prom. E.)
Gravesend Station (Rail) 6A 14
Gravesham Ct. DA12: Grav'nd 7A 14
Gravesham Mus. 6A 14
Grays Farm Rd. BR5: St P 7E 16
Grazeley Cl. DA6: Bex 5B 8
Gt. Queen St. DA1: Dart 7A 10
Green, The BR5: St P 7E 16
DA2: Dart 2E 8
DA7: Bex 1K 7
DA14: Sidc 4D 16
DA16: Well 4B 6
Greenacre DA1: Dart 2J 19
Greenacre Cl. BR8: Swan 4D 26
Greenacres DA14: Sidc 4D 16
Greenbanks DA1: Dart 2K 19
Green Ct. Rd. BR8: Crock 5C 26
Greendale Wlk. DA11: Nflt 3H 23
Grn. Farm La. DA12: Shorne 2K 25
Greenfield Rd. DA2: Dart 5C 18
Greenfinches DA3: Lfield 3E 30
Greenhill Rd. DA11: Nflt 2J 23
GREENHITHE 4J 11
Greenhithe Cl. DA15: Sidc 7B 6
Greenhithe for Bluewater Station (Rail)
. . . . .5J 11
Greening St. SE2 . . . . .4A 4
Green La. DA12: Shorne 6J 25
DA13: Meop 7K 31
Green Mnr. Way DA11: Nflt 4C 12
Greenmead DA18: Erith 3C 4
Green Pl. DA1: Cray 5D 8
Greenside BR8: Swan 2C 26
DA5: Bexl 1H 17
GREEN STREET GREEN 6H 21
Green Street Green Rd. DA1: Dart 1C 20
DA2: Dart 3D 20
Green Va. DA6: Bex 5G 7
Green Wlk. DA1: Cray 5E 8
Green Way DA3: Hart 5B 30
Greenways DA3: Lfield 3G 31
GREENWICH & BEXLEY COTTAGE HOSPICE
. . . . .5A 4
Greenwood Cl. DA15: Sidc 2D 16
Greenwood Rd. DA5: Bexl 4C 18
Gresham Av. DA3: Hart 5C 30
Gresham Cl. DA5: Bexl 6H 7
Gresswell St. DA14: Sidc 3D 16
Greyhound Commercial Cen., The
DA1: Cray 5D 8
Greyhound Way DA1: Cray 5D 8
Grieves Rd. DA11: Nflt 3J 23
Griffin Wlk. DA9: Ghithe 5G 11
Groombridge Cl. DA16: Well 5D 6
Grosvenor Cres. DA1: Dart 5J 9

Grosvenor Rd. DA6: Bex 5G 7
DA17: Belv 6E 4
Grosvenor Sq. DA3: Lfield 3B 30
(off Park Dr.)
Grove, The BR8: Swan 3E 26
DA6: Bex 4G 7
DA10: Swans 5C 12
DA12: Grav'nd 7A 14
DA14: Sidc 5H 17
Grovebury Cl. DA8: Erith 6H 5
Grovebury Ct. DA6: Bex 5A 8
Grovebury Rd. SE2 . . . . .2A 4
Gro. Craft Workshops, The DA3: Fawk 7H 29
Groveherst Rd. DA1: Dart 3A 10
Grovelands Rd. BR5: St P 7D 16
Grove Rd. DA7: Bex 4B 8
DA11: Nflt 5E 12
DA17: Belv 6D 4
GRUBB STREET 1J 29
Guild Rd. DA8: Erith 7K 5
Gulliver Cl. DA15: Sidc 2A 16
Gunfleet Cl. DA12: Grav'nd 7D 14
Gunn Rd. DA10: Swans 6B 12
Gwillim Cl. DA15: Sidc 5D 6
Gwynn Rd. DA11: Nflt 2F 23

H

Haddon Gro. DA15: Sidc 7C 6
Hadley Rd. DA17: Belv 4D 4
Hadlow Rd. DA14: Sidc 4D 16
DA16: Well 7A 4
Hadlow Way DA13: Ist R 7H 23
Haig Gdns. DA12: Grav'nd 7B 14
Hailey Rd. DA18: Erith 2E 4
Hailey Rd. Bus. Pk. DA18: Erith 2E 4
Halcot Av. DA6: Bex 5A 8
Haldane Gdns. DA11: Nflt 1F 23
Haldane Rd. SE28 . . . . .1B 4
Halfway St. DA15: Sidc 7A 6
Halifield Dr. DA17: Belv 3C 4
Hallford Way DA1: Dart 6H 9
Hall Pl. Cres. DA5: Bexl 6B 8
Hall Place & Vis. Cen. 6B 8
Hall Place Gardens 6B 8
Hall Rd. DA1: Dart 4A 10
DA11: Nflt, Sflt 3F 23
Halstead Rd. DA8: Erith 1D 8
Halt Robin La. DA17: Belv 4F 5
Halt Robin Rd. DA17: Belv 4E 4
(not continuous)
Hambledown Rd. DA15: Sidc 7A 6
Hamerton Rd. DA11: Nflt 5E 12
Hamilton Ct. DA8: Erith 7K 5
(off Frobisher Rd.)
Hamilton Rd. DA7: Bex 2H 7
DA15: Sidc 4D 16
Hamilton Wlk. DA8: Erith 7K 5
Hamlet Ho. DA8: Erith 7J 5
Hamlet International Ind. Est.
DA8: Erith 5H 5
Hampton Cres. DA12: Grav'nd 2D 24
Hampton Ho. DA7: Bex 2A 8
(off Erith Rd.)
Hamshades Cl. DA15: Sidc 3C 16
Hanbury Wlk. DA5: Bexl 3D 18
Hanover Pl. DA3: New A 2J 33
Hanover Way DA6: Bex 3G 7
Hansol Rd. DA6: Bex 5H 7
Harbex Cl. DA5: Bexl 7A 8
Harborough Av. DA15: Sidc 7B 6
Harcourt Av. DA15: Sidc 6F 7
Harcourt Rd. DA6: Bex 4H 7
Harden Rd. DA11: Nflt 3J 23
Harding Rd. DA7: Bex 2J 7
Hardwick Cl. DA8: Erith 6H 5
Hardwick Cres. DA2: Dart 6C 10
Hardy Av. DA11: Nflt 2H 23
Hardy Ct. DA8: Erith 7K 5
Hardy Gro. DA1: Dart 4B 10
Harefield Rd. DA14: Sidc 2G 17
Harfst Way BR8: Swan 1B 26
Harland Av. DA15: Sidc 3A 16
Harlequin Ho. DA18: Erith 3C 4
(off Kale Rd.)
Harlington Rd. DA7: Bex 3H 7

Harman Av. DA11: Grav'nd 5A 24
Harman Dr. DA15: Sidc 6C 6
Harmer Rd. DA10: Swans 6C 12
Harmer St. DA12: Grav'nd 6B 14
Harnetts Cl. BR8: Crock 7C 26
Harold Av. DA17: Belv 5D 4
Harold Rd. DA2: Dart 4A 20
Harold Wilson Ho. SE28 . . . . .1A 4
Harris Cl. DA11: Nflt 3J 23
Harris Rd. DA7: Bex 1H 7
Harrowby Gdns. DA11: Nflt 2H 23
Harrow Mnr. Way SE2 . . . . .1A 4
Hart Dyke Rd. BR8: Swan 3C 26
Hart Dyke Rd. BR8: Swan 3C 26
Hartfield Pl. DA11: Nflt 7G 13
Hartford Rd. DA5: Bexl 6K 7
Hartlands Cl. DA5: Bexl 6J 7
HARTLEY 4C 30
Hartley Bottom Rd.
DA3: Hart, Long H, New A, Lfield
. . . . .3K 33 & 7E 30
TN15: New A 6K 33
HARTLEY GREEN 5B 30
HARTLEY HILL 1K 33
Hartley Hill DA3: Hart 1K 33
Hartley Rd. DA3: Lfield 2B 30
DA16: Well 7A 4
Hart Shaw DA3: Lfield 2E 30
Hartshill Rd. DA11: Nflt 2J 23
Hartslock Dr. SE2 . . . . .2B 4
Harvel Cres. SE2 . . . . .5B 4
Harvest Way BR8: Crock 7C 26
Harvill Rd. DA14: Sidc 5H 17
Haslemere Rd. DA7: Bex 2J 7
Hasted Cl. DA9: Ghithe 6K 11
Hatherley Cres. DA14: Sidc 2D 16
Hatherley Rd. DA14: Sidc 4D 16
Hattersfield Cl. DA17: Belv 4D 4
Hatton Cl. DA11: Nflt 3H 23
SE18 . . . . .1A 6
Hattons M. DA9: Ghithe 4K 11
Havelock Rd. DA1: Dart 7G 9
DA11: Grav'nd 1J 23
DA17: Belv 4D 4
Haven Cl. BR8: Swan 3E 26
DA13: Ist R 1J 31
DA14: Sidc 6F 17
Havengore Av. DA12: Grav'nd 7D 14
Haven Hill TN15: Ash 6K 33
Havisham Rd. DA12: Grav'nd 1F 25
Hawkins Av. DA12: Grav'nd 4B 24
HAWLEY 4B 20
Hawley Rd. DA1: Dart 2K 19
DA2: Dart, Sutt H 2K 19
Hawley Ter. DA2: Dart 4B 20
Hawley Va. DA2: Dart 5B 20
Hawthorn Cl. DA12: Grav'nd 4A 24
Hawthorn Cotts. DA16: Well 3D 6
(off Hook La.)
Hawthorn Pl. DA8: Erith 5G 5
Hawthorn Rd. DA1: Dart 2J 19
DA6: Bex 4J 7
Hawthorns DA3: Hart 4C 30
Hawthorn Ter. DA15: Sidc 5C 6
Hayes Rd. DA9: Ghithe 7F 11
Hayes Ter. DA12: Shorne 5K 25
Haynes Rd. DA11: Nflt 3J 23
Hayward Cl. DA1: Cray 5C 8
Hayward Dr. DA1: Dart 3A 20
Hazeldene Rd. DA16: Well 2F 7
Hazel Dr. DA8: Erith 1F 9
Hazel End BR8: Swan 5D 26
Hazel Rd. DA1: Dart 2J 19
DA8: Erith 1F 9
Heath Av. DA7: Bex 6B 4
Heath Cl. BR8: Swan 2D 26
Heathclose Av. DA1: Dart 7G 9
Heathclose Rd. DA1: Dart 1F 19
Heathdene Dr. DA17: Belv 4F 5
Heath End Rd. DA5: Bexl 1D 18
Heatherbank Cl. DA1: Cray 6D 8
Heather Cl. DA14: Sidc 6G 17
Heather Dr. DA1: Dart 7F 9
Heather End BR8: Swan 4C 26
Heatherside Rd. DA14: Sidc 3F 17
Heathfield Pde. BR8: Swan 2B 26
Heathfield Rd. DA6: Bex 4J 7

Heathfield Ter. BR8: Swan 2C 26
Heath Gdns. DA1: Dart 1H 19
Heath Ho. DA15: Sidc 4C 16
Heathlands Ri. DA1: Dart 6G 9
Heath La. Lwr. DA1: Dart 1H 19
Heath La. Up. DA1: Dart 2F 19
Heathlee Rd. DA1: Cray 6D 8
Heath Rd. DA1: Cray 6E 8
　　DA5: Bexl 1B 18
HEATH SIDE .3E 18
Heathside Av. DA7: Bex 1H 7
Heath St. DA1: Dart 7J 9
Heathview Av. DA1: Cray 6D 8
Heathview Cres. DA1: Dart 1F 19
HEATHVIEW DAY CENTRE 6A 4
Heathview Dr. SE2 . . . . .6B 4
Heath Way DA8: Erith 1B 8
Heathwood Gdns.
　　BR8: Swan 2B 26
Heathwood Wlk. DA5: Bexl 1D 18
Hedge Pl. Rd. DA9: Ghithe 6G 11
Hedgerows, The DA11: Nflt 2H 23
Helen Cl. DA1: Dart 7G 9
Hemmings Cl. DA14: Sidc 2E 16
Hemsted Rd. DA8: Erith 7J 5
Henderson Dr. DA1: Dart 4A 10
Henfield Cl. DA5: Bexl 6K 7
Hengist Rd. DA8: Erith 7F 5
Hengrove Ct. DA5: Bexl 1H 17
Henhurst Rd. DA12: Cobh 7D 24
Henley Deane DA11: Nflt 4H 23
Henry Tudor Ct. SE9 . . . . .7A 6
Herald Wlk. DA1: Dart 5A 10
Herbert Rd. BR8: Swan 6G 19
　　DA7: Bex 2H 7
　　DA10: Swans 6C 12
Hereward Lincoln Ho. DA11: Nflt 6G 13
　　　　　　　　　　　　　　(off London Rd.)
Heritage Quay DA12: Grav'nd 6B 14
Hermitage Cl. SE2 . . . . .3A 4
Heron Cres. DA14: Sidc 3B 16
Herongate Rd. BR8: Swan 6D 18
Heron Hill DA17: Belv 5D 4
Heron Ho. DA14: Sidc 3E 16
Hertford Wlk. DA17: Belv 5E 4
Hesketh Av. DA2: Dart 1C 20
Hever Av. TN15: W King 5B 32
Hever Ct. Rd. DA12: Grav'nd 6B 24
Hever Rd. TN15: W King 6B 32
Heversham Rd. DA7: Bex 2K 7
Hever Wood Rd. TN15: W King 7B 32
Hewett Pl. BR8: Swan 4C 26
HEXTABLE 7E 18
Hextable Dance Cen. 1D 26
Hextable Heritage Cen. & Gardens 7D 18
Hibbs Cl. BR8: Swan 2C 26
Hibernia Dr. DA12: Grav'nd 3E 24
Hibernia Point SE2 . . . . .2B 4
　　　　　　　　　　　　(off Wolvercote Rd.)
Highbanks Cl. DA16: Well 1E 6
High Beeches DA14: Sidc 5H 17
High Cft. Cotts. BR8: Swan 4F 27
Highcross Rd. DA13: Sflt 5A 22
Highfield Av. DA8: Erith 6F 5
Highfield Cotts. DA2: Dart 6G 19
Highfield Rd. DA1: Dart 7J 9
　　DA6: Bex 5J 7
Highfield Rd. Nth. DA1: Dart 6J 9
Highfield Rd. Sth. DA1: Dart 7J 9
High Firs BR8: Swan 4D 26
High Gro. SE18 . . . . .1A 6
Highland Rd. DA5: Bexl 5K 7
Highlands Farm Bus. Pk.
　　BR8: Swan 1F 27
Highlands Hill BR8: Swan 1F 27
Highmead SE18 . . . . .1C 6
High Rd. DA2: Dart 3H 19
Highstead Cres. DA8: Erith 1D 8
High St. BR8: Swan 3E 26
　　DA1: Dart 6K 9
　　DA2: Bean 3J 21
　　DA4: Farn 6A 28
　　DA9: Ghithe 4J 11
　　DA10: Swans 5C 12
　　DA11: Grav'nd 6A 14
　　DA11: Nflt 6E 12
High Trees DA2: Dart 6C 10

High Vw. Rd. DA14: Sidc 4E 16
Hilary Cl. DA8: Erith 1A 8
Hilda May Av. BR8: Swan 3D 26
Hilden Dr. DA8: Erith 2K 5
Hill, The DA11: Nflt 6F 13
Hillary Av. DA11: Nflt 3H 23
Hill Brow DA1: Cray 6E 8
Hill Brow Cl. DA5: Bexl 4C 18
Hill Cl. DA13: Ist R 7H 23
Hill Cres. DA5: Bexl 1B 18
Hill Crest DA15: Sidc 7D 6
Hillcrest Dr. DA9: Ghithe 5H 11
Hillcrest Rd. DA1: Dart 7D 8
Hill Ho. Rd. DA2: Dart 7D 10
Hillingdon Rd. DA7: Bex 2B 8
　　DA11: Grav'nd 2A 24
Hill Ri. DA2: Dart 5E 20
Hill Rd. DA2: Dart 2K 19
Hillsgrove Cl. DA16: Well 7A 4
HILLSIDE 4G 5
Hillside DA2: Dart 5F 21
　　DA4: Farn 7A 28
　　DA8: Erith 4G 5
Hillside Av. DA12: Grav'nd 2C 24
Hillside Ct. BR8: Swan 4F 27
Hillside Dr. DA12: Grav'nd 2C 24
Hillside Rd. DA1: Cray 6F 9
Hilltop Gdns. DA1: Dart 5A 10
Hill Vw. Dr. DA16: Well 2B 6
Hillview Ho. DA12: Grav'nd 1B 24
Hill Vw. Rd. DA3: Lfield 3E 30
Hind Cres. DA8: Erith 6H 5
Hinksey Path SE2 . . . . .2B 4
Hive, The DA11: Nflt 6E 12
Hive La. DA11: Nflt 6E 12
　　　　　　　　　　　　　(not continuous)
Hobart Rd. RM18: Tilb 1K 13
Hoblands End BR7: Chst 6B 16
HOCKENDEN .3A 26
Hockenden La. BR8: Swan 3A 26
Hoddesdon Rd. DA17: Belv 5E 4
Hogs La. DA11: Nflt 3G 23
Hogs Orchard BR8: Swan 1G 27
Holbeach Gdns. DA15: Sidc 6B 6
Holbrook La. BR7: Chst 7A 16
Holcote Cl. DA17: Belv 3C 4
Hollands Cl. DA12: Shorne 5K 25
Hollies, The DA3: Lfield 3F 31
　　DA12: Grav'nd 6C 24
Hollies Av. DA15: Sidc 2C 16
Hollingbourne Av. DA7: Bex 1J 7
Hollybrake Cl. BR7: Chst 7A 16
Hollybush Rd. DA12: Grav'nd 2B 24
Holly Ct. DA14: Sidc 4E 16
　　　　　　　　　　　　　　(off Sidcup Hill)
Holly Gdns. DA7: Bex 4B 8
Holly Hill Rd. DA8: Erith 5G 5
　　DA17: Belv, Erith 5F 5
Holly Rd. DA1: Dart 1J 19
Hollytree Av. BR8: Swan 2D 26
Hollytree Pde. DA14: Sidc 6F 17
　　　　　　　　　　　　　　(off Sidcup Hill)
Hollywood Way DA8: Erith 2K 5
Holmbury Mnr. DA14: Sidc 4D 16
Holmes Ct. DA12: Grav'nd 7F 15
Holmesdale Hill DA4: S Dar 1D 28
Holmesdale Rd. DA4: S Dar 1D 28
　　DA7: Bex 2G 7
Holmhurst Rd. DA17: Belv 5F 5
Holmleigh Av. DA1: Dart 5H 9
Holmsdale Gro. DA7: Bex 2D 8
Holstein Way DA18: Erith 3B 4
Holyoake Mt. DA12: Grav'nd 1C 24
Homefield Cl. BR8: Swan 3E 26
Homefield Rd. DA4: Sutt H 1B 28
Home Gdns. DA1: Dart 6K 9
Home Hill BR8: Swan 7E 18
Homemead DA9: Ghithe 6J 11
　　DA12: Grav'nd 7A 14
Home Mead Cl. DA12: Grav'nd 7A 14
Home Orchard DA1: Dart 6K 9
　　　　　　　　　　　　　(not continuous)
Homer Cl. DA7: Bex 1B 8
Homestead, The DA1: Cray 5D 8
　　　　　　　　　　　　(off Crayford High St.)
　　DA1: Dart 6H 9
Homewood Cres. BR7: Chst 6B 16

Honeyden Rd. DA14: Sidc 6H 17
Honeyfield BR8: Swan 6E 18
Honiton Rd. DA16: Well 2C 6
Hookfields DA11: Nflt 3H 23
HOOK GREEN
　　GRAVESEND 6K 31
　　SOUTHFLEET 7D 22
　　WILMINGTON 4F 19
Hook Grn. La. DA2: Dart 3E 18
Hook Grn. Rd. DA13: Sflt 7B 22
Hook La. DA16: Well 4C 6
Hope Rd. DA10: Swans 6C 12
Hopewell Dr. DA12: Grav'nd 5E 24
Horizon Ho. BR8: Swan 4D 26
Horley Cl. DA6: Bex 5K 7
Hornbeam La. DA7: Bex 2B 8
HORNS CROSS 6F 11
Horn Yd. DA12: Grav'nd 6A 14
　　　　　　　　　　　　　　(off Bank St.)
Horsa Rd. DA8: Erith 7F 5
Horsemans Pl. DA1: Dart 7K 9
　　　　　　　　　　　　(off Instone Rd.)
Horsfield Cl. DA2: Dart 7D 10
Horsham Rd. DA6: Bex 5K 7
HORTON KIRBY 4D 28
Horton Kirby Trad. Est. DA4: S Dar 1D 28
Horton Rd. DA4: Hort K, S Dar 4D 28
Horton Way DA4: Farn 7A 28
Hoselands Vw. DA3: Hart 4B 30
Hotham Cl. BR8: Swan 1G 27
　　DA4: Sutt H 7C 20
Hottsfield DA3: Hart 3B 30
Howard Av. DA5: Bexl 1F 17
Howard Rd. DA1: Dart 6B 10
Howbury La. DA8: Erith 2F 9
Howden Cl. SE28 . . . . .1B 4
Howells Cl. TN15: W King 6B 32
Hudson Rd. DA7: Bex 2J 7
Hulsewood Cl. DA2: Dart 3G 19
Humber Rd. DA1: Dart 5J 9
Hume Av. RM18: Tilb 3K 13
Hume Cl. RM18: Tilb 3K 13
Hunters Cl. DA5: Bexl 3D 18
Huntingfield Rd. DA13: Meop 7K 31
Huntley Av. DA11: Nflt 6E 12
Hunt Rd. DA11: Nflt 3H 23
Hurlfield DA2: Dart 3H 19
Hurlingham DA7: Bex 7D 4
Hurst Ct. DA15: Sidc 2D 16
Hurst La. SE2 .5B 4
Hurst La. Est. SE2 . . . . .5B 4
Hurst Pl. DA1: Dart 6H 9
Hurst Rd. DA5: Bexl 1G 17
　　DA8: Erith 1B 8
　　DA15: Bexl, Sidc 2D 16
Hurst Springs DA5: Bexl 1H 17
Hurstwood Av. DA5: Bexl 1H 17
　　DA7: Bex 1D 8
　　DA8: Erith 1D 8
Huxley Rd. DA16: Well 3C 6
Hyde Rd. DA7: Bex 2J 7
Hyndford Cres. DA9: Ghithe 5K 11
　　　　　　　　　　　　(off Calcroft Av.)
Hythe Av. DA7: Bex 7C 4
Hythe St. DA1: Dart 6K 9
　　　　　　　　　　　　　(not continuous)
Hythe St. Lwr. DA1: Dart 5K 9

I

Idleigh Ct. Rd. DA13: Hart, Meop 2K 33
IFIELD 7B 24
Ifield Way DA12: Grav'nd 6C 24
Ightham Rd. DA8: Erith 7E 4
Imperial Bus. Est. DA11: Nflt 6J 13
Imperial Dr. DA12: Grav'nd 5E 24
Imperial Retail Pk. DA11: Grav'nd 6K 13
Imperial Way BR7: Chst 3A 16
Ingess Pk. Av. DA9: Ghithe 4J 11
Inglenorth Ct. BR8: Crock 6B 26
Ingleton Av. DA16: Well 5D 6
Inglewood BR8: Swan 2D 26
Inglewood Rd. DA7: Bex 4C 8
Ingoldsby Rd. DA12: Grav'nd 1D 24
Ingram Rd. DA1: Dart 1K 19
Ingress Gdns. DA9: Ghithe 5A 12

INGRESS PARK 4K 11
Ingress Ter. DA13: Sflt 4B 22
Instone Rd. DA1: Dart 7J 9
Invicta Pde. DA14: Sidc 4E 16
Invicta Rd. DA2: Dart 6C 10
Ionia Wlk. DA12: Grav'nd 3E 24
Iris Av. DA5: Bexl 5H 7
Iris Cres. DA7: Bex 6D 4
Iron Mill La. DA1: Cray 4D 8
Iron Mill Pl. DA1: Cray 4E 8
Irving Wlk. DA10: Swans 7B 12
Irving Way BR8: Swan 2C 26
Isis Reach DA17: Belv 1F 5
ISTEAD RISE 1J 31
Istead Ri. DA13: Ist R 7J 23
Ivedon Rd. DA16: Well 2F 7
Iverhurst Cl. DA6: Bex 5G 7
Ivy Bower Cl. DA9: Ghithe 5J 11
Ivy Cl. DA1: Dart 6B 10
DA12: Grav'nd 4B 24
Ivy Vs. DA9: Ghithe 5H 11
Izane Rd. DA6: Bex 4J 7

J

Jackson Cl. DA9: Ghithe 5G 11
Jacob Ho. *DA18: Erith 2B 4*
(off Kale Rd.)
Jacobs La. DA4: Hort K 3D 28
Jagger Cl. DA2: Dart 7D 10
James Av. *TN15: W King 7B 32*
(off London Rd.)
James Rd. DA1: Dart 7F 9
James Watt Way DA8: Erith 6K 5
Jane Seymour Ct. SE9 7A 6
Jasmine Ct. TN15: W King 7B 32
Jellicoe Av. DA12: Grav'nd 3B 24
Jellicoe Av. W. DA12: Grav'nd 3B 24
Jenner Cl. DA14: Sidc 4D 16
Jenningtree Rd. DA8: Erith 2K 5
Jenningtree Way DA17: Belv 2G 5
Jenton Av. DA7: Bex 1H 7
Jessamine Pl. DA2: Dart 7D 10
Jessett Cl. DA8: Erith 4H 5
JJ's Gun Club 3G 21
John Newton Ct. DA16: Well 3E 6
John's Cl. DA3: Hart 5C 30
JOHN'S HOLE 7D 10
Johnson Cl. DA11: Nflt 3G 23
Johnson's Way DA9: Ghithe 6K 11
John's Rd. DA13: Meop 5J 31
JOYCE GREEN 4A 10
Joyce Grn. La. DA1: Dart 3K 9
(Dunlop Cl.)
DA1: Dart 1J 9
(University Way)
Joyce Grn. Wlk. DA1: Dart 4A 10
JOYDENS WOOD 4C 18
Joydens Wood (Nature Reserve) 4A 18
Joydens Wood Rd. DA5: Bexl 4C 18
Joy Rd. DA12: Grav'nd 1B 24
Jubilee Cl. DA9: Ghithe 6K 11
Jubilee Ct. *DA1: Dart 7J 9*
(off Spring Va. Sth.)
Jubilee Cres. DA12: Grav'nd 2D 24
Jubilee Way DA14: Sidc 2D 16
Judeth Gdns. DA12: Grav'nd 5D 24
Junction Rd. DA1: Dart 6J 9
Juniper Wlk. BR8: Swan 2C 26
Jury St. DA11: Grav'nd 6A 14

K

Kale Rd. DA18: Erith 2B 4
Kaysland Cvn. Pk.
TN15: W King 7B 32
Kay St. DA16: Well 1E 6
Keary Rd. DA10: Swans 7B 12
Keats Gdns. RM18: Tilb 2A 14
Keats Ho. DA1: Cray 5D 8
Keats Rd. DA16: Well 1B 6
DA17: Belv 3G 5
Keightley Dr. SE9 1A 16
Keith Av. DA4: Sutt H 6C 20
Kelso Dr. DA12: Grav'nd 4E 24
Kelvin Rd. DA16: Well 3D 6
RM18: Tilb 2K 13
Kemnal Rd. BR7: Chst 4A 16
(not continuous)
Kempthorne St. DA11: Grav'nd 6A 14
Kempton Cl. DA8: Erith 6G 5
Kemsing Cl. DA5: Bexl 7H 7
Kemsley Cl. DA9: Ghithe 6J 11
DA11: Nflt 4J 23
Kencot Way DA18: Erith 2D 4
Kendall Ct. DA15: Sidc 3D 16
Kenia Wlk. DA12: Grav'nd 3E 24
Kenilworth Ct. *DA2: Dart 6C 10*
(off Bow Arrow La.)
Kenley Cl. DA5: Bexl 7K 7
Kenmere Rd. DA16: Well 2F 7
Kennedy Ho. DA11: Nflt 3H 23
Kennet Rd. DA1: Cray 3F 9
Kennett Ct. *BR8: Swan 3D 26*
(off Oakleigh Cl.)
Kent Av. DA16: Well 5C 6
Kent Cl. TN15: W King 7B 32
Kentish Rd. DA17: Belv 4E 4
Kent Kraft Ind. Est. DA11: Nflt 5C 12
Kent Rd. DA1: Dart 6J 9
DA3: Lfield 2A 30
DA11: Grav'nd 1K 23
Kenwood Av. DA3: Lfield 3F 31
Kenwyn Rd. DA1: Dart 5J 9
Kestlake Rd. DA5: Bexl 6F 7
Keston Cl. DA16: Well 7A 4
Keston Ct. DA5: Bexl 7J 7
Keswick Rd. DA7: Bex 1K 7
Kettlewell Ct. BR8: Swan 2E 26
Keyes Rd. DA1: Dart 4A 10
Keynes Ct. *SE28 1A 4*
(off Attlee Rd.)
Khalsa Av. DA12: Grav'nd 7B 14
Khartoum Pl. DA12: Grav'nd 6B 14
Killigarth Ct. DA14: Sidc 4D 16
Kilndown DA12: Grav'nd 6C 24
Kimberley Dr. DA14: Sidc 2G 17
Kinder Cl. SE28 1B 4
King Edward Av. DA1: Dart 6J 9
King Edward Rd. DA9: Ghithe 5H 11
(not continuous)
Kingfisher Ct. TN15: W King 7B 32
Kingfisher Dr. DA9: Ghithe 6H 11
Kingfisher Pl. DA4: S Dar 2D 28
King Harolds Way DA7: Belv, Bex 7B 4
DA17: Belv 7B 4
King's Cl. DA1: Cray 4D 8
Kingsdale Ct. DA10: Swans 6B 12
Kingsdown Cl. DA12: Grav'nd 1E 24
Kings Dr. DA12: Grav'nd 3A 24
KINGS FARM 3B 24
Kingsfield Ter. DA1: Dart 5J 9
Kingsgate Cl. DA7: Bex 1H 7
Kingsingfield Cl. TN15: W King 7B 32
Kingsingfield Rd. TN15: W King 7B 32
Kingsley Av. DA1: Dart 5B 10
Kingsley Ct. DA6: Bex 4K 7
Kingsmead Cl. DA15: Sidc 2D 16
Kingsridge Gdns. DA1: Dart 6J 9
Kingston Ct. DA11: Nflt 5E 12
King St. DA12: Grav'nd 6A 14
Kingswood Av. BR8: Swan 4E 26
DA17: Belv 4D 4
Kingswood Cl. DA1: Dart 6H 9
Kingswood Ct. TN15: W King 7B 32
Kipling Av. RM18: Tilb 1A 14
Kipling Rd. DA1: Dart 5C 10
DA7: Bex 1H 7
Kirby Rd. DA2: Dart 7E 10
Kirkland Cl. DA15: Sidc 6B 6
Kitchener Av. DA12: Grav'nd 4B 24
Knatts Valley Rd.
TN15: Farn, W King, Knat 6A 32
Knee Hill SE2 4A 4
Kneehill Cres. SE2 4A 4
Knights Cft. DA3: New A 3J 33
Knights Mnr. Way DA1: Dart 5A 10
KNOCKHALL 6K 11
Knockhall Chase DA9: Ghithe 5J 11
Knockhall Rd. DA9: Ghithe 6K 11
Knole, The DA13: Ist R 7H 23
Knole Ga. DA15: Sidc 3B 16
Knole Rd. DA1: Dart 7F 9
Knoll Rd. DA5: Bexl 7K 7
DA14: Sidc 5E 16
Knowle Av. DA7: Bex 7C 4

L

Laburnum Av. BR8: Swan 3B 26
DA1: Dart 1H 19
Laburnum Gro. DA11: Nflt 7G 13
Lacebark Cl. DA15: Sidc 7C 6
Ladbrooke Cres. DA14: Sidc 3G 17
Ladds Way BR8: Swan 4C 26
Ladyfields DA11: Nflt 4J 23
Ladywood Rd. DA2: Dart 5F 21
Lagonda Way DA1: Dart 4H 9
Lake Footpath SE2 2B 4
Lakeside Cl. DA15: Sidc 5F 7
Lakeview Rd. DA16: Well 4E 6
Lambardes DA3: New A 3J 33
Lamb Cl. RM18: Tilb 2B 14
Lambert Ct. *DA8: Erith 6G 5*
(off Park Cres.)
LAMORBEY 1C 16
Lamorbey Cl. DA15: Sidc 1C 16
Lamorbey Swimming Cen. 2D 16
Lamorna Av. DA12: Grav'nd 2C 24
Lamplighters Cl. DA1: Dart 6A 10
Lancaster Ct. DA12: Grav'nd 3B 24
Lance Cft. DA3: New A 2J 33
Lancelot Rd. DA16: Well 4D 6
Lances Cl. DA13: Meop 7K 31
Landale Gdns. DA1: Dart 7H 9
Landseer Av. DA11: Nflt 3G 23
Lane Av. DA9: Ghithe 6K 11
LANE END 4E 20
Lane End DA7: Bex 3A 8
Lanes Av. DA11: Nflt 3J 23
Langafel Cl. DA3: Lfield 2B 30
Langdale Cres. DA7: Bex 7E 4
Langdale Wlk. *DA11: Nflt 3H 23*
(off Landseer Av.)
Langdon Shaw DA14: Sidc 5C 16
Langford Pl. DA14: Sidc 3D 16
Langlands Dr. DA2: Dart 5F 21
Langley Rd. DA16: Well 6A 4
Langmore Ct. DA6: Bex 3G 7
Langworth Cl. DA2: Dart 3J 19
Lanridge Rd. SE2 3B 4
Lansbury Cres. DA1: Dart 5B 10
Lansbury Gdns. RM18: Tilb 1K 13
Lansdowne Av. DA7: Bex 7B 4
Lansdowne Rd. RM18: Tilb 2J 13
Lansdowne Sq. DA11: Nflt 6J 13
Lansdown Pl. DA11: Nflt 1J 23
Lansdown Rd. DA11: Nflt 1J 23
DA14: Sidc 3E 16
Lapis Cl. DA12: Grav'nd 1G 25
Lapwing Cl. DA8: Erith 2K 5
Lapwings DA3: Lfield 3E 30
Lapwings, The DA12: Grav'nd 2C 24
Larch Gro. DA15: Sidc 1C 16
Larch Rd. DA1: Dart 7J 9
Larch Wlk. BR8: Swan 2C 26
Largo Wlk. DA8: Erith 1D 8
Larkfield Rd. DA14: Sidc 3C 16
Larkfields DA11: Nflt 3H 23
Larks Fld. DA3: Hart 4B 30
Larkspur Lodge DA14: Sidc 3E 16
Larkswood Cl. DA8: Erith 1F 9
Larkwell La. DA3: Hart 4C 30
Larner Rd. DA8: Erith 7J 5
Latham Cl. DA2: Dart 2F 21
Latham Rd. DA6: Bex 5K 7
Latona Dr. DA12: Grav'nd 5E 24
Launton Dr. DA6: Bex 4G 7
Laura Dr. BR8: Swan 7F 19
Laurel Av. DA12: Grav'nd 2B 24
Laurel Cl. DA1: Dart 1H 19
DA14: Sidc 3D 16
Laurels, The DA2: Dart 3H 19
DA3: Lfield 3F 31
Lavender Hill BR8: Swan 3C 26
Lavernock Rd. DA7: Bex 2K 7
Lavinia Rd. DA1: Dart 6A 10
Lawford Gdns. DA1: Dart 5H 9

Lawn Cl. BR8: Swan 2B 26
Lawn Rd. DA11: Nflt 6F 13
(not continuous)
Lawns, The DA14: Sidc 4E 16
Lawrance Sq. DA11: Nflt 3J 23
Lawrence Hill Gdns.
DA1: Dart 6H 9
Lawrence Hill Rd. DA1: Dart 6H 9
Lawrence Rd. DA8: Erith 7F 5
Lawson Gdns. DA1: Dart 5J 9
Lawson Rd. DA1: Dart 4J 9
Laymarsh Cl. DA17: Belv 3D 4
Leafield La. DA14: Sidc 3J 17
Leander Dr. DA12: Grav'nd 4E 24
Leas Grn. BR7: Chst 6C 16
Leatherbottle Grn. DA18: Erith 3D 4
Leather Bottle La. DA17: Belv 4C 4
Lea Va. DA1: Cray 4C 8
Leckwith Av. DA7: Bex 6C 4
Leechcroft Av. BR8: Swan 3E 26
DA15: Sidc .5C 6
Leewood Pl. BR8: Swan 4C 26
Lefa Bus. & Ind. Est. DA14: Sidc 6G 17
Leicester Rd. RM18: Tilb 1J 13
Leigh Pl. DA2: Dart 4B 20
DA16: Well .2D 6
Leigh Rd. DA11: Grav'nd 2A 24
Leighton Gdns. RM18: Tilb 1K 13
Leith Pk. Rd. DA12: Grav'nd 1A 24
Lenderyou Ct. DA1: Dart 7J 9
(off Phoenix Pl.)
Lenham Rd. DA7: Bex 6D 4
Lennox Av. DA11: Grav'nd 6J 13
Lennox Ho. DA17: Belv 3E 4
(off Picardy St.)
Lennox Rd. DA11: Grav'nd 6J 13
Lennox Rd. E. DA11: Grav'nd 7K 13
Lenor Cl. DA6: Bex 4H 7
Lensbury Way SE2 . . . . .3A 4
Leonard Av. DA10: Swans 7B 12
Lesley Cl. BR8: Swan 3C 26
DA5: Bexl 7A 8
DA13: Ist R .1J 31
Lesnes Abbey 4B 4
Lesney Farm Est. DA8: Erith 7H 5
Lesney Pk. DA8: Erith 6H 5
Lesney Pk. Rd. DA8: Erith 6H 5
Lessness Av. DA7: Bex 7B 4
LESSNESS HEATH 5F 5
Lessness Pk. DA17: Belv 5D 4
Lessness Rd. DA17: Belv 6E 4
Lewin Rd. DA6: Bex 5H 7
Lewis Ct. DA11: Nflt 2J 23
Lewis Rd. DA10: Swans 6B 12
DA13: Ist R .1J 31
DA14: Sidc .3F 17
DA16: Well .3F 7
Leycroft Gdns. DA8: Erith 1G 9
Leydenhatch La. BR8: Dart, Swan 1B 26
Leyhill Cl. BR8: Swan 5D 26
Leysdown Av. DA7: Bex 4B 8
LEYTON CROSS 2F 19
Leyton Cross Rd. DA2: Bexl, Dart 3E 18
Lighterman's M. DA11: Nflt 7H 13
Lightermans Way DA9: Ghithe 4K 11
Lilac Gdns. BR8: Swan 3C 26
Lilac Pl. DA13: Meop 6K 31
Lila Pl. BR8: Swan 4D 26
Lime Av. DA11: Nflt 7G 13
Lime Gro. DA15: Sidc 6C 6
Lime Rd. BR8: Swan 3C 26
DA18: Erith .3D 4
Lime Row DA18: Erith 3D 4
Limes, The DA1: Dart 7A 10
Limestone Wlk. DA18: Erith 2B 4
Lime Tree Av. DA9: Bluew 7H 11
Limetree Ter. DA16: Well 3D 6
Limewood Rd. DA8: Erith 7G 5
Lincoln Cl. DA8: Erith 2E 8
Lincoln Rd. DA8: Erith 2E 8
DA14: Sidc .5E 16
Lincolnshire Ter. DA2: Dart 4E 20
Linden Av. DA1: Dart 1H 19
Linden Ct. DA14: Sidc 4B 16
Lindisfarne Cl. DA12: Grav'nd 2D 24
Lingey Cl. DA15: Sidc 2C 16
Lingfield Av. DA2: Dart 7C 10

Lingfield Cres. SE9 . . . . .4A 6
Lingfield Rd. DA12: Grav'nd 2A 24
Ling Rd. DA8: Erith 6G 5
Lingwood DA7: Bex 2A 8
Link, The DA3: New A 2J 33
Linley Cl. RM18: E Til 1J 15
Linnet Cl. SE28 . . . . .1A 4
Linsted Ct. SE9 . . . . .6B 6
Linton Cl. DA16: Well 1E 6
Lion Rd. DA6: Bex 4H 7
LIONS HOSPICE, THE 4J 33
Liskeard Cl. BR7: Chst 6A 16
Lisle Cl. DA12: Grav'nd 2G 25
Lister Rd. RM18: Tilb 2K 13
Little Birches DA15: Sidc 2B 16
LITTLE BROOK HOSPITAL 6D 10
LITTLEBROOK BUS. CEN. DA1: Dart 2C 10
LITTLEBROOK INTERCHANGE 4C 10
Littlebrook Mnr. Way DA1: Dart 5B 10
Littlecroft DA13: Ist R 7H 23
Littledale DA2: Dart 3D 20
Lit. Heath Rd. DA7: Bex 1J 7
Lit. Queen St. DA1: Dart 7A 10
Liverymen Wlk. DA9: Ghithe 4K 11
Livingstone Gdns. DA12: Grav'nd 5C 24
LIVINGSTONE HOSPITAL 7A 10
Livingstone Rd. DA12: Grav'nd 5C 24
Loam Ct. DA1: Dart 1K 19
Lochmere Cl. DA8: Erith 6F 5
Lodge Av. DA1: Dart 6H 9
Lodge Hill SE2: Well 7A 4
Lodge La. DA5: Bexl 6G 7
Lombard St. DA4: Hort K 5D 28
Londonderry Pde. DA8: Erith 7H 5
London Intl. Cruise Terminal
RM18: Tilb .4K 13
London Rd. BR8: Swan 1B 26
(Birchwood Rd.)
BR8: Swan .4E 26
(High St.)
London Rd. DA1: Bexl, Cray 5C 8
DA2: Dart, Ghithe, Swans 7C 10
DA4: Farn 6K 27
DA9: Ghithe, Swans 5J 11
DA10: Ghithe, Swans 5J 11
DA11: Nflt .6G 13
RM18: Tilb .6G 13
TN15: W King, Wro, Bor G 5A 32
LONGFIELD 2B 30
Longfield Av. DA3: Lfield 2F 31
LONGFIELD HILL 4G 31
Longfield Rd. DA3: Lfield, Meop 5G 31
DA13: Meop 5G 31
Longfield Station (Rail) 3B 30
LONGLANDS .3A 16
Longlands Ct. DA15: Sidc 2C 16
Longlands Pk. Cres. DA15: Sidc 3B 16
Longlands Rd. DA15: Sidc 3B 16
Long La. DA7: Bex 7B 4
Longleigh La. DA7: Bex 6A 4
SE2 . . . . .6A 4
Longmarsh Vw. DA4: Sutt H 1C 28
Longmead Dr. DA14: Sidc 2G 17
Longmeade DA12: Grav'nd 1E 24
Longmeadow Rd. DA15: Sidc 1B 16
Longreach Rd. DA8: Erith 2K 5
Longtown Rd. DA2: Dart 6C 10
(off Osbourne Rd.)
Longwalk DA13: Ist R 1H 31
Lonsdale Cres. DA2: Dart 1D 20
Lonsdale Rd. DA7: Bex 2J 7
Lord St. DA12: Grav'nd 7A 14
Lordswood Cl. DA2: Dart 4F 21
Lordwood Cl. DA6: Bex 5H 7
Lorton Cl. DA12: Grav'nd 2D 24
Louvain Rd. DA9: Ghithe 7F 11
Lovelace Rd. TN15: W King 6B 32
Love La. DA5: Bexl 6J 7
(not continuous)
DA12: Grav'nd 7B 14
Lovel Av. DA16: Well 2D 6
Lovers La. DA9: Ghithe 5H 11
Low Cl. DA9: Ghithe 5H 11
Lwr. Church Hill DA9: Ghithe 5E 11
Lower Cft. BR8: Swan 4E 26
Lwr. Guild Hall DA9: Bluew 7G 11

Lwr. Higham Rd.
DA12: Grav'nd, Shorne 1E 24
Lower Pk. Rd. DA17: Belv 4E 4
Lwr. Range Rd. DA12: Grav'nd 7D 14
Lower Rd. BR8: Swan 7E 18
DA8: Erith 3F 5
DA11: Nflt .4B 12
(not continuous)
DA12: High'm, Shorne 2K 25
DA17: Belv .3F 5
Lwr. Rose Gallery DA9: Bluew 7G 11
LOWER SHORNE 4K 25
Lwr. Station Rd. DA1: Cray 6D 8
Lwr. Thames Wlk. DA9: Bluew 1G 21
Lowfield St. DA1: Dart 7K 9
Lowry Cl. DA8: Erith 4H 5
Lucas Cres. DA9: Ghithe 4K 11
(off Ingress Pk. Av.)
Lucerne Ct. DA18: Erith 3C 4
Luddesdon Rd. DA8: Erith 7E 4
Luffield Rd. SE2 . . . . .3A 4
Lullingstone Av. BR8: Swan 3E 26
Lullingstone Cl. BR5: St P 7E 16
Lullingstone Cres. BR5: St P 7D 16
Lullingstone Rd. DA17: Belv 6D 4
Lulworth Rd. DA16: Well 2C 6
Lumley Cl. DA17: Belv 5E 4
Lumley Cl. DA17: Belv 5E 4
Lunedale Rd. DA2: Dart 1D 20
Luton Rd. DA14: Sidc 3F 17
Lydd Cl. DA14: Sidc 3B 16
Lydden Ct. SE9 . . . . .6B 6
Lydd Rd. DA7: Bex 7D 4
Lydford Ct. DA2: Dart 6C 10
(off Clifton Wlk.)
Lydia Cotts. DA11: Grav'nd 7A 14
Lydia Rd. DA8: Erith 6K 5
Lyme Rd. DA16: Well 1E 6
Lyminge Cl. DA14: Sidc 4C 16
Lyndean Ind. Est. SE2 . . . . .3A 4
Lynden Way BR8: Swan 3B 26
Lyndhurst Cl. DA7: Bex 3A 8
Lyndhurst Rd. DA7: Bex 3A 8
Lyndhurst Way DA13: Ist R 1H 31
Lyndon Av. DA15: Sidc 5C 6
Lyndon Rd. DA17: Belv 4E 4
Lynmere Rd. DA16: Well 2E 6
Lynsted Cl. DA6: Bex 5A 8
Lynton Rd. DA11: Grav'nd 1K 23
Lynton Rd. Sth. DA11: Grav'nd 1K 23

M

Mabel Rd. BR8: Swan 6F 19
Macaulay Way SE28 . . . . .1A 4
McCudden Rd. DA1: Dart 3A 10
Mackenzie Way DA12: Grav'nd 6C 24
McKillop Way DA14: Sidc 7F 17
Maclean Ter. DA12: Grav'nd 2E 24
McLeod Rd. SE2 . . . . .4A 4
McMillan Cl. DA12: Grav'nd 4B 24
Macmillan Gdns. DA1: Dart 4B 10
Madden Cl. DA10: Swans 6A 12
Maddocks Cl. DA14: Sidc 5H 17
Madison Cres. DA7: Bex 7A 4
Madison Gdns. DA7: Bex 7A 4
Maida Rd. DA17: Belv 3E 4
Maida Va. Rd. DA1: Dart 5F 9
Maiden Erlegh Av. DA5: Bexl 1H 17
Maiden La. DA1: Cray 3F 9
Maidstone Rd. DA14: Sidc, Swan 6G 17
Main Rd. BR8: Crock 6C 26
BR8: Swan .7E 18
DA3: Lfield, Long H 2A 30
DA4: Farn 6K 27
DA4: Fawk . . . . .7B 28 & 3A 32
DA4: Sutt H .6C 28
DA14: Sidc .3A 16
Mall, The BR8: Swan 3D 26
DA6: Bex 4K 7
Mallard Cl. DA1: Dart 5A 10
Mallard Wlk. DA14: Sidc 6F 17
Mallow Cl. DA11: Nflt 4H 23
Mallys Pl. DA4: S Dar 1D 28
Malta Rd. RM18: Tilb 2J 13
Malthouse La. DA3: Shorne 5K 25
Malthouse Rd. TN15: Stans 7J 33

Malthus Path SE28 ....1A 4
Maltings, The DA11: Grav'nd 6K 13
   (off Clifton Rd.)
Maltings Ent. Cen., The
   DA12: Grav'nd 1E 24
Maltings M. DA15: Sidc 3D 16
Malvern Av. DA7: Bex 7C 4
Malvern Ho. DA11: Nflt 6G 13
   (off Laburnum Gro.)
Malvina Av. DA12: Grav'nd 2A 24
Malyons Rd. BR8: Swan 7E 18
Manford Ind. Est. DA8: Erith 1J 5
Mangold Way DA18: Erith 3B 4
Manning Ct. SE28 ....1A 4
   (off Titmuss Av.)
Mannock Rd. DA1: Dart 3A 10
Manor Cl. DA1: Cray 4C 8
  DA2: Dart 3F 19
  DA12: Grav'nd 2G 25
Manor Ct. DA7: Bex 4A 8
Manor Dr. DA3: Hart 6C 30
Manor Fld. DA12: Shorne 5K 25
Manor Forstal DA3: New A 3J 33
Manor Ho. DA3: New A 3J 33
Manor La. DA3: Fawk 7K 29
  DA3: Hart 6D 30
  TN15: Fawk 2F 33
Manor Pk. DA8: Erith 1J 5
Manor Pk. Rd. BR7: Chst 7A 16
Manor Pl. DA1: Dart 1K 19
Manor Rd. DA1: Cray 4D 8
  DA3: Lfield, Long H 5F 31
  DA5: Bexl 1A 18
  DA8: Erith ....6K 5 & 1J 5
  DA10: Swans 6A 12
  DA12: Grav'nd 6A 14
  DA15: Sidc 3C 16
  RM18: Tilb 2K 13
Manorside Cl. SE2 ....4A 4
Manor Vw. DA3: Hart 6D 30
Manor Way DA5: Bexl 1K 17
  DA7: Bex 3C 8
  DA10: Swans 4A 12
Manor Way DA11: Nflt 4A 12
  (not continuous)
Manse Pde. BR8: Swan 4F 27
Manse Way BR8: Swan 4F 27
Mansfield Rd. BR8: Swan 6D 18
Maple Cl. BR8: Swan 2D 26
Maple Cl. DA8: Erith 7K 5
  DA9: Ghithe 7F 11
Maple Cres. DA15: Sidc 6D 6
Mapledene BR7: Chst 5A 16
Maplehurst Cl. DA2: Bexl 2D 18
Maple Leaf Dr. DA15: Sidc 1C 16
Maple Rd. DA1: Dart 1H 19
  DA12: Grav'nd 4B 24
Maples, The DA3: Lfield 2E 30
Maplin Ho. SE2 ....2B 4
  (off Wolvercote Rd.)
Maran Way DA18: Erith 2B 4
Marcet Rd. DA1: Dart 5H 9
Marconi Rd. DA11: Nflt 3G 23
Marcus Rd. DA1: Dart 7F 9
Marden Cres. DA5: Bexl 5B 8
Marechal Niel Av. DA15: Sidc 3A 16
Marechal Niel Pde. DA14: Sidc 3A 16
  (off Main Rd.)
Margaret Barr Row DA10: Swans 7B 12
Margaret Rd. DA5: Bexl 6G 7
Marie Manor Way DA2: Dart 4F 11
Marina Dr. DA1: Dart 1B 20
  DA11: Nflt 7J 13
  DA16: Well 2B 6
Marine Ct. DA8: Erith 7K 5
Mariners Ct. DA9: Ghithe 4J 11
  (off High St.)
Mariners Wlk. DA8: Erith 6K 5
Mariners Way DA11: Nflt 7H 13
Maritime Cl. DA9: Ghithe 5J 11
Maritime Ga. DA11: Nflt 7H 13
Mark Cl. DA7: Bex 1H 7
Market All. DA12: Grav'nd 6A 14
Market Pde. DA14: Sidc 4E 16
Market Pl. DA1: Dart 7K 9
  DA6: Bex 4K 7
  RM18: Tilb 2K 13

Market St. DA1: Dart 7K 9
Mark La. DA12: Grav'nd 7D 14
  (not continuous)
Marks Sq. DA11: Nflt 4J 23
Mark Way BR8: Swan 5F 27
Marlborough Pk. Av. DA15: Sidc 7D 6
Marlborough Rd. DA1: Dart 6H 9
  DA7: Bex 3G 7
Marler Ho. DA8: Erith 2E 8
Marley Av. DA7: Bex 6B 4
Marling Way DA12: Grav'nd 6D 24
Marlowe Cl. BR7: Chst 6A 16
Marlowes, The DA1: Cray 4C 8
Marlwood Cl. DA15: Sidc 2B 16
Marne Av. DA16: Well 3D 6
Marrabon Cl. DA15: Sidc 1D 16
Marriott Rd. DA1: Dart 7A 10
Marriotts Wharf DA11: Grav'nd 5A 14
Marsh St. DA1: Dart 3B 10
  (Chaucer Way)
  DA1: Dart 5A 10
  (Hilltop Gdns.)
  DA1: Dart 2B 10
  (University Way)
Marsh Vw. DA12: Grav'nd 1E 24
Martens Av. DA7: Bex 4A 8
Martens Cl. DA7: Bex 4B 8
Martin Dene DA6: Bex 5J 7
Martin Dr. DA2: Dart 7D 10
Martin Ho. DA11: Nflt 3K 23
Martin Ri. DA6: Bex 5J 7
Martin Rd. DA2: Dart 3H 19
Marwood Cl. DA16: Well 3E 6
Maryfield Cl. DA5: Bexl 3D 18
Maryville DA16: Well 2C 6
Masefield Cl. DA8: Erith 1E 8
Masefield Rd. DA1: Dart 5C 10
  DA11: Nflt 3G 23
Masham Ho. DA18: Erith 2B 4
  (off Kale Rd.)
Mason Cl. DA7: Bex 3A 8
Masthead Cl. DA2: Dart 4D 10
Matfield Rd. DA17: Belv 6E 4
Maude Rd. BR8: Swan 6F 19
Maximfeldt Rd. DA8: Erith 5J 5
Maxim Rd. DA1: Cray 5D 8
  DA8: Erith 4J 5
Maxwell Rd. DA16: Well 3C 6
May Av. DA11: Nflt 1J 23
May Av. Ind. Est. DA11: Nflt 1J 23
  (off May Av.)
Maybury Av. DA2: Dart 1D 20
Mayes Cl. BR8: Swan 4F 27
Mayfair Av. DA2: Dart 1G 7
Mayfair Rd. DA1: Dart 5J 9
Mayfield DA7: Bex 3J 7
Mayfield Rd. DA11: Grav'nd 7J 13
  DA17: Belv 4G 5
Mayfields DA10: Swans 6B 12
Mayfield Vs. DA14: Sidc 6F 17
Maylands Dr. DA14: Sidc 3G 17
Maynard Cl. DA8: Erith 7K 5
Mayor's La. DA2: Dart 4H 19
Mayplace Av. DA1: Cray 4F 9
Mayplace Cl. DA7: Bex 3A 8
Mayplace Rd. E. DA1: Cray 4D 8
  DA7: Bex, Cray 3A 8
Mayplace Rd. W. DA7: Bex 4K 7
MAYPOLE 2C 18
Maypole Rd. DA12: Grav'nd 1E 24
May Rd. DA2: Dart 4A 20
Mead, The DA3: New A 2H 33
Mead Cl. BR8: Swan 5F 27
Mead Cres. DA1: Dart 1J 19
Meadow Bank Cl.
  TN15: W King 7C 32
Meadow Cl. DA6: Bex 5J 7
Meadow La. DA3: New A 2J 33
Meadow Rd. DA11: Grav'nd 2K 23
  DA11: Nflt 1F 23
Meadows Ct. DA14: Sidc 6E 16
Meadowside DA1: Dart 1J 19
Meadow Vw. DA15: Sidc 7E 6
Meadowview Rd. DA5: Bexl 6H 7
Meadow Wlk. DA2: Dart 4H 19
  (not continuous)
Meadow Way DA2: Dart 7D 10

Mead Rd. DA1: Dart 1J 19
  DA11: Grav'nd 2A 24
Medbury Rd. DA12: Grav'nd 1E 24
Medhurst Cres. DA12: Grav'nd 3D 24
Medhurst Gdns. DA12: Grav'nd 3E 24
Medina Ho. DA8: Erith 7J 5
Medlar Ho. DA15: Sidc 3D 16
Medlars, The DA3: Meop 6K 31
Medway Rd. DA1: Cray 3F 9
Megabowl
  Bexleyheath 4J 7
Melanie Cl. DA7: Bex 1H 7
Melba Gdns. RM18: Tilb 1K 13
Melbourne Quay DA11: Grav'nd 6A 14
Melbourne Rd. RM18: Tilb 1H 13
Melliker La. DA13: Meop 6J 31
Melrose Av. DA1: Cray 7D 8
Melville Rd. DA14: Sidc 2F 17
Mendip Rd. DA7: Bex 1D 8
MEOPHAM 7K 31
Meopham Ct. DA13: Meop 7K 31
MEOPHAM STATION 5K 31
Meopham Station (Rail) 5K 31
Mera Dr. DA7: Bex 4K 7
Merchland Rd. SE9 ....1A 16
Merewood Rd. DA7: Bex 2B 8
Meriel Wlk. DA9: Ghithe 4J 11
Merino Pl. DA15: Sidc 6D 6
Merleys Cl. DA3: Lfield 3F 31
Merlin Rd. DA16: Well 4D 6
Merlin Rd. Nth. DA16: Well 4D 6
Mermaid Cl. DA11: Nflt 7G 13
Mermerus Gdns. DA12: Grav'nd 4E 24
Merrilees Rd. DA15: Sidc 7B 6
Merryfields Cl. DA3: Hart 4C 30
Merryweather Cl. DA1: Dart 6A 10
Merton Av. DA3: Hart 4B 30
  (not continuous)
Merton Ct. DA16: Well 2E 6
Mervyn Av. SE9 ....3A 16
Methuen Rd. DA6: Bex 4J 7
  DA17: Belv 4F 5
Mews, The DA3: Lfield 3B 30
  (off Bramblefield Cl.)
  DA14: Sidc 4D 16
Meyer Rd. DA8: Erith 6H 5
Michael Gdns. DA12: Grav'nd 5D 24
Michaels La. DA3: Fawk 2E 32
  TN15: Fawk 2E 32
Mick Jagger Cen., The 6H 9
  (off Shepherd's La.)
Middleham Ct. DA2: Dart 6C 10
  (off Osbourne Rd.)
Middleton Av. DA14: Sidc 6E 16
Middle Way DA18: Erith 3C 4
Midfield Av. BR8: Swan 6F 19
  DA7: Bex 3B 8
Midfield Pde. DA7: Bex 3B 8
Midfield Way BR5: St P 7E 16
Midhurst Hill DA6: Bex 6K 7
Midwinter Cl. DA16: Well 3D 6
Mike Spring Ct. DA12: Grav'nd 4C 24
Mildred Cl. DA1: Dart 6B 10
Mildred Rd. DA8: Erith 5J 5
MILE END GREEN 1A 30
Milestone Ho. DA2: Dart 6C 10
Milford Cl. SE2 ....6C 4
Millbro BR8: Swan 1F 27
Millbrook Av. DA16: Well 4A 6
Mill Cl. DA4: S Dar 2D 28
Millen Ct. DA4: Hort K 4D 28
Miller Ct. DA7: Bex 3B 8
Miller Rd. DA12: Grav'nd 2F 25
Millfield DA3: New A 2H 33
Millfield Dr. DA11: Nflt 2H 23
Millfield La. DA3: New A 2H 33
Millfield Rd. TN15: W King 6A 32
Mill Hill La. DA3: Shorne 5J 25
Mill Pl. DA1: Cray 4F 9
Mill Pond Rd. DA1: Dart 6K 9
Mill Rd. DA2: Dart 4A 20
  DA8: Erith 7G 5
  DA11: Nflt 7H 13
Mill Row DA5: Bexl 1A 18
Millside Ind. Est. DA1: Dart 4J 9
Mill Stone Cl. DA4: S Dar 2D 28
Mill Stone M. DA4: S Dar 1D 28

Milner Wlk. SE9: Sidc 2A 16
Milroy Av. DA11: Nflt 2H 23
MILTON 6B 14
Milton Av. DA12: Grav'nd 1B 24
Milton Ct. DA12: Grav'nd 1B 24
Milton Gdns. RM18: Tilb 1A 14
Milton Hall Rd. DA12: Grav'nd 1C 24
Milton Lodge DA14: Sidc 4D 16
Milton Pl. DA12: Grav'nd 6B 14
Milton Rd. DA10: Swans 6B 12
   DA12: Grav'nd 6A 14
   DA16: Well 1C 6
   DA17: Belv 4E 4
Milton Rd. Bus. Pk. DA12: Grav'nd 7B 14
   (off Milton Rd.)
Milton St. DA10: Swans 6A 12
Minerva Cl. DA14: Sidc 3B 16
Minshaw Ct. DA14: Sidc 4C 16
Miskin Rd. DA1: Dart 7H 9
Miskin Theatre
   Dartford 2H 19
Miskin Way DA12: Grav'nd 6C 24
Mitchell Av. DA11: Nflt 2G 23
Mitchell Cl. DA1: Dart 2K 19
   DA17: Belv 3G 5
   SE2 . . . . .4A 4
Mitchell Wlk. DA10: Swans 7B 12
Mitchem Cl. TN15: W King 7B 32
Moat Ct. DA15: Sidc 3C 16
Moat Cft. DA16: Well 3F 7
Moat La. DA8: Erith 1F 9
Mollison Ri. DA12: Grav'nd 5D 24
Monarch Cl. RM18: Tilb 2A 14
Monarch Rd. DA17: Belv 3E 4
Monica James Ho. DA14: Sidc 3D 16
Monks Cl. SE2 . . . . .4B 4
Monks Orchard DA1: Dart 2J 19
Monks Wlk. DA13: Sflt 6D 22
Monks Well DA9: Ghithe 4K 11
   (off Watermans Way)
Monkton Rd. DA16: Well 2C 6
Monmouth Cl. DA16: Well 4D 6
Montague Cl. DA15: Sidc 3D 16
Montague Pl. BR8: Swan 4E 26
Monterey Cl. DA5: Bexl 2B 18
Montgomery Cl. DA15: Sidc 6C 6
Montgomery Rd. DA4: S Dar 1E 28
Montpelier Av. DA5: Bexl 7G 7
Montreal Rd. RM18: Tilb 3K 13
Montrose Av. DA15: Sidc 7D 6
   DA16: Well 3A 6
Montrose Cl. DA16: Well 3C 6
Moore Av. RM18: Tilb 2A 14
Moore Cl. DA2: Dart 2E 20
Moore Rd. DA10: Swans 6B 12
Moorhen Cl. DA8: Erith 2K 5
Morello Cl. BR8: Swan 4C 26
Moreton Cl. BR8: Swan 2D 26
Moreton Ct. DA1: Cray 3E 8
Moreton Ind. Est. BR8: Swan 4G 27
Morgan Dr. DA9: Ghithe 7F 11
Morland Av. DA1: Dart 5G 9
Mornington Ct. DA5: Bexl 1C 18
Morris Gdns. DA1: Dart 5B 10
Mortimer Rd. DA8: Erith 6H 5
Morvale Ct. DA17: Belv 4D 4
Mossdown Cl. DA17: Belv 4E 4
Moss Way DA2: Dart 4E 20
Mote, The DA3: New A 2J 33
Mottisfont Rd. SE2 . . . . .3A 4
Moultain Hill BR8: Swan 4F 27
Mount, The DA6: Bex 5A 8
Mt. Culver Av. DA14: Sidc 6G 17
Mount Dr. DA6: Bex 5H 7
Mount Pleasant Rd. DA1: Dart 6A 10
Mt. Pleasant Wlk. DA5: Bexl 5B 8
Mount Rd. DA1: Cray 6E 8
   DA6: Bex 5G 7
Mounts Rd. DA9: Ghithe 5J 11
Muggins La. DA2: Shorne 4H 25
Mulberry Cl. DA13: Meop 6K 31
Mulberry Rd. DA11: Nflt 3H 23
Mulberry Way DA17: Belv 2G 5
Mullender Ct. DA12: Grav'nd 1F 25
Multon Rd. TN15: W King 6B 32
Munford Dr. DA10: Swans 7B 12
Mungo Pk. Rd. DA12: Grav'nd 5C 24

Murchison Av. DA5: Bexl 1G 17
Muscovy Ho. DA18: Erith 2C 4
   (off Kale Rd.)
Mussenden La. DA3: Fawk, Hort K 6F 29
   DA4: Hort K 5D 28
Myrtle Cl. DA8: Erith 7J 5
Myrtle Pl. DA2: Dart 7E 10
Myrtle Rd. DA1: Dart 1J 19

N

Nags Head La. DA16: Well 3E 6
Nairn Ct. RM18: Tilb 2J 13
Nansen Rd. DA12: Grav'nd 4C 24
Napier Rd. DA11: Nflt 1J 23
   DA17: Belv 4D 4
Naseby Ct. DA14: Sidc 4C 16
Nash Bank DA13: Meop, Ist R 2J 31
Nash Cft. DA11: Nflt 4H 23
NASH STREET 2J 31
Nash St. DA13: Ist R, Meop 2J 31
Nassau Path SE28 . . . . .1A 4
Nassau Rd. DA12: Grav'nd 4C 24
Neal Rd. TN15: W King 6B 32
Nelson Ct. DA8: Erith 7K 5
   (off Frobisher Rd.)
Nelson Ho. DA9: Ghithe 5A 12
Nelson Pl. DA14: Sidc 4D 16
Nelson Rd. DA1: Dart 6H 9
   DA11: Nflt 2J 23
   DA14: Sidc 4D 16
   DA17: Belv 5D 4
Neptune Ct. DA8: Erith 7K 5
   (off Frobisher Rd.)
Neptune Wlk. DA8: Erith 4H 5
Nethewode Ct. DA17: Belv 3F 5
   (off Lower Pk. Rd.)
Neville Cl. DA15: Sidc 4C 16
Nevill Pl. DA13: Meop 5K 31
NEW ASH GREEN 2J 33
NEW BARN 3F 31
New Barn Rd. BR8: Swan 1D 26
   DA3: Ist R, Lfield 3E 30
   DA13: Ist R, Nflt G, Lfield, Sflt 3F 23
Newbery Rd. DA8: Erith 1E 8
Newbury Cl. DA2: Dart 7C 10
Newbury Ct. DA14: Sidc 4C 16
NEW HOUSE 3J 23
New Ho. La. DA11: Nflt, Grav'nd 3J 23
Newick Cl. DA5: Bexl 6A 8
Newlyn Rd. DA16: Well 2C 6
Newmans Rd. DA11: Nflt 2J 23
Newnham Lodge DA17: Belv 5E 4
   (off Erith Rd.)
Newports BR8: Crock 7C 26
New Rd. BR8: Swan 7E 18
   (Egerton Av.)
   BR8: Swan 5B 10
   (Swanley La.)
   DA4: S Dar 2D 28
   DA11: Grav'nd .6K 13
   DA13: Meop 5J 31
   DA16: Well 2E 6
   SE2 . . . . .4B 4
New Swan Yd. DA12: Grav'nd 6A 14
New Tavern Fort 6B 14
   (in Chantry Heritage Cen.)
Newton Abbot Rd. DA11: Nflt 2J 23
Newton Rd. DA16: Well 3D 6
   RM18: Tilb 3K 13
Newtons Ct. DA2: Dart 4E 10
NEW TOWN 7A 10
Next Generation Club
   Dartford 1B 20
Nickleby Rd. DA12: Grav'nd 1F 25
   (not continuous)
Nicola Ter. DA7: Bex 1H 7
Nightingale Cl. DA11: Nflt 3H 23
Nightingale Gro. DA1: Dart 4B 10
Nightingale Way BR8: Swan 3D 26
Nine Elms Gro. DA11: Grav'nd 7K 13
Noel Ter. DA14: Sidc 4E 16
Nordenfeldt Rd. DA8: Erith 5H 5
Norfield Rd. DA2: Dart 4B 18
Norfolk Cl. DA1: Dart 6B 10
Norfolk Cres. DA15: Sidc 7B 6
Norfolk Gdns. DA7: Bex 1J 7

Norfolk Pl. DA16: Well 2D 6
Norfolk Rd. DA12: Grav'nd 6C 14
   (not continuous)
Norham Ct. DA2: Dart 6C 10
   (off Osbourne Rd.)
Normandy Way DA8: Erith 1D 8
Normanhurst Av. DA7: Bex 1G 7
   DA16: Well 1G 7
Norman Pde. DA14: Sidc 2G 17
Norman Rd. DA1: Dart 1K 19
   DA17: Belv 3F 5
   (not continuous)
Norman's Cl. DA11: Grav'nd 7K 13
Norris Way DA1: Cray 3E 8
Northall Rd. DA7: Bex 2B 8
Nth. Ash Rd. DA3: New A 3H 33
North Cl. DA6: Bex 4G 7
Northcote Rd. DA11: Grav'nd 1J 23
   DA14: Sidc 4B 16
NORTH CRAY 5H 17
Nth. Cray Rd. DA5: Bexl 1A 18
   DA14: Sidc 6H 17
North Cray Woods 4G 17
Northdown Rd. DA3: Lfield 2A 30
   DA16: Well 2E 6
NORTH END 1E 8
Northend Rd. DA1: Cray 1E 8
   DA8: Erith 7K 5
Northend Trad. Est. DA8: Erith 1D 8
Northfield DA3: Hart 3C 30
NORTHFLEET 6E 12
NORTHFLEET GREEN 5F 23
Northfleet Grn. Rd. DA13: Nflt G 6F 23
Northfleet Ind. Est. DA11: Nflt 4C 12
Northfleet Station (Rail) 6E 12
Nth. Glade, The DA5: Bexl 7J 7
Nth. Kent Av. DA11: Nflt 6F 13
North Kent Indoor Bowls Club 3F 5
Nth. Ridge Rd. DA12: Grav'nd 3B 24
North Riding DA3: Lfield 3G 31
North Rd. DA1: Dart 6E 8
   DA17: Belv 3F 5
North Sq. DA3: New A 2J 33
North St. DA1: Dart 7J 9
   DA7: Bex 4K 7
   DA12: Grav'nd .7A 14
Northumberland Av. DA16: Well 4A 6
Northumberland Cl. DA8: Erith 7G 5
NORTHUMBERLAND HEATH 7G 5
Northumberland Pk. DA8: Erith 7G 5
Northumberland Rd. DA13: Ist R 7J 23
Northumberland Way DA8: Erith 1B 8
Northview BR8: Swan 2D 26
North Vw. Av. RM18: Tilb 1K 13
Northwood Pl. DA18: Erith 3D 4
Norvic Ho. DA8: Erith 7K 5
Norwich Pl. DA6: Bex 4K 7
Norwood Ct. DA1: Dart 5B 10
   (off Farnol Rd.)
Norwood La. DA13: Meop 5K 31
Nuffield Rd. BR8: Swan 6F 19
Nursery, The DA8: Erith 7K 5
Nursery Av. DA7: Bex 3J 7
Nursery Cl. BR8: Swan 2B 26
   DA2: Dart 7D 10
Nursery Rd. DA13: Meop 5K 31
NURSTEAD 3J 31
Nurstead Av. DA3: Lfield 4G 31
Nurstead Chu. La. DA13: Meop, Sole S 4J 31
Nurstead Court 4K 31
Nurstead La. DA3: Long H, Meop 4G 31
Nurstead Rd. DA8: Erith 7E 4
Nuthatch DA3: Lfield 3E 30
Nutley Cl. BR8: Swan 1E 26
Nutmead Cl. DA5: Bexl 1B 18
Nuxley Rd. DA17: Belv 6D 4

O

Oak Cl. DA1: Cray .4E 8
Oakdene Av. DA8: Erith 6G 5
Oakenholt Ho. SE2 . . . . .1B 4
Oakfield La. DA1: Bexl 2D 18
   DA1: Dart 2H 19
   DA2: Dart 2G 19
Oakfield Pk. Rd. DA1: Dart 2J 19

Oakfield Pl. DA1: Dart 2J **19**
Oakhouse Rd. DA6: Bex 5K **7**
Oakhurst Av. DA7: Bex 7C **4**
Oakhurst Gdns. DA7: Bex 7C **4**
Oaklands Av. DA15: Sidc 7C **6**
Oaklands Cl. DA6: Bex 5J **7**
TN15: W King 6B **32**
Oaklands Rd. DA2: Dart 1C **20**
DA6: Bex 4J **7**
DA11: Nflt 4J **23**
Oakleigh Cl. BR8: Swan 3D **26**
Oakley Dr. SE9 1A **16**
Oakley Pk. DA5: Bexl 7F **7**
Oak Rd. DA8: Erith 7G **5**
(Mill Rd.)
DA8: Erith 1F **9**
(Moat La.)
DA9: Ghithe 6F **11**
DA12: Grav'nd 3B **24**
Oaks, The BR8: Swan 2D **26**
DA2: Dart 6C **10**
Oak Tree Av. DA9: Bluew 7G **11**
Oakway Cl. DA5: Bexl 6H **7**
Oakwood Cl. DA1: Dart 1C **20**
Oakwood Ct. *BR8: Swan 2B 26*
(off Lawn Cl.)
Oakwood Dr. DA7: Bex 4B **8**
Oakwood Ri. DA3: Lfield 3B **30**
Oast Way DA3: Hart 6B **30**
Ockham Dr. BR5: St P 7D **16**
Ockley Ct. DA14: Sidc 3B **16**
Okehampton Cres. DA16: Well 1E **6**
Old Barn Way DA7: Bex 3C **8**
OLD BEXLEY 7A **8**
Old Bexley Bus. Pk. DA5: Bexl 7A **8**
Old Bexley La. DA1: Bexl 1E **18**
DA5: Bexl, Dart 2C **18**
Old Chapel Rd. BR8: Crock 7B **26**
Old College Ct. DA17: Belv 5F **5**
Old Dartford Rd. DA4: Farn 6A **28**
Old Downs DA3: Hart 5B **30**
Old Farm Av. DA15: Sidc 1A **16**
Old Farm Gdns. BR8: Swan 3E **26**
Old Farm Rd. E. DA15: Sidc 2D **16**
Old Farm Rd. W. DA15: Sidc 2C **16**
Oldfield Rd. DA7: Bex 2H **7**
Old Forge Way DA14: Sidc 4E **16**
Old London Rd. DA14: Sidc, Swan 7K **17**
Old Maidstone Rd. DA14: Sidc 7J **17**
Old Mnr. Dr. DA12: Grav'nd 1B **24**
Old Mnr. Way DA7: Bex 2C **8**
Old Mill Equestrian Cen. 6J **19**
Old Parsonage Yd., The DA4: Hort K 4D **28**
Old Perry St. BR7: Chst 6B **16**
DA11: Nflt 2H **23**
Old Rd. DA1: Cray 5C **8**
Old Rd. E. DA11: Grav'nd 1A **24**
DA12: Grav'nd 1A **24**
Old Rd. W. DA11: Grav'nd 1J **23**
Old School Ct. *BR8: Swan 2D 26*
(off Bonney Way)
Old Watling St. DA11: Grav'nd 5K **23**
Old Yews, The DA3: Lfield 3E **30**
Oliver Cl. RM20: W Thur 1G **11**
Oliver Cl. Ind. Est. RM20: W Thur 1G **11**
Oliver Cres. DA4: Farn 7A **28**
Olive Rd. DA1: Dart 1J **19**
Oliver Rd. BR8: Swan 3C **26**
RM20: W Thur 1G **11**
(not continuous)
Olivers Mill DA3: New A 2H **33**
Olron Cres. DA6: Bex 5G **7**
Olyffe Av. DA16: Well 1D **6**
Olympic Golf & Leisure Cen., The 4G **27**
Onslow Dr. DA14: Sidc 2G **17**
Optima Pk. DA1: Cray 2F **9**
Orbital One DA1: Dart 2C **20**
Orbital One Ind. Est. DA1: Dart 2B **20**
Orchard, The BR8: Swan 2C **26**
Orchard Av. DA1: Dart 7G **9**
DA11: Grav'nd 5A **24**
DA17: Belv 6C **4**
Orchard Cl. DA3: Lfield 2E **30**
DA7: Bex 1H **7**
Orchard Dr. DA13: Meop 5J **31**
Orchard Hill DA1: Cray 5D **8**
Orchard Ho. DA8: Erith 1E **8**
Orchard Lea DA13: Sflt 5C **22**
Orchard Ri. E. DA15: Sidc 5B **6**
Orchard Ri. W. DA15: Sidc 5B **6**
Orchard Rd. DA10: Swans 5B **12**
DA11: Nflt 2F **23**
DA14: Sidc 4B **16**
DA16: Well 3E **6**
DA17: Belv 4E **4**
Orchards Shop. Cen., The DA1: Dart 6K **9**
Orchard St. DA1: Dart 6K **9**
Orchard Ter. DA9: Ghithe 5F **11**
Orchard Theatre, The 6K **9**
Orchard Vs. DA14: Sidc 6F **17**
Orchard Way DA2: Dart 3J **19**
Ordnance Rd. DA12: Grav'nd 6B **14**
Orford Ct. *DA2: Dart 6C 10*
(off Osbourne Rd.)
Orlick Rd. DA12: Grav'nd 1G **25**
Osborne Rd. DA17: Belv 5D **4**
Osbourne Rd. DA2: Dart 6C **10**
Osney Ho. SE2 2B **4**
Osney Way DA12: Grav'nd 2E **24**
Ospringe Ct. SE9 6A **6**
Osterberg Rd. DA1: Dart 4A **10**
Otford Cl. DA5: Bexl 6A **8**
Ottawa Rd. RM18: Tilb 2K **13**
Oval, The DA3: Lfield 3F **31**
DA15: Sidc 7D **6**
Overcliffe DA11: Grav'nd 6K **13**
Overcourt Cl. DA15: Sidc 6E **6**
Overmead BR8: Swan 5D **26**
DA15: Sidc 7A **6**
Over Minnis DA3: New A 3J **33**
Overton Rd. SE2 3A **4**
Overton Rd. E. SE2 3B **4**
Overy St. DA1: Dart 6K **9**
Owen Cl. SE28 1A **4**
Owenite St. SE2 4A **4**
Oxford Cl. DA12: Grav'nd 2E **24**
Oxford M. DA5: Bexl 7K **7**
Oxford Rd. DA14: Sidc 5E **16**
Oxleas Cl. DA16: Well 2A **6**

P

Pacific Cl. DA10: Swans 5B **12**
Packham Rd. DA11: Nflt 3J **23**
Packmores Rd. SE9 5A **6**
Paddock, The DA2: Dart 2F **21**
Paddock Cl. DA4: S Dar 1D **28**
Paddock Rd. DA6: Bex 4H **7**
Paddock Way BR7: Chst 7A **16**
Pageant Cl. RM18: Tilb 1B **14**
Page Cl. DA2: Bean 3K **21**
Page Cres. DA8: Erith 7K **5**
Painters Ash La. DA11: Nflt 3G **23**
Palladian Circ. DA9: Ghithe 4K **11**
Palmar Cres. DA7: Bex 3K **7**
Palmar Rd. DA7: Bex 2K **7**
Palm Av. DA14: Sidc 6G **17**
Palmeira Rd. DA7: Bex 3G **7**
Palmer Av. DA12: Grav'nd 4C **24**
Panter's BR8: Swan 7E **18**
Pantiles, The DA7: Bex 7D **4**
Parade, The DA1: Cray 5E **8**
DA10: Swans 5C **12**
DA12: Grav'nd 2C **24**
DA13: Meop 7K **31**
Parish Ga. Dr. DA15: Sidc 6B **6**
Park, The DA14: Sidc 5D **16**
Park App. DA16: Well 4E **6**
Park Av. DA11: Nflt 1H **23**
DA12: Grav'nd 1B **24**
Parkcliffe Rd. DA9: Ghithe 4K **11**
Pk. Corner Rd. DA13: Sflt 4C **22**
Park Cres. DA8: Erith 6G **5**
Park Cres. Rd. DA8: Erith 6H **5**
Park Dr. DA3: Lfield 3B **30**
Parker Av. RM18: Tilb 1B **14**
Parker Ind. Cen. DA2: Dart 1D **20**
Parkfield DA3: Hart 4B **30**
Park Gdns. DA8: Erith 4H **5**
Park Gro. DA7: Bex 4B **8**
Park Hill DA13: Meop 4H **31**
Park Hill Rd. DA15: Sidc 3B **16**
Parkhill Rd. DA5: Bexl 7J **7**
Parkhurst Gdns. DA5: Bexl 7K **7**
Parkhurst Rd. DA5: Bexl 7K **7**
Park La. BR8: Swan 2H **27**
Park Mead DA15: Sidc 5E **6**
Pk. Pale La. DA12: Shorne 7J **25**
Park Pl. DA12: Grav'nd 6B **14**
Park Rd. BR8: Swan 4E **26**
DA1: Dart 7B **10**
DA10: Swans 6B **12**
DA11: Grav'nd 1A **24**
Park Rd. Ind. Est. BR8: Swan 3E **26**
Parkside DA14: Sidc 2E **16**
Parkside Av. DA7: Bex 2C **8**
RM18: Tilb 2A **14**
(not continuous)
Parkside Cross DA7: Bex 2D **8**
Parkside Lodge DA17: Belv 5G **5**
Parkside Pde. *DA1: Cray 2E 8*
(off Northend Rd.)
Parkside Rd. DA17: Belv 4F **5**
Park Ter. DA9: Ghithe 5K **11**
Parkview DA18: Erith 3B **4**
Park View Road 3F **7**
Park Vw. Rd. DA16: Well 3F **7**
Park Way DA5: Bexl 3D **18**
Parkway DA18: Erith 3C **4**
Parkwood Rd. DA5: Bexl 7J **7**
Paroma Rd. DA17: Belv 4E **4**
Parrock, The DA12: Grav'nd 1B **24**
Parrock Av. DA12: Grav'nd 1B **24**
PARROCK FARM 3C **24**
Parrock Rd. DA12: Grav'nd 1B **24**
Parrock St. DA11: Grav'nd 7A **14**
DA12: Grav'nd 6A **14**
Parsonage La. DA2: Dart, Sutt H 5C **20**
DA4: Dart, Sutt H 6C **20**
DA14: Sidc 4J **17**
Parsonage Manorway DA17: Belv 6E **4**
Parsons La. DA2: Dart 3G **19**
Partridge Rd. DA14: Sidc 3B **16**
Patricia Ct. DA16: Well 1E **6**
Patterdale Rd. DA2: Dart 1E **20**
Patterson Ct. DA1: Dart 5B **10**
Peach Cft. DA11: Nflt 3H **23**
Peacock St. DA12: Grav'nd 7B **14**
Peareswood Rd. DA8: Erith 1E **8**
Pearson Way DA1: Dart 2A **20**
Pear Tree Cl. BR8: Swan 2C **26**
Peartree Cl. DA8: Erith 1C **8**
Pear Tree La. DA12: High'm, Shorne 7K **25**
Pease Hill TN15: Ash 6H **33**
Peatfield Cl. DA15: Sidc 3B **16**
Pedham Pl. Ind. Est. BR8: Swan 5F **27**
Pegasus Ct. DA12: Grav'nd 3B **24**
Pelham Cotts. DA5: Bexl 1A **18**
Pelham Ct. DA14: Sidc 3D **16**
Pelham Rd. DA7: Bex 3K **7**
DA11: Grav'nd 1J **23**
Pelham Rd. Sth. DA11: Grav'nd, Nflt 1J **23**
Pelham Ter. DA11: Grav'nd 7J **13**
Pemberton Gdns. BR8: Swan 3D **26**
Pembroke Pde. DA8: Erith 5G **5**
Pembroke Pl. DA4: Sutt H 1C **28**
Pembroke Rd. DA8: Erith 5G **5**
Pembury Cres. DA14: Sidc 2H **17**
Pembury Rd. DA7: Bex 7C **4**
Pencroft Dr. DA1: Dart 7H **9**
Penda Rd. DA8: Erith 7F **5**
Penenden DA3: New A 2J **33**
Penfold La. DA5: Bexl 2G **17**
(Cotleigh Av.)
DA5: Bexl 1G **17**
(Stansted Cres.)
Pengarth Rd. DA5: Bexl 5G **7**
Penhill Rd. DA5: Bexl 1F **17**
Penney Cl. DA1: Dart 7J **9**
Pennine Way DA7: Bex 1D **8**
DA11: Nflt 3H **23**
Pennis La. DA3: Fawk 6A **30**
Penn La. DA5: Bexl 5G **7**
(not continuous)
Penpool La. DA16: Well 3E **6**
Penshurst Av. DA15: Sidc 6D **6**
Penshurst Cl. DA3: Lfield 2G **31**
TN15: W King 6B **32**
Penshurst Rd. DA7: Bex 1J **7**
Penton Ho. SE2 1B **4**

Pentstemon Dr. DA10: Swans 5B 12	Porchester Cl. DA3: Hart 4C 30	Queenborough Gdns. BR7: Chst 6A 16
Penventon Ct. RM18: Tilb 2K 13	Porchfield Cl. DA12: Grav'nd 2B 24	Queen Elizabeth II Bri. DA1: Dart ..3E 10
(off Dock Rd.)	Port Av. DA9: Ghithe 6J 11	RM20: Dart, W Thur 2E 10
PEPPER HILL 3G 23	Porthkerry Av. DA16: Well 4D 6	QUEEN MARY'S HOSPITAL 5D 16
Pepperhill DA11: Nflt 3F 23	Portland Av. DA12: Grav'nd 2A 24	Queen's Farm Rd.
Pepperhill La. DA11: Nflt 3F 23	DA15: Sidc 6D 6	DA12: Shorne, Grav'nd 2K 25
Pepys Cl. DA1: Dart 4B 10	Portland Pl. DA3: Lfield 3B 30	Queens Gdns. DA2: Dart 1C 20
DA11: Nflt 3G 23	(off Park Dr.)	Queens Rd. DA8: Erith 6J 5
RM18: Tilb 1B 14	DA9: Ghithe 4K 11	DA12: Grav'nd 3B 24
Percy Rd. DA7: Bex 2H 7	Portland Rd. DA11: Nflt 6G 13	DA16: Well 2E 6
Peregrine Ct. DA16: Well 1C 6	DA12: Grav'nd 1A 24	Queen St. DA7: Bex 3J 7
Perkins Cl. DA9: Ghithe 5G 11	Portman Cl. DA5: Bexl 1D 18	DA8: Erith 6J 5
Perpins Rd. SE9 ....6B 6	DA7: Bex 3H 7	DA12: Grav'nd 6A 14
Perran Cl. DA3: Hart 4C 30	Portmeadow Wlk. SE2 ....2B 4	Queenswood Rd. DA15: Sidc 5C 6
Perry Gro. DA1: Dart 4B 10	Portobello Pde. TN15: W King 7D 32	Questor DA1: Dart 2K 19
PERRY STREET 1H 23	Portsea Rd. RM18: Tilb 1B 14	
Perry St. BR7: Chst 6A 16	Pottery Rd. DA5: Bexl 2B 18	
DA1: Cray 4D 8	Pound Bank Cl. TN15: W King 7C 32	
DA11: Nflt 1H 23	Pound Grn. DA5: Bexl 7K 7	
Perry St. Gdns. BR7: Chst 6B 16	Pound Way BR7: Chst 7A 16	R
Perry St. Shaw BR7: Chst 7B 16	Powder Mill La. DA1: Dart 2K 19	
Perth Ho. RM18: Tilb 2K 13	Powell Av. DA2: Dart 2F 21	Rabbits Rd. DA4: S Dar 2E 28
Pescot Av. DA3: Lfield 3D 30	Powerscroft Rd. DA14: Sidc 6F 17	Racefield Cl. DA12: Shorne 7K 25
Peters Cl. DA16: Well 2B 6	(not continuous)	Rackham Cl. DA16: Well 2E 6
Peterstone Rd. SE2 ....2A 4	Power Works DA8: Erith 1F 9	Radfield Dr. DA2: Dart 1D 20
Peter St. DA12: Grav'nd 7A 14	Powys Cl. DA7: Bex 6B 4	Radfield Way DA15: Sidc 7A 6
Petworth Rd. DA6: Bex 5K 7	Poynder Rd. RM18: Tilb 1A 14	(not continuous)
Peveril Ct. DA2: Dart 6C 10	Poyntell Cres. BR7: Chst 7A 16	Radley Ho. SE2 ....2B 4
(off Clifton Wlk.)	Preston Ct. DA14: Sidc 4C 16	(off Wolvercote Rd.)
Phelps Cl. TN15: W King 6B 32	(off Crescent, The)	Radnor Av. DA16: Well 5E 6
Philip Av. BR8: Swan 4C 26	Preston Dr. DA7: Bex 1G 7	Radnor Cl. BR7: Chst 6B 16
Phillips Cl. DA1: Dart 6G 9	Preston Rd. DA11: Nflt 1H 23	Radzan Cl. DA2: Bexl 2D 18
Phoenix Pl. DA1: Dart 7J 9	Pretoria Ho. DA8: Erith 7J 5	Raeburn Av. DA1: Dart 5G 9
Picardy Manorway DA17: Belv 3F 5	Priestlands Pk. Rd. DA15: Sidc ...3C 16	Raeburn Pl. DA10: Swans 5B 12
Picardy Rd. DA17: Belv 5E 4	Priest's Wlk. DA12: Grav'nd 2F 25	Raeburn Rd. DA15: Sidc 6B 6
Picardy St. DA17: Belv 3E 4	Primmett Cl. TN15: W King 6B 32	Raglan Rd. DA17: Belv 4D 4
Pickering Ct. DA2: Dart 6C 10	Primrose Ter. DA12: Grav'nd 1B 24	Railway Pl. DA12: Grav'nd 6A 14
(off Osbourne Rd.)	Prince Charles Av. DA4: S Dar ...2E 28	DA17: Belv 3E 4
Pickford Cl. DA7: Bex 2H 7	Princes Av. DA2: Dart 1C 20	Railway Sidings DA13: Meop 5K 31
Pickford La. DA7: Bex 2H 7	Princes Cl. DA14: Sidc 3G 17	Railway Sidings Ind. Est.
Pickford Rd. DA7: Bex 3H 7	Princes Golf & Leisure Club 1B 20	DA13: Sole S 5K 31
Pickwick Gdns. DA11: Nflt 3G 23	Princes Rd. BR8: Swan 6F 19	Railway St. DA11: Nflt 5D 12
Pickwick Ho. DA11: Nflt 3G 23	DA1: Dart 6F 9	Rainham Cl. SE9 ....6B 6
Pickwick Way BR7: Chst 6A 16	DA2: Dart 1C 20	Raleigh Cl. DA8: Erith ....6K 5 & 1J 5
Pier Rd. DA8: Erith 6J 5	DA12: Grav'nd 4B 24	Raleigh Rd. DA8: Erith 7K 5
(not continuous)	PRINCES ROAD INTERCHANGE .1C 20	Ramillies Rd. DA15: Sidc 6E 6
DA9: Ghithe 4J 11	Princesses Pde. DA1: Cray 5D 8	Ramsden Rd. DA8: Erith 7H 5
DA11: Nflt 6J 13	(off Waterside)	Randall Cl. DA8: Erith 6G 5
Pilgrim's Ct. DA1: Dart 5B 10	Princess Margaret Rd. RM18: E Til ..1J 15	Randolph Cl. DA7: Bex 3B 8
Pilgrims Rd. DA10: Nflt, Swans ...4B 12	Princess Pocahontas Memorial ...6A 14	Ranelagh Gdns. DA11: Nflt 7J 13
Pilgrims Vw. DA9: Ghithe 6K 11	(off Church St.)	Range Rd. DA12: Grav'nd 7D 14
Pilgrims Way DA1: Dart 1B 20	Princes Vw. DA7: Bex 3J 7	Rangeworth Pl. DA15: Sidc 3C 16
Pilots Pl. DA12: Grav'nd 6B 14	DA11: Nflt 6A 14	Ranleigh Gdns. DA7: Bex 7D 4
Pincott Rd. DA6: Bex 5K 7	(not continuous)	Ranworth Cl. DA8: Erith 2D 8
Pincroft Wood DA3: Lfield 3F 31	Princes Vw. DA1: Dart 1B 20	Raphael Av. RM18: Tilb 1K 13
PINDEN 2K 29	Prioress Cres. DA9: Ghithe 4K 11	Raphael Rd. DA12: Grav'nd 7C 14
Pine Av. DA12: Grav'nd 1C 24	Priory Cl. DA1: Dart 5H 9	Rashleigh Way DA4: Hort K 4D 28
Pine Cl. BR8: Swan 4E 26	Priory Ct. DA1: Dart 6J 9	Rathmore Rd. DA12: Grav'nd 7A 14
Pine Ri. DA13: Meop 6K 31	Priory Dr. SE2 ....5B 4	Ravensbourne Rd. DA1: Cray 3F 9
Pinewood Av. DA15: Sidc 1B 16	Priory Gdns. DA1: Dart 5J 9	Ravenswood Rd. DA5: Bexl 1H 17
Pinewood Pl. DA2: Bexl 2D 18	Priory Hill DA1: Dart 6J 9	Rayford Cl. DA1: Dart 5H 9
Pinewood Rd. SE2 ....6B 4	Priory Pl. DA1: Dart 6J 9	Ray Lamb Way DA8: Erith 1K 5
Pink's Hill BR8: Swan 5D 26	Priory Rd. Nth. DA1: Dart 4J 9	Rayner's Ct. DA11: Nflt 5E 12
Pinnacle Hill DA7: Bex 4A 8	Priory Rd. Sth. DA1: Dart 6J 9	Rays Hill DA4: Hort K 4D 28
Pinnacle Hill Nth. DA7: Bex 4A 8	Priory Shop. Cen. DA1: Dart 6K 9	Read Way DA12: Grav'nd 5C 24
Pinnocks Av. DA11: Grav'nd 1A 24	Prospect Cl. DA17: Belv 4E 4	Rebecca Ct. DA14: Sidc 4E 16
Pioneer Way BR8: Swan 3D 26	Prospect Gro. DA12: Grav'nd 7C 14	Recreation Rd. DA15: Sidc 3B 16
Pippins, The DA13: Meop 6K 31	Prospect Pl. DA12: Grav'nd 7C 14	Rectory Bus. Cen. DA14: Sidc 4E 16
Pirrip Cl. DA12: Grav'nd 1E 24	(not continuous)	Rectory Cl. DA1: Cray 4D 8
Pitfield DA3: Hart 4C 30	Prospect Pl. Retail Pk. DA1: Dart ..6K 9	DA14: Sidc 4E 16
Plane Av. DA11: Nflt 7G 13	Providence St. DA9: Ghithe 5H 11	Rectory La. DA14: Sidc 4E 16
Plantation Cl. DA9: Ghithe 6G 11	Prudhoe Ct. DA2: Dart 6C 10	Rectory Mdw. DA13: Sflt 6D 22
Plantation Rd. BR8: Swan 7F 19	(off Osbourne Rd.)	Rectory Rd. DA10: Swans 7B 12
DA8: Erith 1F 9	Pucknells Cl. BR8: Swan 1B 26	Redding Cl. DA2: Dart 2F 21
Plaxtol Rd. DA8: Erith 7E 4	PUDDLEDOCK 6E 18	Reddy Rd. DA8: Erith 6K 5
Pleasant Vw. DA8: Erith 5J 5	Puddledock La. DA2: Dart, Swan ..5D 18	Redhill Rd. DA3: New A 3H 33
Plympton Cl. DA17: Belv 3C 4	Punch Cft. DA3: New A 3H 33	Redhill Wood DA3: New A 3K 33
Plymstock Rd. DA16: Well 7A 4		Red House 4H 7
Pollard Wlk. DA14: Sidc 6F 17		Red Ho. La. DA6: Bex 4G 7
Pondfield La. DA12: Shorne 7K 25		Redleaf Cl. DA17: Belv 6E 4
Poplar Av. DA12: Grav'nd 4B 24	Q	Red Lodge Cres. DA5: Bexl 3C 18
Poplar Mt. DA17: Belv 4F 5		Red Lodge Rd. DA5: Bexl 3C 18
Poplar Pl. SE28 ....1A 4	Quadrant, The DA7: Bex 7B 4	Redpoll Way DA18: Erith 3B 4
Poplars, The DA12: Grav'nd 7D 14	Quakers Cl. DA3: Hart 3B 30	REDSTREET 6E 22
Poplars Cl. DA3: Lfield 3F 31	Quantock Rd. DA7: Bex 2D 8	Red St. DA13: Sflt 5D 22
Poplar Wlk. DA13: Meop 6K 31	Quay La. DA9: Ghithe 4J 11	Redwood Cl. DA15: Sidc 1D 16
Poppy Cl. DA17: Belv 3F 5	Quebec Rd. RM18: Tilb 2K 13	Redwood Ct. DA1: Dart 6B 10
	Queen Anne's Ga. DA7: Bex 3G 7	Reed Ct. DA9: Ghithe 4K 11
		Reeves Cres. BR8: Swan 3C 26

Regency Cl.—St Mary's Cl.

Regency Cl. TN15: W King 6B **32**
Regency Way DA6: Bex 3G **7**
Regents Ct. DA11: Grav'nd 5A **14**
Regent Sq. DA17: Belv 4F **5**
Reinickendorf Av. SE9 6A **6**
Rembrandt Dr. DA11: Nflt 3G **23**
Rennets Cl. SE9 5B **6**
Rennets Wood Rd. SE9 5A **6**
Renshaw Cl. DA17: Belv 6D **4**
Reservoir Cl. DA9: Ghithe 6K **11**
Restons Cres. SE9 6A **6**
Reynolds Health & Fitness 2D **18**
Ribblesdale Rd. DA2: Dart 1D **20**
Ricardo Path SE28 1A **4**
Richardson Cl. DA9: Ghithe 5G **11**
Richmer Rd. DA8: Erith 2J **5**
Richmond Dr. DA12: Grav'nd 2D **24**
Rider Cl. DA15: Sidc 6B **6**
Ridge, The DA5: Bexl 7J **7**
Ridge Av. DA1: Cray 6E **8**
Ridgecroft Cl. DA5: Bexl 1B **18**
Ridge Way DA1: Cray 6E **8**
Ridgeway DA2: Dart 5F **21**
Ridgeway, The DA12: Shorne 7K **25**
Ridgeway Av. DA12: Grav'nd 3A **24**
Ridgeway Bungs.
DA12: Shorne 7K **25**
Ridgeway E. DA15: Sidc 5C **6**
Ridgeway W. DA15: Sidc 5B **6**
Ridgewood DA3: Lfield 2F **31**
RIDLEY 5K **33**
Ridley Rd. DA16: Well 1E **6**
Riefield Rd. SE9 4A **6**
Ripley Rd. DA17: Belv 4E **4**
Ripleys Mkt. DA1: Dart 7K **9**
Rippersley Rd. DA16: Well 1D **6**
Rise, The DA1: Cray 4E **8**
DA5: Bexl 7F **7**
DA12: Grav'nd 4D **24**
Risedale Rd. DA7: Bex 3B **8**
Riverdale Rd. DA5: Bexl 7J **7**
DA8: Erith 5F **5**
Riversdale DA11: Nflt 2H **23**
Riverside App. RM18: Tilb 4J **13**
Riverside Ind. Est. DA1: Dart 5K **9**
Riverside Rail Freight Terminal
RM18: Tilb 4K **13**
Riverside Rd. DA14: Sidc 3H **17**
Riverside Swimming Cen. 5J **5**
Riverside Way DA1: Dart 5K **9**
Riverview *DA1: Dart 4B **10***
(off Henderson Dr.)
RIVERVIEW PARK 4E **24**
Riverview Rd. DA9: Ghithe 5H **11**
River Wharf Bus. Pk. DA17: Belv 1H **5**
Roberts Cl. SE9 1A **16**
Roberts Rd. DA17: Belv 5E **4**
Robina Av. DA11: Nflt 7G **13**
Robina Cl. DA6: Bex 4G **7**
Robina Ct. BR8: Swan 4F **27**
Robin Hood La. DA6: Bex 5H **7**
Robins Cft. DA11: Nflt 3H **23**
Rochester Cl. DA15: Sidc 6E **6**
Rochester Dr. DA5: Bexl 6J **7**
Rochester Rd. DA1: Dart 7B **10**
DA12: Grav'nd 7D **14**
Rochester Way DA1: Dart 7C **8**
SE9 3A **6**
Rodeo Cl. DA8: Erith 1G **9**
Roehampton Cl.
DA12: Grav'nd 7D **14**
Roehampton Dr. BR7: Chst 6A **16**
Rogers Ct. BR8: Swan 4F **27**
Rogers Wood La. DA3: Fawk 4D **32**
Rokesby Cl. DA16: Well 2A **6**
Rollo Rd. BR8: Swan 7E **18**
Roman Rd. DA11: Nflt 3F **23**
Roman Villa Rd.
DA2: Dart, Sutt H, S Dar 5D **20**
DA4: S Dar, Sutt H 5D **20**
Roman Way DA1: Cray 5D **8**
Romney Gdns. DA7: Bex 1J **7**
Romney Rd. DA11: Nflt 3H **23**
Ronaldstone Rd. DA15: Sidc 6B **6**
Rondel Ct. DA5: Bexl 6H **7**
Ron Grn. Ct. DA8: Erith 6H **5**
Roseacre Rd. DA16: Well 3E **6**
Rose Av. DA12: Grav'nd 1D **24**
Rosebank Gdns. DA11: Nflt 1H **23**
Roseberry Gdns. DA1: Dart 7H **9**
Rosebery Av. DA15: Sidc 7B **6**
Rosebery Ct. DA11: Grav'nd 1J **23**
Rosedale Cl. DA2: Dart 7C **10**
Rosedene Ct. DA1: Dart 7H **9**
Rosegarth DA13: Ist R 1H **31**
Rosemary Rd. DA16: Well 1C **6**
Rose St. DA11: Nflt 6E **12**
Rose Vs. DA1: Dart 7C **10**
Rosewood DA2: Dart 4D **18**
Rosewood Cl. DA14: Sidc 3F **17**
Rosher Ho. DA11: Nflt 6J **13**
ROSHERVILLE 6J **13**
Rosherville Way DA11: Nflt 7H **13**
Rossland Cl. DA6: Bex 5A **8**
Ross Rd. DA1: Dart 6F **9**
Rouge La. DA12: Grav'nd 1A **24**
Round Ash Way DA3: Hart 6B **30**
Row, The DA3: New A 3J **33**
Rowan Cl. DA13: Meop 6K **31**
Rowan Cres. DA1: Dart 1H **19**
Rowan Ho. DA14: Sidc 3C **16**
Rowan Rd. BR8: Swan 3C **26**
DA7: Bex 3H **7**
Rowans Cl. DA3: Lfield 2A **30**
Rowanwood Av.
DA15: Sidc 1D **16**
Rowhill Rd. BR8: Swan 6E **18**
DA2: Dart 6E **18**
Rowlatt Cl. DA2: Dart 4H **19**
Rowlatt Rd. DA2: Dart 4H **19**
Rowley Av. DA15: Sidc 7E **6**
Rownmarsh Cl. DA11: Nflt 3G **23**
Rowntree Path SE28 1A **4**
Rowzill Rd. BR8: Swan 6E **18**
Royal Oak Rd. DA6: Bex 5J **7**
(not continuous)
Royal Oak Ter. *DA12: Grav'nd 1B **24***
(off Constitution Hill)
Royal Pde. BR7: Chst 7A **16**
Royal Pde. M. *BR7: Chst 7A **16***
(off Royal Pde.)
Royal Pier M. DA12: Grav'nd 6B **14**
Royal Pier Rd. DA12: Grav'nd 6A **14**
Royal Rd. DA2: Dart 5B **20**
DA14: Sidc 3G **17**
Royston Rd. DA1: Cray 6E **8**
Rudland Rd. DA7: Bex 3A **8**
Ruffets Wood DA12: Grav'nd 6B **24**
Rumania Wlk.
DA12: Grav'nd 3E **24**
Runnymede Ct. DA2: Dart 1D **20**
Rural Va. DA11: Nflt 7H **13**
Rushdene SE2 3B **4**
(not continuous)
Rushetts Rd. TN15: W King 7B **32**
Ruskin Av. DA16: Well 2D **6**
Ruskin Dr. DA16: Well 3D **6**
Ruskin Gro. DA1: Dart 5B **10**
DA16: Well 2D **6**
Ruskin Rd. DA17: Belv 4E **4**
Russell Cl. DA1: Cray 4F **9**
DA7: Bex 4K **7**
Russell Pl. DA4: Sutt H 1B **28**
Russell Rd. DA12: Grav'nd 6C **14**
RM18: Tilb 1H **13**
Russell Sq. DA3: Lfield 3A **30**
Russell Ter. DA4: Hort K 4D **28**
Russets, The DA13: Meop 6K **31**
Russett Way BR8: Swan 2C **26**
Rutland Av. DA15: Sidc 7D **6**
Rutland Cl. DA1: Dart 7J **9**
DA5: Bexl 2G **17**
Rutland Ct. SE9 2A **16**
Rutland Ga. DA17: Belv 5F **5**
RUXLEY 7H **17**
Ruxley Cl. DA14: Sidc 6G **17**
Ruxley Cnr. Ind. Est.
DA14: Sidc 6G **17**
Ruxton Cl. BR8: Swan 3D **26**
Ruxton Ct. BR8: Swan 3D **26**
Rydal Dr. DA7: Bex 1K **7**
Rye Cl. DA5: Bexl 6A **8**
Ryecroft DA3: Long H 4G **31**
DA12: Grav'nd 5D **24**

S

Sackville Rd. DA2: Dart 2J **19**
Saddington St. DA12: Grav'nd 7A **14**
St Aidan's Way DA12: Grav'nd 3D **24**
St Alban's Cl. DA12: Grav'nd 3C **24**
St Alban's Gdns. DA12: Grav'nd 3C **24**
St Alban's Rd. DA1: Dart 7A **10**
St Andrews Ct. BR8: Swan 3D **26**
*DA12: Grav'nd 6A **14***
(off Queen St.)
St Andrew's Gdns. 6A **14**
St Andrew's Rd. DA12: Grav'nd 7A **14**
DA14: Sidc 3G **17**
RM18: Tilb 1H **13**
St Audrey Av. DA7: Bex 2K **7**
St Augustine's Rd. DA17: Belv 4D **4**
St Benedict's Av. DA12: Grav'nd 2C **24**
St Botolph Rd. DA11: Nflt 3G **23**
St Brides Cl. DA18: Erith 2B **4**
St Chad's Dr. DA12: Grav'nd 3D **24**
St Chads Rd. RM18: Grays, Tilb 2K **13**
St Clement's Cl. DA11: Nflt 3J **23**
St Clements Rd. DA9: Ghithe 4K **11**
St Clements Way DA2: Bean 2H **21**
DA2: Bean, Bluew 2H **21**
DA9: Bluew, Ghithe 5H **11**
St Columba's Cl. DA12: Grav'nd 3C **24**
(not continuous)
St David's Cres. DA12: Grav'nd 4C **24**
St Davids Rd. BR8: Swan 6E **18**
St Dunstan's Dr. DA12: Grav'nd 4D **24**
St Edmunds Cl. DA18: Erith 2B **4**
St Edmund's Rd. DA1: Dart 4B **10**
St Fidelis Rd. DA8: Erith 4H **5**
St Francis Av. DA12: Grav'nd 4D **24**
St Francis Rd. DA8: Erith 4H **5**
St George's Cres. DA12: Grav'nd 4C **24**
St Georges Rd. BR8: Swan 4E **26**
(not continuous)
DA14: Sidc 6G **17**
St George's Shop. Cen.
DA11: Grav'nd 6A **14**
St Georges Sq. DA3: Lfield 3B **30**
DA11: Grav'nd 6A **14**
St Gregory's Ct. DA12: Grav'nd 2D **24**
St Gregory's Cres. DA12: Grav'nd 2D **24**
St Helen's Rd. DA18: Erith 2B **4**
St Hilda's Way DA12: Grav'nd 4C **24**
St James Ct. DA9: Ghithe 6G **11**
St James La. DA9: Dart, Ghithe 1F **21**
St James Oak DA11: Grav'nd 7K **13**
St James Pl. DA1: Dart 6J **9**
St James's Av. DA11: Grav'nd 7K **13**
St James Sq. *DA3: Lfield 3B **30***
(off Park Dr.)
St James's Rd. DA11: Grav'nd 6K **13**
St James's St. DA11: Grav'nd 6K **13**
St James Way DA14: Sidc 5H **17**
St John Fisher Rd.
DA18: Erith 3B **4**
St John's Ct. DA8: Erith 4H **5**
St John's Jerusalem Garden 7C **20**
St John's La. DA3: Hart 6C **30**
St Johns Pde. *DA14: Sidc 4D **16***
(off Sidcup High St.)
St John's Rd. DA2: Dart 7D **10**
DA8: Erith 5H **5**
DA12: Grav'nd 7C **14**
DA14: Sidc 4E **16**
DA16: Well 3E **6**
St Katherine's Rd. DA18: Erith 2B **4**
St Leonard's Cl. DA16: Well 3D **6**
St Luke's Cl. BR8: Swan 2C **26**
DA2: Dart 5F **21**
ST MARGARETS 7F **21**
St Margaret's Av. DA15: Sidc 3A **16**
St Margaret's Cl. DA2: Dart 2E **20**
St Margaret's Cres. DA12: Grav'nd 3D **24**
St Margarets Rd. DA2: Dart, S Dar 6F **21**
DA4: S Dar 7F **21**
DA11: Nflt 1H **23**
St Mark's Av. DA11: Nflt 7H **13**
St Martin's Cl. DA18: Erith 2B **4**
St Martin's Rd. DA1: Dart 6A **10**
St Mary's Cl. DA12: Grav'nd 2B **24**

St Mary's Rd. BR8: Swan 4C **26**
DA5: Bexl 1B **18**
DA9: Ghithe 5F **11**
St Mary's Way DA3: Lfield 3B **30**
St Michael's Cl. DA18: Erith 2B **4**
St Michael's Ri. DA16: Well 1E **6**
St Michael's Rd. DA16: Well 3E **6**
St Patrick's Gdns. DA12: Grav'nd 3C **24**
St Paul's Cl. DA10: Swans 7B **12**
St Paul's Cray Rd. BR7: Chst 7A **16**
St Paul's Rd. DA8: Erith 7G **5**
St Paul's Wood Hill BR5: St P 7D **16**
St Peter's Cl. BR7: Chst 7A **16**
DA10: Swans 7C **12**
St Quentin Rd. DA16: Well 3C **6**
St Saviours Wlk. *DA1: Dart* *6K* ***9***
(off Bullace La.)
St Thomas' Almshouses DA11: Grav'nd 1K **23**
St Thomas Ct. DA5: Bexl 7K **7**
St Thomas Rd. DA11: Nflt 2H **23**
DA17: Belv 2G **5**
St Thomas's Av. DA11: Grav'nd 1A **24**
St Vincents Av. DA1: Dart 5B **10**
St Vincents Rd. DA1: Dart 6B **10**
St Vincents Vs. DA1: Dart 6A **10**
Salcote Rd. DA12: Grav'nd 5D **24**
Salem Pl. DA11: Nflt 7G **13**
Salisbury Av. BR8: Swan 4F **27**
Salisbury Rd. DA2: Dart 1D **20**
DA5: Bexl 1K **17**
DA11: Grav'nd 1J **23**
Salmon Rd. DA1: Dart 3A **10**
DA17: Belv 5E **4**
Saltash Rd. DA16: Well 1F **7**
Saltcote Cl. DA1: Cray 6D **8**
Saltford Cl. DA8: Erith 5J **5**
Saltings, The DA9: Ghithe 4K **11**
Sampson Cl. DA17: Belv 3B **4**
Sanctuary, The DA5: Bexl 6G **7**
Sanctuary Cl. DA1: Dart 6H **9**
Sandalwood Ho. DA15: Sidc 2C **16**
Sandbanks Hill DA2: Bean, Dart 6J **21**
Sandcliff Rd. DA8: Erith 4H **5**
Sanderling Ct. SE28 1A **4**
Sanderling Way DA9: Ghithe 5H **11**
Sandford Rd. DA7: Bex 4H **7**
Sandgate Rd. DA16: Well 7A **4**
Sandhurst Rd. DA5: Bexl 5G **7**
DA15: Sidc 3C **16**
RM18: Tilb 2B **14**
Sandown Rd. DA12: Grav'nd 6B **24**
Sandpiper Cl. DA9: Ghithe 6H **11**
Sandpiper Dr. DA8: Erith 2K **5**
Sandpipers, The DA12: Grav'nd 2C **24**
Sandpit Rd. DA1: Dart 4H **9**
Sandringham Ct. DA15: Sidc 6C **6**
Sandringham Dr. DA2: Bexl 2D **18**
DA16: Well 2B **6**
Sandy Bank Rd. DA12: Grav'nd 1A **24**
Sandy La. BR5: St P 7G **17**
DA2: Bean, Sflt 2K **21**
(not continuous)
DA14: Sidc 7G **17**
Sapho Pk. DA12: Grav'nd 4E **24**
Sara Cres. DA9: Ghithe 4J **11**
Sara Ho. DA8: Erith 7J **5**
Sara Pk. DA12: Grav'nd 4D **24**
Saunders Cl. DA11: Nflt 2H **23**
Saunders Way DA1: Dart 2A **20**
Savoy Rd. DA1: Dart 5J **9**
Saxon Cl. DA11: Nflt 3F **23**
Saxon Pl. DA4: Hort K 5D **28**
Saxon Rd. DA2: Dart 4K **19**
Saxon Wlk. DA14: Sidc 6F **17**
Sayer Cl. DA9: Ghithe 5H **11**
Scadbury Pk. Nature Reserve 7C **16**
School Cl. DA13: Meop 7K **31**
School Cres. DA1: Cray 4E **8**
School La. BR8: Swan 1G **27**
DA2: Bean 4K **21**
DA3: Fawk, S Dar 5F **29**
DA4: Hort K, Fawk, S Dar 4D **28**
DA16: Well 3E **6**
School Rd. DA12: Grav'nd 3B **24**
Schooner Ct. DA2: Dart 4D **10**
Scott Cres. DA8: Erith 1E **8**
Scott Ho. DA17: Belv 5D **4**
Scott Rd. DA12: Grav'nd 5C **24**
Scratchers La. DA3: Fawk 2A **32**
Scudders Hill DA3: Fawk 6J **29**
Seacourt Rd. SE2 2B **4**
Seaton Rd. DA1: Dart 7F **9**
DA16: Well 7A **4**
Sedcombe Cl. DA14: Sidc 4E **16**
Sedgemere Rd. SE2 3A **4**
Sedley DA13: Sflt 6D **22**
Selah Dr. BR8: Swan 1B **26**
Selborne Av. DA5: Bexl 1H **17**
Selborne Rd. DA14: Sidc 4E **16**
Selbourne Cl. DA3: Lfield 3G **31**
Selkirk Dr. DA8: Erith 1D **8**
Selsey Cres. DA16: Well 1G **7**
Selwyn Cres. DA16: Well 3E **6**
Selwyn Rd. RM18: Tilb 2J **13**
Sermon Dr. BR8: Swan 3B **26**
Seven Acres BR8: Crock 6C **26**
DA3: New A 3H **33**
Sevenoaks Cl. DA7: Bex 4A **8**
Sevenoaks Way BR5: St P 7F **17**
DA14: Sidc 7F **17**
Sewell Rd. SE2 2A **4**
Sexton Rd. RM18: Tilb 1J **13**
Seymour Rd. DA11: Nflt 1J **23**
RM18: Tilb 1J **13**
Seymour Wlk. DA10: Swans 7B **12**
Shaftesbury La. DA1: Dart 4C **10**
Shaftsbury Ct. *DA8: Erith* *1E* ***8***
(off Selkirk Dr.)
Shakespeare Av. RM18: Tilb 2A **14**
Shakespeare Rd. DA1: Dart 4B **10**
DA7: Bex 1H **7**
Shamrock Rd. DA12: Grav'nd 7D **14**
Sharland Rd. DA12: Grav'nd 2B **24**
Sharman Ct. *DA14: Sidc* *4D* ***16***
(off Carlton Rd.)
Sharnbrooke Cl. DA16: Well 3F **7**
Sharp Way DA1: Dart 3A **10**
Shaw Cl. SE28 1A **4**
Shaw Cres. RM18: Tilb 1A **14**
Shaw Ho. DA17: Belv 5D **4**
Shears Cl. DA1: Dart 2H **19**
Shears Grn. Ct. DA11: Nflt 2K **23**
Shearwater DA3: Lfield 3E **30**
Shearwood Cres.
DA1: Cray 3E **8**
Shelbury Cl. DA14: Sidc 3D **16**
Sheldon Rd. DA7: Bex 1J **7**
Shellbank La. DA2: Bean, Dart 6H **21**
Shelley Dr. DA16: Well 1B **6**
Shelley Pl. RM18: Tilb 1A **14**
Shenley Rd. DA1: Dart 6B **10**
Shenstone Cl. DA1: Cray 4C **8**
Shepherds Grn. BR7: Chst 7A **16**
Shepherd's La. DA1: Dart 1F **19**
Shepherds Leas SE9 4A **6**
Shepherd St. DA11: Nflt 7G **13**
Sheppey Cl. DA8: Erith 2K **5**
Sheppy Pl. DA12: Grav'nd 7A **14**
Sherbourne Cl. TN15: W King 6B **32**
Sherbrooke Cl. DA6: Bex 4K **7**
Sheridan Cl. BR8: Swan 4E **26**
Sheridan Ct. DA1: Dart 4B **10**
Sheridan Rd. DA7: Bex 3H **7**
DA17: Belv 4E **4**
Shermanbury Pl. DA8: Erith 7K **5**
Sherwood Cl. DA5: Bexl 6F **7**
Sherwood Pk. Av. DA15: Sidc 7D **6**
Sherwood Rd. DA16: Well 2B **6**
Shieldhall St. SE2 4A **4**
Shinglewell Rd. DA8: Erith 7E **4**
Ship La. BR8: Swan 1J **27**
DA4: Sutt H, Swan 1J **27**
Shire Ct. DA18: Erith 3B **4**
Shirehall Rd. DA2: Dart 5H **19**
Shirley Av. DA5: Bexl 7G **7**
Shirley Cl. DA1: Dart 4H **9**
DA12: Grav'nd 2G **25**
Shirley Rd. DA15: Sidc 3B **16**
Shooters Hill DA16: Well 2A **6**
Shore, The DA11: Nflt 5F **13**
Shoreham Cl. DA5: Bexl 1G **17**
SHORNE 5K **25**
Shorne Cl. DA15: Sidc 6E **6**
Shorne Ifield Rd. DA12: Shorne 6F **25**
Shornells Way SE2 4A **4**
SHORNE RIDGEWAY 6K **25**
Shorne Wood Country Pk. 7G **25**
Shorne Wood Country Pk. Vis. Cen. 7H **25**
Shortlands Cl. DA17: Belv 3D **4**
Showcase Cinema
Bluewater 1G **21**
Shrimp Brand Cotts. DA13: Grav'nd 5K **23**
Shrubbery Rd. DA4: S Dar 1E **28**
DA12: Grav'nd 1A **24**
Shurlock Av. BR8: Swan 2C **26**
Shuttle Cl. DA15: Sidc 7C **6**
Shuttlemead DA5: Bexl 7J **7**
Shuttle Rd. DA1: Cray 3F **9**
Sibley Cl. DA6: Bex 5H **7**
SIDCUP 4D **16**
Sidcup By-Pass BR5: Sidc, Swan, St P 6D **16**
BR7: Chst, Sidc 3A **16**
DA14: Sidc 6D **16**
Sidcup High St. DA14: Sidc 4D **16**
Sidcup Hill DA14: Sidc 4E **16**
Sidcup Hill Gdns. DA14: Sidc 5F **17**
Sidcup Place 5D **16**
Sidcup Pl. DA14: Sidc 5D **16**
Sidcup Rd. SE9 3A **16**
Sidcup Station (Rail) 2D **16**
Sidcup Technical Cen. DA14: Sidc 5G **17**
Sidewood Rd. SE9 1A **16**
Sidmouth Ct. *DA1: Dart* *1C* ***20***
(off Churchill Cl.)
Sidmouth Rd. DA16: Well 7A **4**
Silecroft Rd. DA7: Bex 1K **7**
Silver Birch Cl. DA2: Dart 4D **18**
Silverdale DA3: Hart 4C **30**
Silverdale Rd. DA7: Bex 2A **8**
Silver Rd. DA12: Grav'nd 2D **24**
Silver Spring Cl. DA8: Erith 6F **5**
Simmonds Dr. DA3: Hart 5D **30**
Sinclair Way DA2: Dart 4E **20**
SINGLEWELL 5C **24**
Singlewell Rd. DA11: Grav'nd 1A **24**
Sirdar Strand DA12: Grav'nd 5E **24**
Siri Guru Nanak Sports Cen. & Arts Studio
7B **14**
Skinney La. DA4: Hort K, S Dar 3E **28**
Skippers Cl. DA9: Ghithe 5J **11**
Slade Gdns. DA8: Erith 1E **8**
SLADE GREEN 1F **9**
Slade Grn. Rd. DA8: Erith 2K **5** & 2J **5**
Slade Green Station (Rail) 1F **9**
Slades Dr. BR7: Chst 4A **16**
Sloane Sq. DA3: Lfield 3B **30**
Slocum Cl. SE28 1A **4**
Small Grains DA3: Fawk 3E **32**
Smarden Cl. DA17: Belv 5E **4**
Smarts Rd. DA12: Grav'nd 3A **24**
Smugglers Wlk. DA9: Ghithe 5J **11**
Smythe Rd. DA4: Sutt H 1B **28**
Snelling Av. DA11: Nflt 2H **23**
Snipe Cl. DA8: Erith 2K **5**
Somerhill Av. DA15: Sidc 7E **6**
Somerhill Rd. DA16: Well 2E **6**
Somerset Av. DA16: Well 5C **6**
Somerset Rd. DA1: Dart 6G **9**
Somersham Rd. DA7: Bex 2H **7**
Somerville Rd. DA1: Dart 6A **10**
Sorrel Way DA11: Nflt 4H **23**
Sounds Lodge BR8: Crock 6B **26**
Sth. Ash Rd. TN15: Ash 7G **33**
Southbank BR8: Swan 7E **18**
South Cl. DA6: Bex 4G **7**
Southcroft Av. DA16: Well 3B **6**
SOUTH DARENTH 1D **28**
Southdowns DA4: S Dar 2E **28**
Southern Pl. BR8: Swan 4C **26**
Southey Wlk. RM18: Tilb 1A **14**
Southfields BR8: Swan 7D **18**
Southfields Rd. TN15: W King 7C **32**
SOUTHFLEET 5D **22**
Southfleet Av. DA3: Lfield 2E **30**
Southfleet Rd. DA2: Bean 4K **21**
DA10: Swans 7C **12**
DA11: Nflt 1J **23**
Sth. Gipsy Rd. DA16: Well 3G **7**
Sth. Glade, The DA5: Bexl 1J **17**
Sth. Hall Cl. DA4: Farn 7A **28**
Sth. Hill Rd. DA12: Grav'nd 1B **24**

Sth. Kent Av. DA11: Nflt .6F **13**
South Rd. DA8: Erith .7K **5**
Southspring DA15: Sidc .7A **6**
South St. DA12: Grav'nd .7A **14**
South Ter. DA4: Farn .7A **28**
South Vw. Av. RM18: Tilb .1K **13**
South Vw. Cl. DA5: Bexl .6J **7**
Southview Cl. BR8: Swan .4F **27**
South Vw. Rd. DA2: Dart .3J **19**
Southwold Rd. DA5: Bexl .6A **8**
Sovereign Ct. *DA4: Sutt H .1C 28*
(off Ship La.)
Sparepenny La.
DA4: Eyns, Farn .7K **27**
Sparrows La. SE9 .1A **16**
Speedgate Hill DA3: Fawk .2D **32**
Spencer St. DA11: Grav'nd .7K **13**
Spencer Wlk. RM18: Tilb .2K **13**
Spielman Rd. DA1: Dart .4A **10**
Spindles RM18: Tilb .1K **13**
Spinney, The BR8: Swan .2D **26**
DA14: Sidc .5H **17**
Spire Cl. DA12: Grav'nd .1A **24**
Spires, The DA1: Dart .2J **19**
Spital St. DA1: Dart .6J **9**
Splashworld .4G 7
Springcroft DA3: Hart .6D **30**
Spring Cross DA3: New A .3K **33**
Springfield Av. BR8: Swan .4E **26**
Springfield Rd. DA7: Bex .4A **8**
DA16: Well .3E **6**
Spring Gro. DA12: Grav'nd .1A **24**
Springhead Ent. Pk.
DA11: Nflt .1E **22**
Springhead Rd. DA8: Erith .6K **5**
DA11: Nflt .2F **23**
Spring Va. DA7: Bex .4A **8**
DA9: Ghithe .6K **11**
Spring Va. Cl. BR8: Swan .1E **26**
Springvale Ct. DA11: Nflt .2F **23**
Spring Va. Nth. DA1: Dart .7J **9**
Spring Va. Sth. DA1: Dart .7J **9**
Sprucedale Cl. BR8: Swan .2D **26**
Spurrell Av. DA5: Bexl .4C **18**
Square, The BR8: Swan .3C **26**
Squires Fld. BR8: Swan .1F **27**
Squires Way DA2: Dart .4C **18**
Stacey Cl. DA12: Grav'nd .5D **24**
Stacklands Cl. TN15: W King .6B **32**
Stack La. DA3: Hart .5B **30**
Stack Rd. DA4: Hort K .4E **28**
Stadium Way DA1: Cray .5D **8**
Stafford Cl. DA9: Ghithe .5G **11**
Stafford Rd. DA14: Sidc .4B **16**
Staines Wlk. DA14: Sidc .6F **17**
Stanbrook Rd.
DA11: Grav'nd .1J **23**
Standard Rd. DA6: Bex .4H **7**
DA17: Belv .5E **4**
Stanham Pl. DA1: Cray .4F **9**
Stanham Rd. DA1: Dart .5H **9**
Stanhill Cotts. DA2: Dart .7C **18**
Stanhope Rd. DA7: Bex .2H **7**
DA10: Swans .6C **12**
DA15: Sidc .4D **16**
Stanley Cl. DA9: Ghithe .5F **11**
Stanley Cotts. DA2: Dart .5F **21**
Stanley Cres. DA12: Grav'nd .5C **24**
Stanley Rd. DA10: Swans .6C **12**
DA11: Nflt .2H **23**
DA14: Sidc .3D **16**
Stanley Ter. DA6: Bex .4K **7**
Stanmore Rd. DA17: Belv .4G **5**
Stansted Cres. DA5: Bexl .1G **17**
Staple Cl. DA5: Bexl .3C **18**
Staples, The BR8: Swan .1G **27**
Stapleton Rd. DA7: Bex .7D **4**
Stapley Rd. DA17: Belv .5E **4**
Starboard Av. DA9: Ghithe .6J **11**
Star Hill DA1: Cray .5D **8**
Starling Cl. DA3: Lfield .3E **30**
Station App. BR8: Swan .4D **26**
DA1: Cray .6E **8**
DA1: Dart .6K **9**
DA5: Bexl .1K **17**
DA7: Bex .2B **8**
(Barnehurst Rd.)
Station App. DA7: Bex .2H **7**
(Pickford La.)
DA13: Meop .5K **31**
DA16: Well .2D **6**
(not continuous)
Station App. Nth. DA15: Sidc .2D **16**
Station Pde. *DA7: Bex .2H 7*
(off Pickford La.)
DA8: Erith .5J **5**
DA15: Sidc .2D **16**
Station Rd. BR8: Swan .4D **26**
DA1: Cray .7E **8**
DA3: Lfield .3B **30**
DA4: S Dar .2C **28**
DA7: Bex .3H **7**
DA9: Ghithe .5H **11**
(not continuous)
DA11: Nflt .6E **12**
DA13: Meop .5K **31**
DA13: Sflt .4C **22**
DA15: Sidc .2D **16**
DA17: Belv .3E **4**
Station Rd. Nth. DA17: Belv .3F **5**
Stedman Cl. DA5: Bexl .3D **18**
Steele Av. DA9: Ghithe .5G **11**
Steele Wlk. DA8: Erith .7F **5**
Stelling Rd. DA8: Erith .7H **5**
Stephen Rd. DA7: Bex .3B **8**
Stephenson Av. RM18: Tilb .1K **13**
Sterndale Rd. DA1: Dart .7A **10**
Stevannie Ct. DA17: Belv .5D **4**
Stevedale Rd. DA16: Well .2F **7**
Stevens Cl. DA2: Dart .5F **21**
DA5: Bexl .4C **18**
Stevenson Cl. DA8: Erith .2K **5**
Steynton Av. DA5: Bexl .2G **17**
Stickland Rd. DA17: Belv .4E **4**
Stiles Cl. DA8: Erith .5F **5**
Stirling Cl. DA14: Sidc .4B **16**
Stock La. DA2: Dart .3H **19**
Stokesay Ct. *DA2: Dart .6C 10*
(off Osbourne Rd.)
STONE .5F **11**
Stonebridge Road .5D 12
Stonebridge Rd. DA11: Nflt .5D **12**
Stone Ct. DA8: Erith .5K **5**
Stonecroft Rd. DA8: Erith .7G **5**
Stone Crossing Station (Rail) .5F 11
Stonefield Cl. DA7: Bex .3K **7**
STONEHILL GREEN .7B **18**
Stonehill Woods Pk.
DA14: Sidc .6A **18**
STONE HOUSE HOSPITAL .6D 10
Stone Pl. Rd. DA9: Ghithe .5F **11**
Stones Cross Rd. BR8: Crock .5B **26**
Stone St. DA11: Grav'nd .6A **14**
STONEWOOD .3A **22**
Stonewood DA2: Bean .3K **21**
Stonewood Rd. DA8: Erith .5J **5**
Stony Cnr. DA13: Meop .4H **31**
Stornaway Strand
DA12: Grav'nd .3E **24**
Stour Rd. DA1: Cray .3F **9**
Stow Ct. DA2: Dart .7D **10**
Strand Cl. DA13: Meop .7K **31**
Stratton Cl. DA7: Bex .3H **7**
Stratton Rd. DA7: Bex .3H **7**
Strawberry Flds. BR8: Swan .1D **26**
Stream Way DA17: Belv .6D **4**
Street, The DA4: Hort K .4C **28**
DA12: Shorne .5K **25**
TN15: Ash .5G **33**
Strickland Av. DA1: Dart .3A **10**
(not continuous)
Struttons Av. DA11: Nflt .2J **23**
Stuart Cl. BR8: Swan .7E **18**
Stuart Evans Cl. DA16: Well .3F **7**
Stuart Mantle Way
DA8: Erith .7H **5**
Stuart Rd. DA11: Grav'nd .6K **13**
DA16: Well .1E **6**
Studios, The *DA3: New A .2J 33*
(off Row, The)
Studland Cl. DA15: Sidc .3C **16**
Studley Ct. DA14: Sidc .5E **16**
Studley Cres. DA3: Lfield .2F **31**
Sturges Fld. BR7: Chst .6A **16**
Suffolk Rd. DA1: Dart .6K **9**
(not continuous)
DA12: Grav'nd .6C **14**
DA14: Sidc .6F **17**
Sullivan Cl. DA1: Dart .6G **9**
Sullivan Rd. RM18: Tilb .1K **13**
Summerhill Rd. DA1: Dart .7J **9**
Summerhouse Dr. DA2: Dart .4C **18**
DA5: Bexl, Dart .4C **18**
Sun Ct. DA8: Erith .2E **8**
Sundridge Av. DA16: Well .2A **6**
Sundridge Cl. DA1: Dart .6B **10**
Sun Hill DA3: Fawk .3D **32**
Sunland Av. DA6: Bex .4H **7**
Sun La. DA12: Grav'nd .2B **24**
Sunninghill DA11: Nflt .2H **23**
Sun Rd. DA10: Swans .6C **12**
Sunset Cl. DA8: Erith .2K **5**
Surrey Cl. TN15: W King .7B **32**
Sussex Cl. TN15: W King .7B **32**
Sussex Rd. DA1: Dart .7B **10**
DA8: Erith .7F **5**
DA14: Sidc .5E **16**
Sutcliffe Rd. DA16: Well .2F **7**
Sutherland Av. DA16: Well .4B **6**
Sutherland Cl. DA9: Ghithe .5G **11**
DA12: Grav'nd .2G **25**
Sutherland Rd. DA17: Belv .3E **4**
SUTTON AT HONE .7C **20**
Swaisland Dr. DA1: Cray .5E **8**
Swaisland Rd. DA1: Dart .5G **9**
Swalecliffe Rd. DA17: Belv .5F **5**
Swaledale Rd. DA2: Dart .1D **20**
Swale Rd. DA1: Cray .4F **9**
Swallow Cl. DA8: Erith .1D **8**
DA9: Ghithe .5G **11**
Swallowfields DA11: Nflt .3H **23**
Swanbridge Rd. DA7: Bex .1K **7**
Swan Bus. Pk. DA1: Dart .4J **9**
Swan La. DA1: Dart .7E **8**
SWANLEY .3D **26**
Swanley By-Pass BR8: Swan .1A **26**
DA14: Swan .1A **26**
Swanley Cen. BR8: Swan .3D **26**
SWANLEY INTERCHANGE .5G **27**
Swanley La. BR8: Swan .3E **26**
Swanley Rd. DA16: Well .1F **7**
Swanley Station (Rail) .4C 26
SWANLEY VILLAGE .1G **27**
Swanley Village Rd. BR8: Swan .1G **27**
SWANSCOMBE .5C **12**
Swanscombe Bus. Cen.
DA10: Swans .5B **12**
Swanscombe Leisure Cen. .6A 12
Swanscombe Skull Site Nature Reserve
.6A 12
Swanscombe Station (Rail) .5C 12
Swanscombe St. DA10: Swans .7B **12**
Swanton Rd. DA8: Erith .7E **4**
Swaylands Rd. DA17: Belv .6E **4**
Sweyne Rd. DA10: Swans .6B **12**
Swiller's La. DA12: Shorne .5K **25**
Swinburne Gdns. RM18: Tilb .2A **14**
Swingate La. SE18 .1B **6**
Sycamore Av. DA15: Sidc .6C **6**
Sycamore Cl. DA12: Grav'nd .7C **14**
RM18: Tilb .2K **13**
Sycamore Ct. *DA8: Erith .5H 5*
(off Sandcliff Rd.)
DA9: Ghithe .7F **11**
Sycamore Dr. BR8: Swan .3D **26**
Sycamore M. *DA8: Erith .5H 5*
(off St John's Rd.)
Sycamore Rd. DA1: Dart .1J **19**
Sydney Rd. DA6: Bex .4G **7**
DA14: Sidc .4B **16**
RM18: Tilb .2K **13**
SE2 .3A **4**
Sylvan M. *DA9: Ghithe .4J 11*
(off Watermans Way)
Symonds Cl. TN15: W King .5B **32**

T

Tallents Cl. DA4: Sutt H .7C **20**
Tamesis Strand DA12: Grav'nd .5D **24**

Tanhurst Wlk. SE2 . . . . .3B 4
(off Alsike Rd.)
Tanyard Cotts. DA12: Shorne 6K 25
Tanyard Hill DA12: Shorne 6K 25
Tanyard La. DA5: Bexl 7K 7
Tarling Cl. DA14: Sidc 3E 16
Tates Orchard DA3: Hart 6C 30
Taunton Cl. DA7: Bex 2C 8
Taunton Rd. DA11: Nflt 5D 12
Taunton Va. DA12: Grav'nd 3C 24
Tavistock Rd. DA16: Well 1F 7
Tavy Bri. SE2 . . . . .2A 4
Taylor Row DA2: Dart 3G 19
Taylors Cl. DA14: Sidc 3C 16
Teardrop Cen. BR8: Swan 5G 27
Teesdale Rd. DA2: Dart 1D 20
Teeswater Ct. DA14: Sidc 3B 4
Teignmouth Rd. DA16: Well 2F 7
Telford Rd. SE9 .2A 16
Templar Dr. DA11: Grav'nd 5K 23
Templars Ct. DA1: Dart 5B 10
TEMPLE HILL 5A 10
Temple Hill DA1: Dart 6A 10
Temple Hill Sq. DA1: Dart 5A 10
Tenby Rd. DA16: Well 1G 7
Tennants Row RM18: Tilb 2H 13
Tennyson Cl. DA16: Well 1B 6
Tennyson Ho. DA17: Belv 5D 4
Tennyson Rd. DA1: Dart 5B 10
Tennyson Wlk. DA11: Nflt 3G 23
   RM18: Tilb 2A 14
Tensing Av. DA11: Nflt 3H 23
Terence Cl. DA12: Grav'nd 1E 24
Terence Ct. DA17: Belv 6D 4
(off Stream Way)
Terrace, The DA11: Grav'nd 6A 14
(not continuous)
   DA12: Grav'nd 6A 14
(not continuous)
Terraces, The DA2: Dart 7D 10
Terrace St. DA12: Grav'nd 6A 14
Teviot Cl. DA16: Well 1E 6
Teynham Rd. DA2: Dart 1D 20
Thackeray Av. RM18: Tilb 1A 14
Thames Ga. DA1: Dart 5B 10
Thamesgate Shop. Cen.
   DA11: Grav'nd 6A 14
Thames Ho. DA1: Cray 3F 9
Thameside Aviation Mus. 1J 15
THAMESMEAD EAST 2E 4
THAMESMEAD SOUTH 2B 4
Thames Rd. DA1: Cray 2E 8
Thames Way DA11: Nflt, Grav'nd 5D 12
Thanet Ho. DA11: Nflt 1J 23
Thanet Rd. DA5: Bexl 7K 7
   DA8: Erith 7J 5
Thanington Ct. SE9 . . . . .6B 6
Thatcher Ct. DA1: Dart 7J 9
Thelma Cl. DA12: Grav'nd 5E 24
Third Av. DA11: Nflt 1H 23
Thirlmere Rd. DA7: Bex 1B 8
Thirza Rd. DA1: Dart 6A 10
Thistlebrook SE2 . . . . .3A 4
Thistlebrook Ind. Est. SE2 . . . . .3A 4
Thistle Ct. DA1: Dart 1C 20
(off Churchill Cl.)
Thistledown DA12: Grav'nd 6C 24
Thistlefield Cl. DA5: Bexl 1G 17
Thistle Rd. DA12: Grav'nd 7D 14
Thomas Dr. DA12: Grav'nd 2C 24
THONG 6F 25
Thong La. DA12: Grav'nd, Shorne 4E 24
Thorne Cl. DA8: Erith 6F 5
Thornton Rd. DA17: Belv 4F 5
Three Corners DA7: Bex 2A 8
Three Gates Rd. DA3: Fawk 3C 32
Thrift, The DA2: Bean 3K 21
Throwley Cl. SE2 . . . . .3A 4
(not continuous)
Thurrock Yacht Club 1E 12
Thursland Rd. DA14: Sidc 5H 17
Thwaite Cl. DA8: Erith 6G 5
Ticehurst Cl. BR5: St P 7D 16
Tickford Cl. SE2 .2A 4
Tidford Rd. DA16: Well 2C 6
TILBURY 2J 13
Tilbury Bowls & Squash Cen. 2K 13

Tilbury Fort 4B 14
Tilbury Go-Karting Track 1J 13
Tilbury Leisure Cen. 2A 14
Tilbury Town Station (Rail) 2J 13
Tilehurst Point SE2 . . . . .2B 4
(Blewbury Ho.)
   SE2 . . . . .2A 4
(Tavy Bri.)
Tile Kiln La. DA5: Bexl 2B 18
Till Av. DA4: Farn 7A 28
Tillet Pl. RM18: Tilb 1A 14
Tilmans Mead DA4: Farn 7A 28
Timothy Cl. DA6: Bex 5H 7
Timothy Ho. DA18: Erith 2C 4
(off Kale Rd.)
Titmuss Av. SE28 . . . . .1A 4
Tivoli Gdns. DA12: Grav'nd 1A 24
Tolcairn Ct. DA17: Belv 5E 4
Tollgate Rd. DA2: Dart 7E 10
Tooley St. DA11: Nflt 7G 13
Top Dartford Rd. BR8: Swan 7E 18
   DA2: Dart 7E 18
Torbrook Cl. DA5: Bexl 6H 7
Toronto Rd. RM18: Tilb 2K 13
Torrens Wlk. DA12: Grav'nd 5D 24
Tor Rd. DA16: Well 1F 7
Totnes Rd. DA16: Well 7A 4
Tourist Info. Cen.
   Bexley 6B 8
   Bexleyheath .4K 7
   Gravesend 6A 14
   Gravesend 7A 14
   Swanley 3D 26
Tower Cl. DA12: Grav'nd 5D 24
Tower Pk. Rd. DA1: Cray 5E 8
Tower Retail Pk. DA1: Cray 5E 8
Tower Rd. DA1: Dart 7H 9
   DA7: Bex 4K 7
   DA17: Belv 4G 5
Towers Wood DA4: S Dar 1E 28
Townfield Cnr. DA12: Grav'nd 1B 24
Townley Rd. DA6: Bex 5J 7
Townshend Ct. DA14: Sidc 6E 16
Town Sq. DA8: Erith 6J 5
Tradescant Dr. DA13: Meop 6K 31
Trafalgar Ct. DA8: Erith 7K 5
(off Frobisher Rd.)
Trafalgar Rd. DA1: Dart 2K 19
   DA11: Grav'nd 7K 13
Tranquil Ri. DA8: Erith 5J 5
Trebble Rd. DA10: Swans 6B 12
Tredegar Rd. DA2: Dart 2F 19
Treetops DA12: Grav'nd 5A 24
Treetops Cl. SE2 . . . . .5C 4
Trefoil Ho. DA18: Erith 2C 4
(off Kale Rd.)
Trevelyan Cl. DA1: Dart 4A 10
Trevithick Dr. DA1: Dart 4A 10
Trewsbury Ho. SE2 . . . . .1B 4
Triangle, The DA15: Sidc 7D 6
(off Burnt Oak La.)
Trinity Ct. DA1: Dart 1C 20
(off Churchill Cl.)
Trinity Gdns. DA1: Dart 6J 9
Trinity Pl. DA6: Bex 4J 7
Trinity Rd. DA12: Grav'nd 7B 14
Trivett Cl. DA9: Ghithe 5H 11
Trosley Av. DA11: Grav'nd 2A 24
Trosley Rd. DA17: Belv 6E 4
Trunks All. BR8: Swan 2A 26
Truro Rd. DA12: Grav'nd 3C 24
Tudor Cl. DA1: Dart 6G 9
   DA11: Nflt 1H 23
Tudor Ct. DA8: Erith 7B 26
   DA14: Sidc 3D 16
Tudor Wlk. DA5: Bexl 6H 7
Tufnail Rd. DA1: Dart 5H 9
Tunstock Way DA17: Belv 3C 4
Turnball Cl. DA9: Ghithe 7F 11
Turner Ct. DA1: Dart 5H 9
Turner Rd. DA2: Bean 3J 21
Turners Cl. TN15: W King 6B 32
Turners Oak DA3: New A 3H 33
Turners Pl. DA4: S Dar 2D 28
Turnpike Cl. DA6: Bex 4G 7
Turnstone DA3: Lfield 3D 30
Turnstones, The DA12: Grav'nd 2C 24

Turpin La. DA8: Erith 1J 5
Twigg Cl. DA8: Erith 7J 5
Twistleton Ct. DA1: Dart 6J 9
Tyeshurst Cl. SE2 . . . . .5C 4
Tyler Cl. DA8: Erith 7F 5
Tyler Gro. DA1: Dart 4A 10
(not continuous)
Tylers Grn. Rd. BR8: Crock 6B 26
Tyndall Rd. DA16: Well 3C 6
Tynedale Cl. DA2: Dart 1E 20
Tyron Way DA14: Sidc 4B 16
Tyrrell Av. DA16: Well 5D 6

U

Unicorn Wlk. DA9: Ghithe 5G 11
University Gdns. DA5: Bexl 7J 7
University of Greenwich
   Avery Hill Campus 6A 6
University Pl. DA8: Erith 7G 5
University Way DA1: Dart 4C 10
Updale Rd. DA14: Sidc 4C 16
Upland Rd. DA7: Bex 3J 7
Up. Abbey Rd. DA17: Belv 4D 4
Upper Av. DA13: 1st R 1H 31
Up. Church Hill DA9: Ghithe 5F 11
Upper Gro. Rd. DA17: Belv 6D 4
Up. Guild Hall DA9: Bluew 7G 11
Up. Holly Hill Rd. DA17: Belv 5F 5
Upper Pk. Rd. DA17: Belv 4F 5
Up. Rose Gallery DA9: Bluew 7H 11
UPPER RUXLEY 7K 17
Up. Sheridan Rd. DA17: Belv 4E 4
Upper St. Nth. DA3: New A 2J 33
(off Row, The)
Upper St. Sth. DA3: New A 2J 33
(off Row, The)
Up. Thames Wlk. DA9: Bluew 1G 21
Upperton Rd. DA14: Sidc 5C 16
Up. Wickham La. DA16: Well 1E 6
UPTON 5G 7
UPTON CENTRE 4H 7
Upton Cl. DA5: Bexl 6J 7
Upton Rd. DA5: Bexl 4H 7
   DA6: Bex 4H 7
Upton Rd. Sth. DA5: Bexl 6J 7
Upton Vs. DA6: Bex 4H 7
Ursula Lodges DA14: Sidc 5E 16

V

Valence Rd. DA8: Erith 7H 5
Valentine Av. DA5: Bexl 2H 17
Vale Rd. DA1: Dart 1G 19
   DA11: Nflt 7G 13
Valley Cl. DA1: Cray 6E 8
Valley Dr. DA12: Grav'nd 4C 24
Valley Gdns. DA9: Ghithe 6J 11
Valley Hgts. DA1: Dart 4A 10
Valley Rd. DA5: St P 7E 16
   DA1: Cray 6E 8
   DA3: Fawk 1E 32
   DA8: Erith 4G 5
   DA17: Belv 4F 5
Valley Vw. DA9: Ghithe 6J 11
Valley Vw. Ter. DA4: Farn 7A 28
Valliers Wood Rd. DA15: Sidc 1B 16
Vanessa Cl. DA17: Belv 5E 4
Vanessa Wlk. DA12: Grav'nd 5E 24
Vanessa Way DA5: Bexl 3C 18
Vanquisher Wlk. DA12: Grav'nd 3E 24
Vaughan Rd. DA16: Well 2C 6
Vauxhall Cl. DA11: Nflt 7J 13
Vauxhall Pl. DA1: Dart 7K 9
Venners Cl. DA7: Bex 2D 8
Venture Cl. DA5: Bexl 7H 7
Veritas Ho. DA15: Sidc 2D 16
(off Station Rd.)
Vernon Cl. TN15: W King 7C 32
Vernon Rd. DA10: Swans 6C 12
Veroan Rd. DA7: Bex 2H 7
Verona Ho. DA8: Erith 7K 5
Vestry Cotts. DA3: Lfield 4F 31
Viaduct Ter. DA4: S Dar 2D 28

Via Romana DA12: Grav'nd 1G **25**
Vicarage Cl. DA8: Erith 6G **5**
Vicarage Ct. DA12: Grav'nd 1F **25**
Vicarage Dr. DA11: Nflt 6F **13**
Vicarage La. DA12: Grav'nd 2F **25**
Vicarage Rd. DA5: Bexl 1A **18**
Vickers Rd. DA8: Erith 5H **5**
Victoria Av. DA11: Grav'nd 7A **14**
Victoria Dr. DA4: S Dar 2E **28**
Victoria Hill Rd. BR8: Swan 1E **26**
Victoria Pk. Ind. Est. DA1: Dart 5K **9**
Victoria Rd. DA1: Dart 5J **9**
DA6: Bex 4K **7**
DA8: Erith 6J **5**
(not continuous)
DA11: Nflt 1J **23**
DA15: Sidc 3C **16**
Victoria Scott Ct. DA1: Cray 3D **8**
Victoria St. DA17: Belv 5D **4**
Victory Ct. *DA8: Erith 7K 5*
(off Frobisher Rd.)
Victory Way DA2: Dart 4D **10**
View, The SE2 5C **4**
Viewfield Rd. DA5: Bexl 1F **17**
Vigilant Way DA12: Grav'nd 5E **24**
Viking Rd. DA11: Nflt 3F **23**
Viking Way DA8: Erith 3G **5**
TN15: W King 5B **32**
Villa Cl. DA12: Grav'nd 2G **25**
Villa Ct. DA1: Dart 2K **19**
Village, The DA9: Bluew 7G **11**
Village Cres., The DA9: Bluew 7G **11**
Village Grn. Rd. DA1: Cray 4F **9**
Vincent Cl. DA15: Sidc 1B **16**
Virginia Wlk. DA12: Grav'nd 6C **24**
Vista, The DA14: Sidc 5C **16**
Voce Rd. SE18 1A **6**
Vyne, The DA7: Bex 3A **8**

W

Wadard Ter. BR8: Swan 5H **27**
Wadeville Cl. DA17: Belv 5E **4**
Waid Cl. DA1: Dart 6A **10**
Wakefield Rd. DA9: Ghithe 5K **11**
Wakefield St. DA11: Grav'nd 6A **14**
Waldeck Rd. DA1: Dart 7A **10**
Walden Cl. DA17: Belv 5D **4**
Waldrist Way DA18: Erith 2D **4**
Walker Cl. DA1: Cray 3E **8**
Walkley Rd. DA1: Dart 5G **9**
Wallace Cl. SE28 1B **4**
Wallace Gdns. DA10: Swans 6B **12**
Wallhouse Rd. DA8: Erith 2K **5**
Wallis Cl. DA2: Dart 3E **18**
Wallis Pk. DA11: Nflt 5E **12**
Walnut Hill Rd. DA13: Meop, Ist R 3H **31**
Walnut Tree Av. DA1: Dart 2K **19**
Walnut Tree Cl. BR7: Chst 7A **16**
Walnut Tree Rd. DA8: Erith 5J **5**
Walnut Tree Way DA13: Meop 6K **31**
Walnut Way BR8: Swan 2C **26**
Walsingham Wlk. DA17: Belv 6E **4**
Waltham Cl. DA1: Dart 6F **9**
Walton Rd. DA14: Sidc 2F **17**
Wansbury Way BR8: Swan 5F **27**
Wansunt Rd. DA5: Bexl 1B **18**
Ward Cl. DA8: Erith 6H **5**
Wardona Ho. DA10: Swans 6C **12**
Wardour Ct. *DA2: Dart 6C 10*
(off Bow Arrow La.)
Waring Rd. DA14: Sidc 6F **17**
Warland Rd. SE18 1A **6**
TN15: W King 7C **32**
Warne Pl. DA15: Sidc 6E **6**
Warren, The DA12: Grav'nd 4C **24**
Warren Cl. DA6: Bex 5K **7**
Warren Hastings Ct. *DA11: Nflt 6J 13*
(off Pier Rd.)
Warren Rd. DA1: Dart 3K **19**
DA6: Bex 5K **7**
DA13: Sflt 5E **22**
DA14: Sidc 3F **17**
Warrens, The DA3: Hart 6C **30**
Warren Vw. DA12: Shorne 5K **25**
Warrior Av. DA12: Grav'nd 4B **24**
Warwick Cl. DA5: Bexl 7J **7**
Warwick Ct. DA8: Erith 7K **5**
Warwick Ho. BR8: Swan 4D **26**
Warwick Pl. DA11: Nflt 5E **12**
Warwick Rd. DA14: Sidc 5E **16**
DA16: Well 3F **7**
Warwick Way DA1: Dart 2K **19**
Watchgate DA2: Dart 5E **20**
(not continuous)
Water Cir. DA9: Bluew 1G **21**
Waterdales DA11: Nflt 2F **23**
Waterfield Cl. DA17: Belv 3E **4**
Waterhead Cl. DA8: Erith 7J **5**
Water La. DA14: Sidc 2J **17**
Waterloo St. DA12: Grav'nd 7B **14**
Watermans Way DA9: Ghithe 4J **11**
Watermeadow Cl. DA8: Erith 1G **9**
Water Mill Way DA4: S Dar 2C **28**
Waters Edge Ct. DA8: Erith 5K **5**
Waterside DA1: Cray 5D **8**
DA11: Nflt 6H **13**
Waterton BR8: Swan 4C **26**
Waterton Av. DA12: Grav'nd 7D **14**
Watery La. DA14: Sidc 6E **16**
Watling St. DA1: Dart 7B **10**
(Brent, The)
DA1: Dart 6G **9**
(Dartford Rd.)
DA1: Dart 7A **10**
(East Hill)
DA2: Bean, Dart, Ghithe, Bluew 1E **20**
DA6: Bex 4A **8**
DA11: Grav'nd, Nflt G, Nflt 3F **23**
DA11: Sflt, Cobh 2D **22**
DA12: Grav'nd 7F **25**
Watson Cl. RM20: W Thur 1H **11**
Watts Bri. Rd. DA8: Erith 6K **5**
Wavell Dr. DA15: Sidc 6B **6**
Wayfield Link SE9 6A **6**
Waylands BR8: Swan 4E **26**
Wayville Rd. DA1: Dart 7C **10**
Way Volante DA12: Grav'nd 4D **24**
Weald Cl. DA13: Ist R 7H **23**
Weardale Av. DA2: Dart 2D **20**
Weavers Cl. DA11: Grav'nd 1K **23**
Weavers Orchard DA13: Sflt 6D **22**
Webber Cl. DA8: Erith 2K **5**
Wedgewood Ct. DA5: Bexl 7J **7**
Weird Wood DA3: Lfield 3F **31**
Weir Rd. DA5: Bexl 7A **8**
Welbeck Av. DA15: Sidc 1D **16**
Weldon Way DA9: Ghithe 5J **11**
Wellan Cl. DA15: Sidc 5E **6**
Wellcome Av. DA1: Dart 4K **9**
Well Fld. DA3: Hart 4C **30**
WELLING 3E **6**
Welling High St. DA16: Well 3E **6**
Welling Station (Rail) 2D **6**
Wellington Av. DA15: Sidc 6D **6**
Wellington Pde. DA15: Sidc 5D **6**
Wellington Rd. DA1: Dart 6H **9**
DA5: Bexl 5G **7**
DA17: Belv 5D **4**
RM18: Tilb 2K **13**
Wellington St. DA12: Grav'nd 7B **14**
Welling United FC 3F **7**
Welling Way DA16: Well 3A **6**
SE9 3A **6**
Welton Rd. SE18 1B **6**
Wendover Way DA16: Well 5D **6**
Wentworth Cl. DA11: Grav'nd 5K **23**
Wentworth Dr. DA1: Dart 6F **9**
Wenvoe Av. DA7: Bex 2A **8**
Wessex Dr. DA8: Erith 2D **8**
Wessex Wlk. DA2: Bexl 2D **18**
Westbourne Rd. DA7: Bex 7B **4**
Westbrooke Cres. DA16: Well 3F **7**
Westbrooke Rd. DA15: Sidc 2A **16**
DA16: Well 3E **6**
Westcott Av. DA11: Nflt 3J **23**
WESTCOURT 2C **24**
Westcourt La. DA12: Grav'nd 1E **24**
Westcourt Pde. DA12: Grav'nd 3D **24**
West Cres. Rd. DA12: Grav'nd 6A **14**
Wested La. BR8: Crock 7F **27**
(not continuous)
Westergate Rd. SE2 6C **4**
Westerham Dr. DA15: Sidc 6E **6**
Western Cross Cl. DA9: Ghithe 6K **11**
Westfield DA3: New A 4J **33**
Westfield Cl. DA12: Grav'nd 6B **24**
Westfield Rd. DA7: Bex 3B **8**
Westgate Rd. DA1: Dart 6J **9**
Westharold BR8: Swan 3C **26**
WEST HEATH 6B **4**
W. Heath Cl. DA1: Cray 6E **8**
W. Heath Rd. DA1: Cray 6E **8**
SE2 6A **4**
West Hill DA1: Dart 6J **9**
Westhill Cl. DA12: Grav'nd 1A **24**
W. Hill Dr. DA1: Dart 6H **9**
W. Hill Ri. DA1: Dart 6J **9**
West Holme DA8: Erith 1B **8**
W. Kent Av. DA11: Nflt 6F **13**
WEST KINGSDOWN 6B **32**
W. Kingsdown Ind. Est. TN15: W King 7B **32**
West Mill DA11: Grav'nd 6J **13**
Westmoreland Av. DA16: Well 3B **6**
West Shaw DA3: Lfield 2A **30**
West St. DA7: Bex 3J **7**
DA8: Erith 4H **5**
DA11: Grav'nd 6K **13**
West Ter. DA15: Sidc 1B **16**
West Vw. Rd. BR8: Crock 6C **26**
BR8: Swan 4F **27**
DA1: Dart 6A **10**
WESTWOOD 7A **22**
Westwood La. DA15: Sidc 5D **6**
DA16: Well 3C **6**
Westwood Rd. DA13: Sflt 7B **22**
West Woodside DA5: Bexl 7H **7**
WEST YOKE 3H **33**
West Yoke TN15: Ash 2G **33**
W. Yoke Rd. DA3: New A 3H **33**
Wharf, The DA9: Ghithe 4H **11**
Wharfedale Rd. DA2: Dart 1D **20**
Wharf Rd. DA12: Grav'nd 6D **14**
Wharfside Cl. DA8: Erith 5K **5**
Wharnecliffe DA9: Ghithe 6J **11**
Wheatley Cl. DA9: Ghithe 5H **11**
Wheatley Ter. Rd. DA8: Erith 6K **5**
Wheatstone Rd. DA8: Erith 5H **5**
Wheelock Cl. DA8: Erith 7F **5**
Whenman Av. DA5: Bexl 2B **18**
Whernside Cl. SE28 1A **4**
Whinfell Way DA12: Grav'nd 4E **24**
Whitby Cl. DA9: Ghithe 5H **11**
White Av. DA11: Nflt 3J **23**
White Cft. BR8: Swan 2D **26**
Whitegates Av. TN15: W King 6B **32**
Whitehall La. DA8: Erith 2E **8**
Whitehall Pde. DA12: Grav'nd 3B **24**
Whitehead Cl. DA2: Dart 3H **19**
Whitehill La. DA12: Grav'nd 3B **24**
Whitehill Rd. DA1: Cray 5F **9**
DA3: Dart, Lfield 2A **30**
DA12: Grav'nd 2B **24**
DA13: Sflt 2A **30**
White Oak Ct. BR8: Swan 3D **26**
White Oak Gdns. DA15: Sidc 7C **6**
White Oak Leisure Cen. 2C **26**
White Oak Sq. *BR8: Swan 3D 26*
(off London Rd.)
White Post Hill DA4: Farn 7B **28**
White Post La. DA13: Sole S 4K **31**
Whites Cl. DA9: Ghithe 6K **11**
Whitewebbs Way BR5: St P 7C **16**
Whitfield Cres. DA2: Dart 7D **10**
Whitfield Rd. DA7: Bex 7D **4**
Whitney Wlk. DA14: Sidc 6H **17**
Wickham St. DA16: Well 2B **6**
Wickhams Way DA3: Hart 5C **30**
Wicksteed Cl. DA5: Bexl 3C **18**
Widgeon Rd. DA8: Erith 2K **5**
Wilberforce Way DA12: Grav'nd 5C **24**
Wilde Cl. RM18: Tilb 2B **14**
Wilde Rd. DA8: Erith 7F **5**
Wilfred St. DA12: Grav'nd 6A **14**
Wilkinson Cl. DA1: Dart 4A **10**
(not continuous)
Wilks Av. DA1: Dart 2A **20**
Willersley Av. DA15: Sidc 1C **16**
Willersley Cl. DA15: Sidc 1C **16**
William Cory Prom. DA8: Erith 5J **5**

William Ho. DA12: Grav'nd 7A **14**
William Smith Ho. *DA17: Belv* *3E 4*
(*off Ambrooke Rd.*)
William St. DA12: Grav'nd 7A **14**
Williams Way DA2: Bexl 2C **18**
Willis Rd. DA8: Erith 4G **5**
Willow Av. BR8: Swan 3E **26**
DA15: Sidc 6D **6**
Willow Cl. DA5: Bexl 6J **7**
Willow Grange DA14: Sidc 3E **16**
Willow Rd. DA1: Dart 1H **19**
DA8: Erith 1F **9**
Willow Tree Ct. DA14: Sidc 5D **16**
Willow Wlk. DA1: Cray 4H **9**
DA1: Dart 5H **9**
Willrose Cres. SE2 . . . . .5A **4**
Wilmay Copse Nature Reserve 2D 32
WILMINGTON **3H 19**
Wilmington Ct. Rd. DA2: Dart 3F **19**
Wilmot Rd. DA1: Dart 5F **9**
Wilson La. DA4: S Dar 2G **29**
Wilton Rd. SE2 . . . . .4A **4**
Wiltshire Cl. DA2: Dart 7E **10**
Winchelsea Av. DA7: Bex 7D **4**
Winchester Cres. DA12: Grav'nd 3C **24**
Winchester Rd. DA7: Bex 2G **7**
Wincrofts Dr. SE9 . . . . .4A **6**
Windermere Cl. DA1: Dart 1G **19**
Windermere Rd. DA7: Bex 2B **8**
Windhover Way DA12: Grav'nd 4D **24**
Windmill Grange TN15: W King 7B **32**
Windmill St. DA11: Grav'nd 7A **14**
(not continuous)
DA12: Grav'nd 6A **14**
(not continuous)
Windsor Dr. DA1: Dart 6F **9**
Windsor Rd. DA6: Bex 4H **7**
DA12: Grav'nd 3A **24**
Wingate Rd. DA14: Sidc 6F **17**
Wingfield Bank DA11: Nflt 2F **23**
Wingfield Ct. DA15: Sidc 2C **16**
Wingfield Rd. DA12: Grav'nd 7A **14**
Winifred Rd. DA1: Dart 5G **9**
DA8: Erith 5J **5**
Winston Cl. DA9: Ghithe 6G **11**
Wintergarden Cres. DA9: Bluew 7H **11**
Winters Cft. DA12: Grav'nd 6C **24**
Winton Ct. BR8: Swan 4D **26**
Wise's La. TN15: Ash, Stans 7G **33**
Wisley Rd. BR5: St P 7D **16**
Wisteria Gdns. BR8: Swan 2C **26**
Wodehouse Rd. DA1: Dart 4B **10**
Wolsley Cl. DA1: Cray 5D **8**
Wolvercote Rd. SE2 . . . . .2B **4**
Wombwell Gdns. DA11: Nflt 2H **23**
WOMBWELL PARK **2G 23**
Woodberry Gro. DA5: Bexl 3C **18**
Woodbine Rd. DA15: Sidc 1B **16**
Woodchurch Cl. DA14: Sidc 3A **16**
Wood Cl. DA5: Bexl 3D **18**
Wood End BR8: Swan 4B **26**
Woodfall Dr. DA1: Cray 4D **8**
Woodfield Av. DA11: Grav'nd 1A **24**
Woodgers Gro. BR8: Swan 2E **26**
Woodland Av. DA3: Hart 5C **30**
Woodland Cl. DA3: Lfield 3F **31**
Woodlands DA6: Bex 5A **8**
Woodlands Av. DA15: Sidc 1B **16**
Woodlands Cl. BR8: Swan 3E **26**
Woodlands La. DA12: Shorne 7J **25**
Woodlands Pk. DA5: Bexl 4C **18**
Woodlands Ri. BR8: Swan 2E **26**
Woodlands Rd. DA7: Bex 3H **7**
Woodlands Ter. BR8: Crock 6A **26**
Woodland Way DA9: Ghithe 5H **11**
SE2 . . . . .4B **4**
Wood La. DA2: Dart 4E **20**
(not continuous)
Woodlea DA3: Lfield 3F **31**
Woodman Vs. DA3: Fawk 3E **32**
Woodmount BR8: Crock 7C **26**
Woodpecker Rd. SE28 . . . . .1A **4**
Woodside Cl. DA7: Bex 4C **8**
Woodside Cres. DA15: Sidc 3B **16**
Woodside Dr. DA2: Dart 4D **18**
Woodside La. DA5: Bexl 6G **7**
Woodside Pde. DA15: Sidc 3B **16**
Woodside Rd. DA7: Bex 4C **8**
DA15: Sidc 3B **16**
Woodstock Cl. DA5: Bexl 7J **7**
Wood St. BR8: Swan 2H **27**
Woodview DA2: Dart 6H **21**
Woodview Cl. TN15: W King 6B **32**
Woodview Rd. BR8: Swan 2B **26**
Woodville Gro. DA16: Well 3D **6**
Woodville Halls Theatre *7A 14*
(*off Woodville Pl.*)
Woodville Pl. DA11: Grav'nd 7A **14**
DA12: Grav'nd 7A **14**
Woodward Ter. DA9: Ghithe 6F **11**
Woolbrook Rd. DA1: Cray 6D **8**
Woolf Wlk. RM18: Tilb 2B **14**
Woollett Cl. DA1: Cray 4F **9**
Woolwich Rd. DA7: Bex 3K **7**
DA17: Belv 6B **4**
SE2 . . . . .6B **4**
Worcester Cl. DA9: Ghithe 4J **11**
DA13: Ist R 7J **23**
Wordsworth Cl. RM18: Tilb 2B **14**
Wordsworth Rd. DA16: Well 1B **6**
Wordsworth Way DA1: Dart 4B **10**
(not continuous)
Worsley Grange BR7: Chst 6A **16**
Wren Rd. DA14: Sidc 4F **17**
Wrens Cft. DA11: Nflt 4H **23**
Wren Wlk. RM18: Tilb 1A **14**
Wright Cl. DA10: Swans 6A **12**
Wrotham Rd. DA11: Grav'nd, Nflt 4K **23**
DA16: Well 1F **7**
Wrott & Hill Ct. DA4: Sutt H 1C **28**
Wyatt Rd. DA1: Cray 3E **8**
Wycliffe Cl. DA16: Well 1C **6**
Wycliffe Ho. *DA11: Nflt* *1J 23*
(*off Wycliffe Row*)
Wycliffe Row DA11: Nflt 1J **23**
(not continuous)
Wye Rd. DA12: Grav'nd 2C **24**
Wyfold Ho. *SE2* *2B 4*
(*off Wolvercote Rd.*)
Wykeham Cl. DA12: Grav'nd 6D **24**
Wyncham Av. DA15: Sidc 1B **16**
Wyncham Ho. *DA15: Sidc* *2D 16*
(*off Longlands Rd.*)
Wynford Pl. DA17: Belv 6E **4**
Wynn's Av. DA15: Sidc 5C **6**
Wyvern Cl. DA1: Dart 7H **9**

Y

Yarnton Way DA18: Belv, Erith 3D **4**
SE2 . . . . .2A **4**
Yews, The DA12: Grav'nd 2C **24**
Yew Tree Cl. DA3: Lfield 2G **31**
Yewtree Cl. DA16: Well 1D **6**
York Av. DA15: Sidc 2B **16**
Yorkland Av. DA16: Well 3C **6**
York Rd. DA1: Dart 7A **10**
DA11: Nflt 7G **13**
DA12: Grav'nd 3B **24**
York Ter. DA8: Erith 1B **8**

Z

Zion Pl. DA12: Grav'nd 7A **14**

The representation on the maps of a road, track or footpath is no evidence of the existence of a right of way.

The Grid on this map is the National Grid taken from Ordnance Survey mapping with the permission of the Controller of Her Majesty's Stationery Office.